Polly Toynbee is an award-winning *Guardian* columnist and former social affairs editor for the BBC. Her previous books include *Hard Work: Life in Low-pay Britain*. Polly is chair of the Brighton Festival. David Walker was director of public reporting at the Audit Commission and founding editor of Guardian Public. Together they wrote *Unjust Rewards: Exposing Greed and Inequality in Britain*, *The Verdict: Did Labour Change Britain?* and *Cameron's Coup: How the Tories Took Britain to the Brink*.

Dismembered

How the attack on the state harms us all

POLLY TOYNBEE & DAVID WALKER

gff

First published in 2017
by Guardian Books, Kings Place, 90 York Way, London N1 9GU
and Faber & Faber Ltd, Bloomsbury House,
74–77 Great Russell Street, London WC1B 3DA

Typeset by seagulls.net

Printed and bound by CPI Group (UK) Ltd, Croydon, CR0 4YY

A CIP record for this book is available from the British Library

ISBN 978–1–78335–120–6

2 4 6 8 10 9 7 5 3 1

Contents

Introduction

Our Better Selves

They care for stroke victims, guard the borders, patrol children's crossings, rescue people from fires (and stop them breaking out), teach English in further education colleges, check restaurants are clean and weights and measures accurate, monitor brimming river levels and perform a thousand other unsung but indispensible tasks. They are essential if we are to hold together as a society and thrive. This book is a paean of praise to these people, to public service and, behind them, the state.

Pen-pushers and bean counters may be the butt of the tabloids and the trolls, but they too are equally essential, along with tax inspectors, regulators and enforcers and the operators of surveillance CCTV and speed cameras. Unseen and vital are the monitors who ensure that Wessex Water (aka the private company YTL Power International of Kuala Lumpur) flushes the sewers as it is supposed to and that transport giant First Group's 15 per cent operating profit has not been puffed up by axing buses, cancelling trains or colluding on prices.

Public service is about prevention and assurance. Without the protection of public service, we come to harm – take, for instance, the Financial Conduct Authority without which we would pay over the odds for mortgages or even not be able to get them at all. Free enterprise only thrives within a strong public realm.

For the state is our security. When their credit ran out and their financial nakedness was exposed, the bankers in the Canary Wharf skyscrapers turned automatically to the government; they were ungrateful then and since, perhaps because they were witnessing a fundamental truth, that private profitmaking depends on public power. It's the backstop when Tata threatens to pull out of Port Talbot and the steel mills in Hartlepool go cold.

The 'it' is what the Romans called *res publica*, the space within which collective decisions were made and implemented, armies sent to march, taxes levied and bridges built. Theirs was an empire. Over the centuries, its shape has largely settled on the nation state, within which is preserved much of our sense of who we are, certainly far more than any identity offered by global companies or giant internet corporations, however bloated their marketing budgets.

In our case, Britishness, the national fabric, is woven from interlinked identities. With increasing devolution the UK state has become harder to decipher as commitments, values and spending levels diverge across Scotland, Wales and Northern Ireland – though all are subject to the Tory austerity drive. Visit the permanent secretary of the Welsh government at Cathays Park in Cardiff and the campus around her feels like the headquarters of a small state. The relative size of government in Northern Ireland has been maintained, while its counterpart in England has continued to shrink. And Nicola Sturgeon's Scottish Nationalist government has talked a fine game on growing public services – although so far it has not dared raise taxes in order to support its greater spending than England.

For all that, we can't tell ourselves much about our common past or what faces us tomorrow without also narrating government. Who are 'we', in these times of confused identity, exposed in the Brexit vote? Public services used to define who we are, from the NHS to the British Army, National Grid and elemental water and energy services. Some have been sold, bought by foreign companies and run for private profit. Others have been broken up into competing units, defying common understanding of who does what in whose name. 'Public spirit' is evaporating.

In Theresa May's Cabinet the communities secretary, Sajid Javid, dislikes government, wants to shrink spending and reduce regulation; his bedtime novels are said to be the libertarian fantasies of Ayn Rand. As business secretary he famously banned the phrase 'industrial policy', declaring it oxymoronic. But confronted with questions about integration and values in modern Britain, his response is to turn to … the state. In order to tighten citizenship requirements, to administer oaths: who else is going to define 'Britishness'? What he has to accept is that Britishness and the health of the British state are co-determined; to dismember the latter is to diminish exactly what he says he wants to extol. Charities have the potential to bind people in a sense of national common endeavour but they too are in crisis, overloaded, underfunded and, now, under political and regulatory attack; the Big Society is a failed fantasy of an already half-forgotten prime minister.

It's not too late; cuts and dislocation have not yet inflicted permanent damage. We can say that because the 'public thing' is in large measure the people who work for it and for us and their spirit has not been extinguished: dimmed and guttering the flame may be but it still burns. You will meet some of them in the pages of this book: NHS podiatrists, trading standards enforcers, police officers, water regulators, council chief executives, people at work within government agencies, local authorities, Whitehall departments. Of course they are not all moral heroes; some may even be knaves. But together, they embody an ethos built around the idea of the common good: the frustrations they express almost always concern cuts and obstacles to doing their job as well as they otherwise could.

They would rarely use such hifalutin terms as 'ethos' and that is because they are usually highly focused. They define themselves by a specific job: border control, community programmes, running a Whitehall department, managing a sexual health clinic. Citizens also tell pollsters they value specifics – their children's teacher, their GP, local police officers and home carers. Nurses top the polls for public respect, with an array of public servants close behind in esteem;[1] but what happens when the same question is posed of the NHS or the local council or other public body as a whole? The institutions themselves seem to find it harder to command the citizens' respect. We moan about service. We swap tales of shortcomings. Yet the engine of state is greater than the sum of its working parts and extends beyond the immediate here and now, stretching across the decades, to pay our and our children's pensions. Without reminders and encouragement to take pride, citizens themselves may end up undermining the wider thing that binds us in common purpose.

Dismembered

It's not just the recent cuts. The UK state has been pulled apart, partially rebuilt, then deconstructed time and again during the past 30 years. Few of these 'reforms' have been backed by evidence of organisational effectiveness; most have been based on dogma, hunch or the discovery by newly arrived ministers that, far easier than changing society or economy, they could just pull a lever and reconfigure the machinery of state. The result has been confusion and public mistrust.

In the Thatcher and Major era, the Tories sold the family silver and privatised the state's capacity to contribute directly to the economy in energy and the utilities, transport and communications. They straitjacketed councils but also created ramshackle executive agencies as part of a programme to bring business into the heart of government. But Tory ministers were not themselves prepared to be businesslike. In 1995, Home Secretary Michael Howard said he wanted the prisons run as if they were freestanding companies, then sacked the chief executive of the prisons agency, Derek Lewis, because he was behaving like an executive manager.

After 1997, a jungle of zones and semi-autonomous bodies sprang from a welter of well-intentioned Blair government initiatives. Ministers wanted to do things, but their enthusiasm produced overlap and befuddlement. Under the New Deal for Communities, local boards took on substantial sums of public money for estate regeneration and jobs. But when we chronicled one such project in Clapham Park for our book *The Verdict* we could see how puzzling the structures were. The project wasn't run by Lambeth Council, nor the (confusingly named) Office of the Deputy Prime Minister;

the initiative was part voluntary, part enforced. As blocks were refurbished and training schemes started, great potential benefits were proffered to residents, but they were unlabelled. Money was spent, there was some physical and some social renewal, but no one was claiming agency over it; the government certainly got no credit.

From 2010, the cuts were accompanied by tinkering; austerity with administrative anarchy. (Chaos is deliberate, said the Tory ideologue Oliver Letwin; if public staff are disorientated, they will be easier to get rid of.) Cameron swung about like a mad axeman, lopping off regional development agencies and sundry commissions whose usefulness he hadn't bothered to ask about. He also redisorganised health and education, creating hundreds of new quangos and 'trusts'.

In the Cameron coalition and afterwards, Tory ministers let rip. Civil servants were 'enemies of enterprise', echoing dark Thatcherite invocations of the 'enemy within'.[2] Liam Fox attacked 'pen-pushers'; Andrew Lansley disparaged the very managers whom he was asking to make his incomprehensible health scheme work. In the case of education, Michael Gove's apparatchik Dominic Cummings and special advisers around Theresa May at the Home Office (now with her in Downing Street) insulted officials to their faces. Gove called them 'The Blob'. Communities Secretary Eric Pickles banged on about useless town hall officials and 'bureaucrats in government departments who concoct ridiculous rules and regulations'.

We need to push back this relentless denigration of government. One of the sacred beasts to be slaughtered is belief in another great monster, Leviathan, Thomas Hobbes' characterisation of the state. In fact, impotence is a better characterisation of 21st-century British government. Successive reports by parliamentary committees show governmental incompetence related to inadequate resources and refusal to look ahead, and all of them are bound up with a philosophy that despises planning, activism and the mobilisation of collective resources. Thanks to austerity, public service increasingly lacks people and skills. A month after the EU referendum, Amyas Morse, the Comptroller and Auditor General – head of the National Audit Office (NAO) – looked at the resources and people that are going to be needed to handle Brexit, while simultaneously dealing with the rest of the UK's jostling 'to do' list, which includes energy and power stations, transport, roads and railways, as well as looking after growing numbers of older citizens, reskilling redundant workers and so on. Unusually, for he is ultra-cautious, Morse was outspoken in his pessimism. When the Institute for Government reviewed state capacity seven months later, its conclusion was even darker.[3]

This is the age of 'me'. Polls show that people, the young especially, want individual service, preferably on demand. Queuing and sharing feel counter cultural. Individualism beats old-fashioned collectivism. Younger people may doubt the value for money of services that they aren't using at this current stage in their life, for across the lifecourse there is a natural mismatch between contributing and taking out. But Generation Y is also generation rent: its cohorts want somewhere to live. Markets won't oblige: councils and development corporations alone can do the planning and, given a fair wind, muster the resources in order to build. Then there is the fact that even hale young people get sick; accidents happen; they may get knocked off their bikes by Uber drivers. Only when they begin to have children do they realise who provides the maternity unit, the nursery and school place, or helps with a child who is difficult or disabled.

Prophets who proclaim the triumph of individualism never quite explain how each 'me' lives with every other 'me' in tolerable harmony. And this ostensibly personal world is also highly collectivised. It is ruled by mega corporations, which patently don't have the individual's interests at heart. Against their might the power of 'us' needs to be asserted.

Some will need convincing that the state can revive common purpose and deal effectively with the multiple challenges ahead: Brexit, an ageing population, energy, productivity and the rest. Their ranks include those who in their dealings with government have experienced delays, unanswered phones, poor customer service and, sometimes, rank maladministration. A debilitating attribute of government is silo working. Officials retreat into their own departments, agencies and professional specialisms, failing to join together. Healthfulness, for example, depends on exercise, income and housing as well as on GPs, pharmacists and the wider NHS. Joining them together requires money, yes, but also a strong sense of shared aims.

The way forward isn't 'reform' as preached by those who want to further weaken government by bringing in yet more consultants and private firms. The way forward starts with an end to what we are calling dismemberment – how government in recent times has been chopped up, contracted out, rebadged and confusingly branded, as if its people were pulling apart rather than together. First we stop this civic vivisection, then can we slough off the ideology that says 'me', that says 'markets can do it all', and relegitimise the belief – based on the evidence of history, what other countries accomplish and everyday experience – that a powerful and well-resourced state is a necessary condition of our wellbeing.

Chapter 1

What a State We're in

After 40 years of ideological assault, the state is in trouble. Once, the path towards general social improvement was well paved and signposted. Now protections for old and young are weakening, the health service is in peril, environmental standards are slipping and road deaths blipping up again for the first time in years. Social services caseloads are on the rise – between 2010 and 2015 there was a 17 per cent rise in the number of children having to be looked after by statutory authorities in England. Old people die at home alone. Powys Council, cash strapped, proposes closing all its day centres: users must 'fit in what we can offer, not what would best suit his or her needs'.[1] David Cameron's fantasies about voluntary activity have run away with the fairies. As charities buckle, there is no substitute for public provision.

It's not just the social state that's threadbare. Other functions are dilapidated, including defence. Once they retire, generals and admirals become vocal and lately have been, warning that the UK can no longer defend itself from obvious threats. Missiles misfire. The Home Office does not have the staff to 'take back control'; Brexit will require thousands extra to operate more immigration booths at Heathrow and more customs sheds at Dover. Oddly, those most alarmed by migration have often been those most eager to diminish and dismantle government – refusing, for example, to see the necessity of public investment to help communities adapt to troubling social and cultural change. That runs parallel to the failure to admit that trends in the economy, such as divisive inequality or failure to export goods, demand more not less state intervention.

Bigger is Better

There is no optimal size for government, no single, sustainable level for tax in relation to GDP. There is no perfect recipe for balancing taxes on income and wealth against tax on sales and value added. However, we can empirically show when basic standards are harmed, when cutbacks become dysfunctional and self-defeating, and when society is damaged and economic functioning impaired. That is before bringing to bear values that challenge inequality and unfairness or assert minimum standards of welfare and wellbeing.

Anti-statists constructed a strong conventional wisdom, blaming Big Government for impeding economic growth. The charge does not stand up.[7] Economists can't be said to be in complete agreement but surveys by the Organisation for Economic Co-operation and Development (OECD) and the International Monetary Fund find no reliable association between smaller government and expansion of GDP. On the contrary, indices of wellbeing and fairness as well as GDP per head, point to bigger government being better. For the OECD neither higher tax nor increased redistribution impede growth as long as government can make labour markets more efficient – by helping get people into work and boosting productivity, for example, through good infrastructure investment.[3] The international evidence suggests 'larger and more effective governments reduce inequality' – which in turn can benefit productivity and the functioning of markets.[4]

Government Has Got Harder

The state is in trouble for two reasons. The first, which we look at in Chapter 3, is ideological assault. A battle of ideas is being waged and the anti-statists have big guns and can pay for squads of intellectual mercenaries. It's maybe also that government has become more difficult, more intellectually and technically challenging as the range of problems expands at home and abroad and the political and managerial resources available to deal with them stretch and (as a permanent secretary put it) lose their pep.

Delivering IT, plugging holes in social relationships (by extracting child maintenance payments from absent fathers, for example), planning energy supplies as the planet heats up ... the list of challenges is long. To meet them people are needed with the highest technical skills, but who also have political imagination and the ability to run complex administrative systems. These talents are often undervalued, especially by business types. But bring those captains of commerce into complex government and they soon realise how easy it is to operate with a single target, the bottom line, compared with fulfilling the multiple obligations that fall on the public sector.

The state needs virtuosi, skilled in IT, accountancy, statistics, risk analysis and the law, who understand politics and social media and are accomplished drafters of official papers open to public inspection through Freedom of Information. Certain skills are missing across the economy, among them project management. The arguments for the state that we present in this book are not blind to these gaps, or to differences between the temperament demanded by political success and the mindset for successful public management. But as the historian Peter Hennessy and others have shown, close and fruitful cooperation between ministers and public servants is possible, provided we start with basic belief in the necessity and potential of state action.

The State's Billions

At the time of writing, in 2016–17, the UK state is a £772bn entity. It is in the red, with spending overshooting the proceeds from tax by some £56bn. Longstanding loans (the national debt) will be worth £1,638bn in March 2017. Which sounds a lot but is less than the UK's GDP, the total value of transactions generated within the economy, which stands at £1,943bn. As a matter of arithmetic, each of the UK's 65 million population shares £25,200 of the national debt. They also enjoy average individual wealth of £135,000, or five times as much. But averages tell us nothing much about how we live now, or how wealth is shared. Politicians promoting austerity try to frighten voters with the scale of the national debt. The analogy with a household is inadequate, but easier to grasp. A family happily accepts a huge mortgage debt that would bankrupt the family to repay now, but which becomes manageable when repaid over 30 years.

Similarly, the state exists in time, across centuries; its debt is a transaction between generations. Government borrowing over the decades is mostly in the form of National Savings bonds and the like. It's a debt to one another for mutual benefit, as citizens, taxpayers, pensioners, newborn infants, students, earners and so on through the multiple roles we occupy during the course of our lives.

Government debt gets compared to maxing out a credit card as if it were an individual's borrowings. But government debt is unique. Since the 2008 crash the Bank of England has been able, safely, through its quantitative easing programme, to do what pundits had for centuries said was a recipe for immediate ruin – it has been able to print money.

The state's official balance sheet demands careful reading. It excludes 'goodwill', vast accumulated trust and what we take for granted from public services, let alone the value of precious objects in museums, areas of outstanding natural beauty protected by planning regimes, the maintenance of intergenerational solidarity through pension payments, public edifices built to last, defence and security against domestic and foreign threats … and so on.

The British pride themselves on practicality and empiricism. Not for us Gallic or German theorising. *They* talk about *l'état* and read Hegel, while we muddle through with ambiguous notions such as the Crown and ministers' use (and abuse) of the royal prerogative. We get by, we tell ourselves, eschewing definitions and hifalutin concepts.

But it's a conceit. In recent decades we have been more driven by ideologies than our neighbours in Europe. Powerful theories have been propagated and imposed by ideas merchants and thinktankers in the pay of American business interests. Certainly how we think about the public realm and what we practise in central and local government is freighted by abstractions such as markets and competition, all the more insidious because they go unrecognised or pass as 'common sense'.

Our Untidy State

The state is desperately untidy and UK public space is littered with anomalies. People can't tell who runs the ambulance service, councils, the NHS or other bodies. Go to Sellafield in your anti-radiation suit and try to sort the mess of organisations and private companies involved with its sheds, pipes and pools. The debatable land between central government and councils lacks maps. Boundaries between Whitehall departments and arm's-length agencies befuddle even the wonks. Semi-autonomous bodies abound, these days including thousands of academies and free schools. Chief constables answer in part to elected commissioners, in part to the Home Office. The NHS in England is broken into a hotchpotch of trusts, commissioners and specialist bodies, some privatised. The UK state is also made up of governments in Edinburgh, Cardiff and Belfast that themselves have state-like attributes.

From the monarchy derive the mysterious Crown prerogatives and powers wielded by ministers and officials – often in conflict with the rights claimed by elected MPs in the Commons. Post Brexit, the Supreme Court has had to act as referee. Rules of statecraft are often informal and tacit. In England and Wales common and statute law intermingle; rights and duties are often implied rather than expressed.

England has a state church; Scotland a national church. Unlike the moderator of the latter, the Archbishop of Canterbury is a sort of civil servant. The monarch is head of the Anglican Church, defender of the faith, the prelates of which bizarrely sit in the UK legislature as lawmakers. That's one bit of the state. Network Rail is another and pretty anomalous, too. Tory governments have tried to figure out how the private sector could be made responsible for track, signalling and stations as it was when the Major government sold the railways off, but Railtrack came to a sticky end in 2001 when Labour had no choice but to renationalise. They and Tory successors tried to keep Network Rail's borrowing off the public accounts, obfuscating its finances with payments from private train operators who were simultaneously being subsidised by the Department of Transport to lease rolling stock.

In another neck of the woods there's the BBC. The broadcaster is widely seen as a national glory, a source of pride at home and a remarkable influence abroad, a creative engine and fair reflector of an increasingly fissiparous society. As long, that is, as BBC hierarchs exercise a sense of proportion and, with other senior managers, are prepared to say out loud that this handsome salary plus perks and pension is justified – really justified – by recruitment needs and the 'going rate', if there is one. With public service must come a measure of public humility.

Not M&S

Some of this complexity around government is inevitable, the fruit of long history. Complication comes from the division between legislative, judicial and executive functions and from ensuring accountability and fairness in services. But in an age when attention spans are shortening and civics is not a compulsory school exam, over-elaboration has consequences. It pushes those making the case for government and the tax to pay for it on the back foot, unable to give a pat answer to those brandishing analogies with the market.

Why can't government services be like Marks and Spencer, asked Margaret Thatcher (only a few years before that company nearly went bust and appointed a succession of bosses unable to arrest long-term decline in sales). The answer then and now is that the state is not selling knickers or sandwiches; caring for people and maintaining prison services, making communities more cohesive and the economy more productive, these services take a vastly different set of skills and values to those of commerce. In commerce, all that matters is the bottom line; public services, on the other hand, have hosts of difficult, divergent objectives. The response to those who call citizens 'customers' and demand personalisation is that this is not shopping. The public sector operates within a mutual social contract that relies on a wider conception of who 'we' are, beyond 'me, me'. First in line in such a situation is not the one with the deepest wallet, but the one with most pressing need.

Public vs Private

A pernicious myth has been spread that business alone generates wealth. In this story public employees drag on innovation, the state crowds out growth and, despite years of austerity, is forever in need of pruning. Breitbart London and the *Daily Mail* sneer and tell lies about public sector pay and pensions that get echoed unquestioningly on social media. For years now public staff have been up against it. Margaret Thatcher liked to ask officials, why don't you get a proper job? Even as he expanded services, Tony Blair paraded the 'scars on his back' from dealing with them.[5] Under the cuts enforced by

George Osborne from 2010, many have felt less like valued professionals than like enemies within.

By contrast, so the story goes, the private sector is bustling and striving and would thrive if only it were freer of regulators and obstructors. Blessed are the profit makers, sings the conventional wisdom. Will Hutton justly complained of the 'determined way the national conversation is skewed towards the inadequacies of the public sector, without any parallel focus on the inadequacies of the private'; prime ministers and chancellors change but this relentless drumbeat hammers on.[6]

Yet private enterprise depends on government. Not just government as guarantor of property and contractual rights, but as builder, manager of schools and administrator of the tax credits that allow households to enter the labour market at below-survival pay. Even some rightwingers reluctantly come thus far. But their red line is any suggestion that the state could be an effective owner or provider of goods and services. Over that threshold, they say, lie the corpses of nationalised industries, the rusting hulks of civil service-directed firms stranded in a desert of planned enterprise or expensive services paying staff above rock-bottom market rates. The state lacks the wit and wisdom to understand market dynamics, they claim, and its officials the temperament and fleetness of foot to survive competitively.

This is wrong. Competitive free markets are figments of the imagination of ideologues and academics: in the real world, firms collude and directors fix their own pay while short-term investors chase the fastest bucks, regardless of a company's long-term potential. Only government keeps capitalism on the straight and narrow and prevents it from eating itself. State and markets are symbiotic: they need each other to survive.

The Self-Interested State

The individualist impulse to get and keep things has been officially sanctified over these Thatcher-inflected decades. Look after you and yours, stand on your own two feet and despise those who can't manage without help. Social suspicion and fear of being cheated by lead-swingers have been nurtured in order to spread mistrust of collective effort. Yet empowering the state to help others is self-interest: take care of others by paying the tax and supporting good social programmes and you will be taken care of in turn if your luck or your health runs out, spreading out the risk across generations, across the life-cycle, between good times and bad. No private insurance can offer as much. Give a decent start in life to other people's deprived children, and they will grow up to contribute to everyone's productivity and growth, instead of costing everyone more in mental health services or prison sentences.

The insulated rich may imagine they can live in wealth-protected bubbles in gated compounds, paying their accountants huge sums to avoid tax. But the 1 per cent also rely on the security the state provides, as enforcer of the legal framework protecting their property rights. It guarantees their air is breathable, their water drinkable. Who keeps the roads safe for their Lamborghinis and the A&E ready for when they crash? The state fosters the arts, culture and civic grandeur they may enjoy, while conscientious planners protect views of the countryside from their estates. On a humbler but no less important scale, it even looks after the nation's lower limbs.

Rotting From the Feet up

Throughout the book, we will dip into public services, sampling their condition, watching the effects of dismemberment and shrinkage. The NHS provides alarming examples of both, not just in its great flagship hospitals and their much-reported A&E units, but in nooks and crannies where the spotlight rarely shines on the creeping erosions. Things once taken for granted slip away. Podiatry is not glamorous, but as diabetes takes an ever-heavier toll, cuts to the service make a good example of the consequences of shrinking provision.

————————

Every week 135 people have limbs amputated because diabetes has caused their feet to rot: their circulation goes, and so does the feeling in their feet, so they don't notice damage caused by rubbing shoes, stubbing toes or stepping on nails. They get ulcers that, if left untreated for too long, turn gangrenous and then they lose their foot or their leg. Many of these amputations are preventable — or would be if there were the podiatrists to treat the first signs of foot ulcers. But the number of podiatrists is falling almost as fast as the number of diabetes sufferers is rising. There are now nearly 3 million diabetics across the UK.

In his surgery, the head of podiatry for Solent NHS Trust, Graham Bowen, is unwrapping the foot of a life-long diabetic to reveal a large missing chunk of heel and foot, a great red hole through to the bone where much of the foot should be. This patient has already had some toes amputated. He has been having treatment with maggots, bandaged into his wound to eat up the dead skin and help healing — and his condition is improving. All the patients Bowen now sees are similarly high-risk. Incipient ulcers, the ones that need to be caught early (and cheaply) don't get NHS treatment: 'On the NHS, we're essentially firefighting the worst ones now,' says Bowen. 'We are going through our lists and discharging all non-high-risk patients.'

But not even all these patients get the same optimal treatments, due to the vagaries of the Cameron coalition's 2012 NHS Act. Five different commissioning groups pay for Solent, a community trust, covering Southampton, Portsmouth and West Hampshire. But each commissioning group has their own criteria for what they will pay for. The most effective treatment, an instant plaster-cast, cures an ulcer in eight weeks, but some commissioners refuse the extra cost for their patients, opting for a less effective treatment that takes 52 weeks to work, with risks that it may not work at all. That's an example of the increasingly dismembered NHS, broken into a fragmented postcode lottery of treatments.

Good podiatry delivers more quality life years than hip replacements. The NHS needs 12,000 practitioners, but has fewer than 3,000 – and that's falling, despite 65,000 high-risk diabetics needing weekly appointments. If diabetic foot damage is caught early, most amputations are preventable, but they are rising annually, to over 7,000.

Bowen's clinic has had to lose four podiatry posts to save money as commissioners budget less for feet: as patient numbers soar, especially diabetics, his budget has been frozen for years. 'Doing more for less,' he says, with the same sigh you hear echoing through all public services. As Bowen goes through the clinic's books removing all but the most acute cases, he is turning away those diabetics who should be seen in order to catch problems early.

What happens to those people now? 'They have to go private, if they can afford it. If not, then nothing.' He used to send them to Age UK, but the charity has shut their clinic too for lack of funds.

Another sign of the times – this NHS clinic has now set up its own private podiatry service for those not serious enough to meet the ever-tightening NHS criteria for treatment. Their private clinic, for those who can afford it, channels any profits back into their NHS work. In Bowen's circumstances, it's not an unreasonable response but from there it's only a short step to means testing, even though all the evidence shows that universal services tend to be better quality, and maintaining broad support for services targeted on 'them' not 'us' gets more and more difficult.

What Went Wrong?

Shortfalls in the NHS budget may be making the news now but it wasn't always that way. Public spending rose by 3.2 per cent a year on average between 1956 and 2010 and by even more, 4.7 per cent, in the Labour years to 2010. That did not necessarily mean the state got bigger. Some of the additional spending went in (justifiable) increases in pay for teachers and soldiers.

The Labour years were good for public services, both for staff and for those benefiting from them. The general government pay bill grew from £111bn (in 2009 prices) in 1998 to £182bn in 2009 – though public sector weekly earnings increased broadly at the same rate as earnings in the private sector. This increase in the pay bill mainly reflected urgently needed extra staff, especially in schools and hospitals. Labour increased the government workforce by 14 per cent, from 4.8 million to 5.4 million: more doctors, nurses, teaching and healthcare assistants; civil service numbers went up 2 per cent.

At its most recent high point in 2010, the public sector employed about 6.1 million people. This followed an increase of about 700,000 in the absolute size of the public workforce since 1998–99. But remember these were also years in which the population of the UK was rising, so the public sector's share of the total workforce only increased from 20 per cent to 21 per cent. Remember too that Labour was inheriting 18 years of public neglect: some schools still had outside toilets, some hospitals still used wartime Nissen huts.

Missed Opportunity

In retrospect, Blair–Brown missed a great opportunity – not only to enthuse the public with better services but also to win acceptance of the higher taxation those services relied on. Much was accomplished. With devolution, the state has become more coherent in Wales, Scotland and Northern Ireland. The Labour government tried to re-equilibrate citizens' rights through freedom of information and human rights legislation, and to equip the state with new regulatory powers to oversee the good running of services.

But more staff and improved services did not bring enough public approval. Spending went unappreciated. Labour ministers failed to talk up the success of evidence-based programmes such as Every Child a Reader. For our book *Unjust Rewards* we visited a school in Wythenshawe in Manchester that was part of the programme and were knocked out by its results, which were independently attested; the programme was speeding up the pupils' learning and boosting their chances of better earnings later in life. Come Cameron, it withered, becoming just another council-funded scheme that the council couldn't afford.

A golden age came and went without core attitudes shifting. Labour leaders never dared take on the prevalent anti-statist culture, especially over tax, afraid to seem too old-fashioned. Instead they talked up 'reform' as a kind of punishment for public servants, which served only to undermine trust in the public sector. By failing to win hearts and minds for their best programmes, Labour allowed their successors to use the financial crisis as an excuse to uproot and roll back much of what they had achieved.

Public service professionals bear some responsibility, too. They never took upon themselves the vocational challenge of enlisting the public in their services. Public managers often neglected what patients, parents and planning applicants *felt* about a complex relationship that involves two-way notions of service, authority, accountability and scarcity. Instead Blair encouraged the citizen to think like a shopper: when he promised to make booking hospital appointments as easy as booking an air ticket, he failed to remind citizens of the difference between purchasing from an unending commercial supply that grows to meet demand, and sharing in a collective but always limited public good.

Austerity

In 2010, Osborne jammed on the brakes and ever since we have been living through 'the most prolonged period of spending restraint since the Second World War', according to the House of Commons library.[7] The Bank of England, economists and budget analysts say plainly that crisis and recession were not caused by Labour tax and spend – although public finances could have been stronger when the train hit the buffers, had

Labour dared tax more. The jump in public spending to 48.1 per cent of GDP by 2010 was caused by the crash and bailout. The budget deficit – the annual gap between government income and outlays – ballooned to £159bn, or 11.2 per cent of GDP, in 2009–10, which was big, but still less than in the US and Japan. This wasn't 'socialism' or 'Labour excess' but the price of rescuing capitalism from itself.

Neither austerity nor the way it was implemented was inevitable and unavoidable: there is always a choice. Conservatives, on the testimony of their Liberal Democrat collaborator Vince Cable, saw 'fiscal consolidation as cover for an ideologically driven "small state" agenda'.[8] That was the path they took.

Sustained cuts in public spending since 2010 have not provoked revolt. After 2010, pollsters noted with surprise that respondents even said some services had improved, despite fewer staff and less maintenance. On local services public opinion remained remarkably constant in England through 2014 – either reflecting genuine satisfaction or a reflection of reduced expectations that resulted from widespread belief in Osborne's trope that the country had 'maxed out' its credit card. Over the years the mood darkened. By 2016 surveys found at least half of British adults were anxious about the effects of the cuts on themselves and two-thirds were anxious about their community, with many more supportive of increased spending, even if that meant (as it would) tax rises.

Polls also show diminishing trust in politics and public affairs; turnout is low at local and crime commissioner elections. The EU referendum showed how attracted many are to slogans, simplifications and downright lies – or to promises of fairy money, as in the case of that notorious £350m a week for the NHS.

Pessimists might fear no one noticing as the public realm floats away. New parents do not know the potential for better care that they are missing out on – that health visitors used to visit more often, or that nurseries that too often just warehouse children once had teachers, or that midwives had time to watch out for postnatal depression, but now send mothers home a few hours after a birth. As children's centres shut, shrinking services are wedged below the political radar, as they are used for only a short time in a family's life.

But the absence of the state and its diminution explain many Brexit votes; a growing perception of inadequate services – housing, GP appointments, school places – turned into blaming new migrants, even in areas where migrant populations were low. As pay fell and stubbornly failed to return to pre-crash levels, the laissez-faire attitude taken towards wages, insecure jobs and gig-economy working conditions said the state was failing to protect and provide for its citizens. Support for further cuts dropped steadily after the 2015 election.

Attrition

We hear from Sir Jeremy Heywood the cabinet secretary and fellow panjandrums that the civil service is hale and hearty, weathering the storm and fighting the good fight. It's his job to keep whistling, of course. But he must see indicators of failing quality in public administration, caused by cuts in budgets and overstretch. The Treasury had to recognise that the quality of the economic statistics on which it relies had been adversely affected by spending cuts, so they stumped up extra to help the Office for National Statistics do better, chasing up facts on the growing online economy and changes in employment. That's a welcome but sadly one-off admission that the world doesn't stand still and government therefore needs persistent investment.

Public service still attracts good people. A permanent secretary tells us the brightest and best graduates are still eager to sit the tough competitive civil service exams, and they are still committed to ideals of public service. But the rate of attrition is high, as career paths and pensions are disrupted and respect is scarce; organisational turmoil and redundancies are frequent. We want more not less such disruption, say the 'creative destroyers' who still buzz around the thinktanks and get recruited as special advisers to Tory ministers. States are old fashioned, they say: the future lies with Uber and Amazon, corporations bigger than medium-sized nations and yet hollow, relying – as with courier and delivery companies – on artificial self-employment. Uber's boss, Travis Kalanick, is another unabashed admirer of Ayn Rand who seeks nothing less than the destruction of public services – post, transport, healthcare – and their replacement with low-waged workers permanently available online. Some American local authorities are already offering rebates on taxes to citizens who use Uber instead of social services minibuses to get to clinics and clubs.

Under Siege

Look back beyond the cuts and the austerity imposed since 2010. The state and public services have been under ideological siege for decades. Long before the Cameron coalition began the disastrous dissection of the NHS, 'reform' was the stick used by ministers to prove themselves in control, as they atomised public organisations, enforcing competition. Now, thinking like private companies, academy schools try to slough off children with disabilities. NHS trusts spend thousands bidding against each other or chasing up the 'debts' owed them by other NHS trusts.

The self-belief of public sector leaders has suffered. Many feel they have been subjects of a giant experiment. You continue to give your all, to maintain the public interest, but meanwhile we'll introduce private sector modes of working along with private firms securing profits, and we'll split you up into warring units and leave you to pick up the pieces as things fall apart. Oh, and at the same time we'll unleash and collude with the *Daily Mail* and the tabloids in their incessant campaign of denigration and calumny against the public sector, especially you managers.

As we talk to people working in the public sphere, you hear corrosive fear. The political triumph of the Tories, public reluctance to pay taxes, media sniping and business opportunism have all sapped morale. That's why retaining the best of senior teachers and nurses is so hard, with a dearth of head teachers; why good people desert Whitehall after a few years; why chief constables express profound doubts about the future of the police.

The story we tell in this book is about how and why anti-government forces have gained ground. Meanwhile, from the centre as well as the nationalist fringes of politics have come demands for devolution, one effect of which has been to further break down the sense of common standards and purposes with a patchwork of services; the lottery of where you live increasingly determines what you get. Does it make sense that families with disabled children move to the council districts best equipped to provide for them, upending those councils' ability to go on providing well for the inrush of escapees from bad councils?

But those families with disabled children, like all families, rely on government. What lies ahead demands more not less of the public sector – if those children are to be educated and prosper, if the economy is to grow, if society is to remain coherent, if we are to live in reasonable security.

Since the crash, and with renewed anxiety after Brexit and Trump's election, commentators have struggled to piece together a narrative for our times. Rich countries, especially the UK, have become more unequal; relative conditions at work and at home for many have worsened. Resentment has fuelled voting. Government – delegitimised by business, which refuses to pay tax and lobbies to undermine policy – tries to put the pieces in some sort of order. Markets disrupt expectations, destabilise communities and, to maximise profit, employ robots in place of bodies.

Contending with market forces doesn't mean sacrificing the dynamism of acquisitiveness that at best marries with the entrepreneur's desire to build and create; it does mean seeking to channel and temper them and forcing the winners and the owners to share some of the proceeds of their fortune in order to keep the show on the road.

There Is No Alternative to the State

The state not only can do it, it has to do it. But it's not just about spending settlements or improving quantitative easing to use the money for building railways, housing or wind farms. The people need to be re-engaged with the possibilities. Public service has not only to be made attractive to technologists, engineers, people with talent, but their employment has to be grounded in approval from the wider public. No one is going to take on big government jobs when ministers and their media allies do nothing but carp and snipe or, worse, avow their principled objection to government as an activity.

It's a big ask – and it hinges on public belief in the necessity of taxation, trusting that a more muscular state can make the Britain of the 2020s and 2030s a better place for our children and grandchildren by willingness to raise the share of income going to those collective purposes. The balance between direct and indirect tax, between tax on income, property, wealth and deterrent taxes on smoking or planet-warming fuel, will always be the stuff of debate. But the public would have to assent to a rise, abandoning the shoddy language of 'tax burden'. The first thing is to let sunlight in on that tax language and dismiss the never-ending political race to the bottom in taxes. The great review of taxation commissioned from Sir James Mirrlees by the Institute for Fiscal Studies (IFS) noted how there is a 'more limited discussion and debate about tax policy within government, and as part of the legislative process, than in other areas of policy'.[9]

We aren't naïve about public attitudes, which are broadly resistant to paying more except, possibly, for health, and are suspicious if not downright negative about existing let alone increasing commitments on welfare. Yet expectations remain high. Mixed as it is, the polling evidence permits a positive conclusion. Our society has become more diverse and less deferential as overall standards of living have risen. Despite everything, public belief in and attachment to universal provision of public services, particularly health and basic welfare, remain strong. People are worried by postcode lotteries and favour countrywide standards, though they often tell pollsters they want more local control. Asked questions about ownership, people do say they want more state involvement, for example providing trains and buses.

We are not talking revolution here, but marginal increases in public resources. Compare the Tory aim of lowering net public spending excluding investment to 36 per cent of GDP (by 2020) with what the state might accomplish by raising its sights to a German 44 per cent level, paid for by taxation, with a smarter attitude towards borrowing in order to invest. The real revolution would be in marrying a regenerated public confidence in the good state with a fresh sense of purpose in demoralised public servants. Practical arrangements for schools, the NHS, policing, social care and the rest need to be refounded on a shared understanding of the public's interest. We called this book *Dismembered*, but as we look ahead the severed limbs of public services can be joined together again, strengthening the state's functions to occupy a bigger and warmer place in the national imagination.

Chapter 2

The Public Realm

The UK state shifts shapes and may have too many facets for its own good: the public may no longer be able to see the common core of services and functions. People don't necessarily know – or care to find out – what connects broadcasting, paving and potholes, security online, connectivity between cities and countries and so on. But even taking these services for granted denotes a belief in the order of things; it is an aspect of feeling secure. Technology, markets and society are not changing as rapidly as it suits some, not least those flogging new products and services, but nonetheless our lives do need anchoring. Public services provide, often silently and out of sight, a platform and predictability. They are our heritage and our future. Damage this anchor and anxiety and distrust may grow, and with them the tendency to lash out politically, as shown in the Brexit referendum.

Big Government?

The Office for Budget Responsibility (OBR) is part of the state and since we rely on its numbers, we ought to introduce it.

Employing a small team of bright people, it keeps the government honest by checking the cost of commitments. Created by George Osborne, it was the best thing he did; the second best was to appoint Robert Chote to run it. Formerly director of the Institute for Fiscal Studies, Chote is ascetic without being a puritan, clever without being academic. Reliably independent, the OBR works on the same raw data as the Treasury so the chancellor and mandarins cannot get away with obfuscation as easily as they used to.

The OBR says that in 2015–16, tax amounted to 36 per cent of the total economy or GDP, which is one approximation of the size of the state. Income tax and National Insurance are familiar to most and they amounted to one in every £7 generated in the economy. Despite the name, NI isn't insurance nor, as many people still think, does it pay for the NHS: its proceeds mix in with other taxes. As well as Value Added Tax, significant revenue comes from corporation tax, duties on fuel, business rates and council taxes. One pound out of every £8 paid in tax is derived from the financial services sector, in corporation tax, the bank levy and employees' income tax and NI.

In 2015–16, income from tax undershot the amount spent by government, the gap covered by borrowing. Roughly half of spending goes on welfare, debt interest and pensions and half on goods, services and the operating cost of departments. 'Welfare' – recently made to sound so pejorative by the political right – is tax credits, housing and disability benefits and payments to older citizens. In 2015–16 they totalled £173.4bn, well over half of which went to pensioners.

Propagandists try to scare us with lurid graphs showing the mountain peaks of spending: they have tried to import into the UK the American notion of Big Government, a sort of paranoid mash-up of *The X-Files*, the Pentagon, park rangers and speed limits. Back in the real world, the state has expanded as a proportion of GDP over the post-war period, reflecting demography, the changing economy and public expectations. Across the western world, the greater size of government isn't because there are more officials or teachers but because for the sake of stability let alone fairness, the state does more transferring of cash from one group to another. The ratio between tax, spend and GDP is not sacrosanct. The recession and financial crash pushed it to 45 per cent in 2010; in 2017 it's 39 per cent. The Osborne scheme, endorsed by his successor, is to cut further to 36 per cent of GDP by 2020. We say too far, too fast, hence this book. Judge for yourselves. Is the work of the people described in these pages really so dispensable?

The Balance Sheet

Government employees are far fewer than the ideologues would have you believe. Armed forces personnel, teachers, refuse collectors included, they are now well below one in five of the total UK workforce. And they get paid less than editors and social media commentators assert. Median earnings in the civil service in 2014–15 were £24,980, more than in the private sector (£21,792), but a higher proportion of public staff are professionals and highly skilled now that many blue-collar jobs have been contracted out to the private sector.

The Whole of Government Accounts, published by the Treasury each year, are the best we have by way of a balance sheet for the state. They list assets and liabilities, which include pensions to be paid in the future as well as an estimate of £160bn for cleaning up decommissioned nuclear plants (the costs of Hinkley Point and any new reactors are extra). As of March 2015, the UK's total liabilities, to be funded by future revenues, amounted to £2,103bn. That's equivalent to just over a year's GDP.

Auditors and statisticians argue about boundaries and what properly belongs where. Like strips of no man's land, further education colleges have been won and lost for the state in recent years. While the public, students and lecturers experience it as essentially public, Further Education is now in fact excluded from the official state in England ... but not in Northern Ireland, Scotland or Wales. Similarly, non-profit housing associations, which often depend on grants or guarantees, have been bounced around between public and private sectors. However, these definitions aren't just technical.

Take the obscure but vital Financial Reporting Council (FRC), which is chaired by Sir Winfried Franz Wilhelm Bischoff, former chair of Lloyds Banking Group after its collapse and post-Brexit cheerleader for the City's line that everything in the garden is rosy. The FRC oversees how auditors report on companies and because stock markets depend on their veracity, this regulator is notionally responsible for the good housekeeping of £2,900bn worth of market capitalisation. But the FRC is itself a company, funded by a voluntary levy, which 'belongs' to the City, even though the Department for Business, Energy and Industrial Strategy appoints its directors. It feels mulish.

Opaque accountability is non-accountability. The fifty shades of grey swallow up our sense of who we are, what we know and what we can do about our country and government. The public–private divide is fundamental to politics, and must always be in a state of flux, shrinking one and expanding the other. We discuss in Chapter 3 the ascendancy of the shrinkers.

'The State'

What constitutes 'the state'? The list of components is loose and baggy. Perhaps that's why 'the state' won't mean much to many people. For the Treasury it's a set of allocations to departments – defence, intelligence, the Home Office, Scotland, justice, HMRC, arm's-length bodies and so on. These departments can in turn be broken down by category: staff costs, computers, grants, subsidies to companies, pensions. But the economic analysis only goes so far. The spreadsheets don't capture the importance of state-sanctioned rules and its role in shaping behaviour – for example, police officers, courts, inspectors and regulators all work to prevent crime, malfunction and disorder.

For many, the state is the NHS. Its 2015–16 budget of £116.4bn paid for nearly 23 million A&E attendances (the highest number ever); 14 million GP referrals to acute hospitals; almost 6 million hospital admissions; 19 million outpatient attendances; and more than 9 million calls to ambulance switchboards. Local authorities spent £13.8bn on adult social care services, covering short- and long-term support for more than a million people.

Watched by millions, the state also includes Channel 4, paid for by advertising but retaining public cultural and newsgathering purposes. A longstanding target of the mean-minded right is the British Council, which teaches (British) English across the globe, for which it earned £568m in 2015–16, exceeding its £541m cost. The UK state is also represented by the 1,500 Foreign Office staff serving abroad and 8,000 locally engaged staff working in embassies, delegations and consulates.

Room on the canvas has to be found for local authorities, for they too are part of the state. Subtle brush strokes alone

will capture their autonomy – councillors command democratic legitimacy to match MPs' – but also their dependence
on central government grants, because people expect common
standards of service wherever they live. Council staff are not
paid extravagantly, whatever the propagandists say: median
earnings in 2013–14 were £19,582, below the private sector.
Local and parochial, this branch of the state is also utterly
necessary. For instance, councils dealt with just over 81,000
stray dogs in 2015, 37,000 of which remained unclaimed and
had to be put down, despite more being microchipped.[1] Here
the state has to sweep up after shifts in attitudes (we no longer
think it acceptable to let a dog take care of itself) and owners'
careless behaviour.

   These dogs are emblematic of the 'daily' state. It provides
bin-emptying, courts, road surfaces, training, search-and-
rescue helicopters, healthcare and park keepers, occupying a
space in our common life and imagination that often extends
well beyond the nominal cost of staff and procurement.
'Imagination' may strike you as odd. The state, at least in the
shape of its managers, has not often been kindly handled by
writers of fiction, whether it's the Ministry of Magic or Charles
Dickens' beadles; the Circus employing Le Carré's spies is not
much better treated. Positive depictions such as George Eliot's
heroic public health physician in *Middlemarch* are exceptional.
Maybe novelists tend towards individualism but what would
they or we do without the Oxfordshire Constabulary, employers
of Inspector Morse, or Anthony Powell's Welch Regiment?
The state is ubiquitous, though not always recognised.

Civic Heritage

The state comprises land, buildings, plant, ports and transport. In some instances, these can be easily valued: to replace Network Rail's assets would cost £280bn; Jobcentre Plus had 713 offices across the UK in 2016; major roads are estimated to be worth £306bn.

Balance sheets may miss important valuations, however. Take parks, which provide health and wellbeing, estimated at £1.2bn according to one study.[2] Counting up the extent of the state in hectares or square metres of building is tricky but we know, for example, that councils in England own around £170bn worth of housing, land and buildings. Many of them are irreplaceable markers of place and identity, Manchester Town Hall, Hillingdon Civic Centre and County Hall, Hertford among them. Sheffield's Grade II-listed central library and gallery, says city native Michael Palin, was built to give education and literacy a prominent place at the heart of the city; no wonder the austerity-driven plan to sell it to the Sichuan Guodong Corporation and turn it into a hotel shakes South Yorkshire. What does the sale of the art deco Hornsey Town Hall in north London and its conversion into a 'boutique hotel' or the proposed closure of Wisbech town museum say about belonging and recognition in those areas? Accountants give a notional value (£3.6bn in 2013–14) to the castles, parks and the contents of museums in local authority care while acknowledging the cash value doesn't begin to match the emotional and civic importance of such heritage.

The public realm is wide and dappled, like light through the trees of the New Forest falling on the beech mast. Indeed, the horses, cattle and pigs that graze there, along with turf cutting, are under a special regime upheld by a unique statutory body called the Verderers. Supported by the Forestry Commission, they hold court in Lyndhurst in Hampshire in an old panelled room underneath, fittingly, a pair of mounted deer antlers. Divergent interests have to be reconciled – walkers, cyclists, tree lovers, conservationists, farmers – and money has to be spent.

With the Verderers, the state links the past, present and future in a way no company can. A business is subject to the disruption and uncertainty of markets. Shares and titles are sold to the highest bidder. If privately owned, corporate fate depends on family bloodlines and feuds. In recent times, public bodies have been subjected to similar pressures, deprived of core funds and forced to focus on revenue-raising. Public bodies have to rebrand themselves as their purpose changes – remember that daft but indicative slogan from the Victoria and Albert Museum? *An ace caff with quite a nice museum attached.* But it's not just the Victoria and Albert: the museums, galleries, landscapes and great edifices of our nation all face commercial repurposing. And with it our identity as a nation changes; our sense of ourselves as a defined community existing in time depends on these state institutions. What might be the answer to 'who are we?' if those charged with curating the past and preserving our common inheritance in the future become more interested in the revenue from sandwiches and souvenirs than the significance or care of artefacts or ancient stones?

Past and Present

In 2014, the trust that looked after Hadrian's Wall closed for lack of funds, following the abolition of the regional development agency that backed it. A miracle of survival over the centuries, the wall needs constant attention; without it, this piece of our heritage will crumble. In 2016, Anglesey council pleaded with voluntary groups to take over the 19th-century gaol and courthouse in Beaumaris as well as Wales' only working windmill, citing 'significant financial pressures'.[3]

The past can also be productive business, supporting jobs across the UK's regions and nations, in large part through tourism. Tourists coming to England have been increasing, but of the 31 million who now arrive each year, 16 million never leave London. Without quangos such as Visit England or Visit Britain, who is going to campaign to attract them away from the capital? Not firms certainly, many of whom are too small to chip in, while others are unwilling to join forces with other firms in promoting their wares in common. However, they are all happy enough to take a free ride if the government pays.

No state, no patrimony – except what is retained in private hands for restricted viewing for those with a credit card to cover the admission fee. The National Trust exemplifies magnificent charitable endeavour, but it relies on the customer's ability to pay and volunteers' dedicated efforts, as well as state spending otherwise known as tax relief. But charities are private bodies and can be opaque and unaccountable, unlike the Verderers of the New Forest and most state institutions, where decisions are subject to review and challenge and where all business is conducted in the sight of elected councillors and MPs.

Out of Sight, Out of Mind

Charities have become accomplices of the state shrinkers, as public assets are privatised in their favour. The rationale behind the creation of the Canal and River Trust was to shrink headcount in public sector employment and get rid of a quango, British Waterways. The significance is profound. Hundreds of miles of cuttings, tunnels and willows, loved by boaters, cyclists and walkers, have been abandoned to the charity sector. Of course they were mostly built by private adventurers in that extraordinary burst of capitalist development in the later 18th and early 19th century – though in nearly every case in close collaboration with the state.

Charities are supposed to confer public benefit – although this definition appears wide enough to accommodate Eton and Charterhouse and their exclusive benefits. The Canal and River Trust inherited experienced staff, many of them dedicated to keeping the waterways open to all; it promises to mobilise extra volunteers. But running the canals means adjudicating between competing and perhaps incommensurable interests, for example those on the towpath vs those on the water. If this charity is entrepreneurial and innovative (as the privatising Tories say it must be), it may favour the property developers sniffing around urban canal basins and, for the sake of the bottom line, let locks silt up on stretches of water where narrow boats are rarely seen. The charity's trustees affirm their good intent but England's canals are now theirs, not ours.

Privatisation has been the fate of other important aspects of our national inheritance too. English Heritage, the quango looking after monuments and castles, including Stonehenge – a site famous enough to attract a cultured president of the United States into making a detour from the 2014 NATO summit – is becoming an endowed charity. The stones of old England are formally to remain in public ownership, with the charity being given a long contract to extract revenue from charges, cafes, car parks and shops. It will receive an endowment, a one-off payment of £80m. Since that sum is not going to be enough to keep the heritage in good condition, the new body is bound to be tempted to look at raising entry fees, expanding shopping, charging more for parking, letting out its sites for parties and commercial events – with the potential effect of thinning out the public's sense of belonging and common ownership of communal assets.

Parks and Recreation

Parkrun is the brand for local organisers striding out on Saturday mornings. It gets people out huffing and puffing, enhancing wellbeing and expending calories. Parkrun, surely, is an example of a self-organising, non-state activity; it's a million miles away from government with its forms and taxes. But Parkrun is dependent. It could not take place without open spaces where the grass is cut and undergrowth trimmed, where paths are maintained and access made easy. It depends on parks and public authorities. Parkrun has provoked opposition in some places, from dog walkers and other park people who dislike the sweaty gangs bearing down on them. Councils have to adjudicate, trying to balance conflicting interests within a framework of accountability.

In an increasingly overweight Britain, maintaining open spaces should surely be a priority. The total number of walking and cycling trips we make each year has been in decline since 1995. Used regularly by over 37 million people each year, 'good quality parks are' – or ought to be – 'the places where we can tackle many of today's greatest challenges, from childhood obesity to our changing climate'.[4] Britain's 27,000 public parks 'provide places for people to play and to reconnect with nature and the seasons, as well as with each other'.[5]

But with the number of park staff cut, park managers fear for the future: there is a growing gap between rising use and declining resources. An increasing proportion of councils are contemplating selling their parks. Between 2013 and 2016, half of all councils in England transferred outdoor sports facilities to non-public management – a pocket park here is taken over by the adjacent coffee chain store, additional closures there are needed to bump up revenue from money-making private events, with no one keeping an eye on the aggregate losses. Local campaigns may succeed, as in Hammersmith when locals protested against the previous Tory council's attempt to sell parkland to a private sports company. Private gyms and pools not only charge more, thus excluding the poorest who may need exercise the most, but they also baffle attempts to join up community schemes to combat obesity, to lower the incidence of Type 2 diabetes, keep older people fitter longer and reduce the strain on the NHS.

Without the state we are going to get sicker quicker. Another way to get ill is to eat food in dodgy restaurants when they are not inspected sufficiently by environmental health officers.

Who's Inspecting for Public Safety?

Workaday arms of the state often go unnoticed until they disappear. We expect weights and measures to be checked, health and safety laws to be enforced, kitchens to be inspected, poisons to be eradicated, regulations observed. If the maître d' swears the chicken tikka masala contains no peanuts, who does the checking? If you have severe allergies, your life may depend on it.

Environmental health officers are a quiet lot, meticulous, pedestrian, precise – and now in short supply. Huntingdonshire

District Council has lost a third of its environmental health officers (EHOs) in the past five years. Yet the hazards have not diminished, far from it: pollution increases; air quality falls; resulting illness and mortality rises. The Cambridgeshire district had three automatic air quality monitoring stations, now it has just one, despite the increase in buildings, cars and pollutants.

Then there's landfill and contaminated land, industrial waste, sites of disused gas works and toxic factories to be checked before new building starts – and unfortunately old local knowledge is lost when experienced EHOs are let go. Pest control is on the wane. Pollution comes from every direction, fumes and smoke and noise … from neighbours, dogs and industry. Officers no longer follow up most complaints. The out-of-hours anti-social noise service was cut: you can complain about late-night parties in vain.

With food hygiene, the rules have not changed but the way they are administered has. A category A high-risk kitchen should be checked every six months, category B every year, down to category E every three years. As staff are cut, fewer places are rated category A or B. 'How long,' asks Keith Lawson, Huntingdon's chief EHO, 'before everyone we used to check on relaxes their standards when they realise we probably won't come knocking any more? They'll save money, cut corners, not check their chemicals, if they don't think we're looking.'

New staff are in short supply. 'We no longer take in a trainee every year, as we did. It's not funded any more. They have to pay for themselves now, costing them £15,000 to train over four years. When the local authority paid for training, you did it on the job. No longer.' Lawson himself trained over five years on day release, gaining an environmental health degree. Now fewer train and there are fewer jobs. He wonders where the next generation of expertise will come from.

Out on the main road by a roundabout is a petrol station with a shop, a seedy hotel and a basic restaurant, much used by truck drivers, a zone fallen on hard times following the closure of an air base nearby. Andy Agass, EHO, knows his patch well and knows what to look for as we visit the restaurant unannounced. The owner is absent but dashes to the scene once alerted: he and the inspector know each other. Agass examines the records every kitchen has to keep, the food hygiene safety certificate, the files listing suppliers and staff and their training: here all are level 2, which is a course lasting a few hours that costs £27. He checks the food store, noting the staff's outdoor clothing piled on the floor; the floor and guttering are not quite clean enough; the unwrapped lasagne trays are not as they should be. He sticks a thermometer in the freezer and checks how well the microwave heats – everything here is pre-prepared. What are those bread rolls in the fridge doing next to the meat? He checks the servicing update on extractor fans, the gas certificate and the anti-micro-bial spray used for cleaning kitchen surfaces. The owner admits he hasn't yet got his head round the allergy regulations.

All is reasonably well, with advice given and taken in good heart: the inspector is not heavy-handed. But just as he reaches the end of the inspection, he spots the pies. A stack of them is on a bottom shelf in the storeroom, not in the chiller. You can see a flicker of alarm in the owner's face. Pies are big on his menu. He sighs. 'Well, it's complicated,' he says, and the story of the pies unfolds. They used to be made by so-and-so but the company owners split acrimoniously into two different manufac-turers, arguing over the rights to the brand name and recipes.

'Ah yes,' says the inspector. 'I know this story.' He has the local knowledge and as he probes and prods, the restaurant owner admits a bit sheepishly that the pies arrive with a scrappy piece of paper, no official invoice, no list of contents, paid for in cash off the back of a lorry.

The number of food businesses the EHOs have to check is rising – and so is the turnover in their ownership. 'They can change several times a year. We have over 1,300 food premises on our patch, over 200 new ones selling food last year, quite a churn. But we've had to lose staff, and with them out goes a lot of local knowledge. Public expectations rise, but our capacity falls.'

A parallel story could be told about many workplaces. Since 2010, the downwards trend in injury and ill health has come to a halt, which may reflect the claim by union safety reps that inspection visits to factories and workplaces have decreased.[6] Employers cannot be relied on; safety depends on the state.

The Security State

Environmental and safety officers protect us. So do spies and security operatives. The UK's 'security state' has expanded in recent years: MI5 now has a staff of 4,000, up from 1,600 at the turn of the century, and a budget near £1bn a year. This is an aspect of the state that the political right traditionally favours.

But you can no longer, if indeed you ever could, isolate threat from social circumstances. The Security Service has more work to do because Jihadist threat levels have risen and they have a significant domestic component, related to housing, economic opportunity, language classes, discrimination, cultural aggression, dogmatic faith and lack of social integration. Security is not just a matter for police, surveillance and counter terrorism, but has social and civic dimensions that bring in local authorities, teachers and an array of arms of the state.

In this book we make no dogmatic calculation of the precise contours of government nor do we fix on a number for the staff it should employ. Needs shift, rise and fall. Take the police, who live on the sharp end of social change. Crime has been falling across a range of categories, from some 18 million incidents a year in the mid 1990s to just 6.5 million in 2015. But cyber fraud and online aggression is rising. Mirrored right across the west, this drop in traditional crime may have to do with young people staying on longer at school. Cultural and behavioural shifts play their part: young people prefer Xbox gaming, cars are harder to nick and homes have fewer valuables worth burgling. Home secretaries, Labour as well as Tory, claim the UK's exceptionally high prison population keeps wrong-doers off the streets but they can't explain why crime falls as fast in countries such as the Netherlands where they are closing scores of prisons. Should we also be closing prisons? Do we need as many police? As then-Home Secretary Theresa May told the Police Federation, they could well manage their hefty cut.[7]

Police service cuts have been deep: 17,000 or 12 per cent fewer police officers in 2015 compared with 2010. Add to that a loss of 15,877 civilian support staff and 4,587 uniformed police community support officers and the size of the force has returned to roughly what it was in 2001.

But when we talked to the former chief constable of Gloucestershire, Tim Brain, the story becomes one about misperception. Knife crime in his county is trivial – about 50 recorded offences a year. Yet the citizens of Cheltenham and Stroud seem to believe lurid stories in the local papers about an epidemic of violence. 'Maybe people just got used to the idea that crime goes on rising, even though it stopped a decade ago.'

The police service deals with much more than crime. As the rest of the public services shrink, the police spend more of their time picking up the pieces in safety nets full of gaping holes. The force acts as a last resort when other agencies and mechanisms to deal with problems have been exhausted. And police numbers affect public confidence and perceptions of security. As station managers, bus conductors and other uniformed guardians of day-to-day orderliness are replaced by machines, people prize the visibility of the police even more. According to the polls, people say they are seeing fewer officers around than they did five years ago, and this worries them.

Scraping Up

We spent a Friday night in the Luton and Bedfordshire police control room then went out in a patrol car with Olly Martins, the Police and Crime Commissioner. No, there was not a lot of crime, but there were all kinds of social distress.

People call in tears, some scream. Oscar One, who's been a control room officer for 15 years, makes the life and death decisions: early that night he already had 18 calls he judged serious enough to need attending, but he only had 11 officers to send out. That triaging of calls, trying to estimate who is most at risk, is one of the hardest jobs.

They get an average of four possible suicides reported every night here. Some are frivolous, such as the call about a boy missing for seven hours, whose mental state was precarious, although he was later found larking about in a nightclub. But how can they tell which ones will prove deadly? Dealing with mental health problems overwhelms their daily work, accounting for 60 per cent of all those they take into custody.

'We scrape up,' said Oscar One brutally. 'There's no one else to do it.' The public expects the police to answer every distress call, to reassure, to save, to solve problems but the crime statistics ignore all this chaos.

That night, a man was reported going into a wood with a rope, threatening suicide. Two cars dashed to the scene and officers searched through the trees, joined soon by an ambulance and then a police helicopter with heat-seeking equipment. Over the radio we heard them find him as the helicopter crew guided those on the ground to the right tree – dead or alive, no one knew. The man was found sitting on a branch but he wouldn't budge; next, the fire brigade arrived with a ladder and down he came.

Another call was a domestic, neighbours reporting bloodcurdling shrieks from the stairwell in a council block. When we got there, the couple were back in their flat with a young baby lying on the floor in a scene of chaos. After long conversations, checks on the radio, talking to the mother alone to see what she said, we left with an uneasy sense that the police were not best placed to deal with this on their own. But there was no one else. Using the police is an extravagant way to plug the gaps left by inadequate mental health, social work and youth services.

What alarms officers is that they no longer patrol neighbourhoods as they did, listening to local people and earning local trust. In the past, a neighbourhood tip-off from a local Muslim led them to a machete-wielding extreme Islamicist, a convert from the Jehovah's Witnesses. But building these contacts, creating the trust to receive information from inside communities, takes time they often now lack. Neighbourhood policing is the eyes and ears of counter-terrorism, they say, which extra recruits to MI5 can't replace.

Finding ways to cope with funding cuts from central government, police and crime commissioner Martins tried to raise the small portion of council tax that goes to the police. But the government required him to hold a referendum asking a question of Whitehall's devising which he says may have misled voters into thinking their whole council tax bill would rise by 15 per cent and the vote was lost. Next he tried to raise money by threatening zero tolerance speed-enforcement cameras on his stretch of the M1, to collect £35 each from drivers obliged to attend speed awareness courses. But the Alliance of British Drivers stirred up such an outcry from the tabloids and the transport secretary that he was forced to abandon it.

Trust, rule enforcement, community, neighbourhood, social dysfunction … policing is an example of how the shape of the state has to shift in response to social changes. Officers' skills and aptitude will have to evolve, too, but in Luton and Bedfordshire, as elsewhere, they stand in the front line, between us and anarchy.

The Queen's Head

The sale of Royal Mail from 2013 was the latest loss to the public patrimony. With this privatisation a significant element in British public identity is lopped off; the queen's head becomes part of a commercial brand, added to a company's 'goodwill' to bump up its asset price when hedge funds start hovering.

The Tories still call themselves Conservatives and yet they have no visible wish to conserve. The nature of a state-guaranteed universal system of post delivery with all the stamps and the forms help us identify ourselves as citizens of the UK who are equal not as consumers but as members of the civic community and nation. Don't worry, they say, regulations will ensure letters are still delivered to far-flung addresses (adding, beneath their breath, it won't be long before the internet finally kills off the anachronistic business of sticking stamped envelopes in letter boxes). But regulators are fallible; they get captured or they start recruiting from the business they are supposed to be regulating. Business finds ways of cutting corners. Ministers talk up competition. What this means is that just after the Royal Mail postman calls, a bunch of envelopes (mainly advertising) drops on the mat, pushed through by a bedraggled DHL or Whistl worker. Roads are clogged and air polluted by thousands of delivery vans, where once a unified service delivered for all. London traffic has slowed to an average of seven miles an hour, with delivery drivers and Uber drivers largely to blame. Push the state back and no one tries to hold the ring and sort out the destructive dysfunctions of commercial competition.

Next up is that staple of the high street, the crown Post Office. Don't worry, say ministers, this elemental branch of the state will still be available … as a franchise inside WH Smith. Public functions – passport forms, paying the road fund tax, collecting pensions – shrink into a corner next to the sandwiches and the hobbyists' magazines. Who pays car licences over the counter these days, they ask, now that DVLA has gone online? The counter argument is not just that many people are not and may never get online or that, even if you can apply online, it's worth preserving choice. It's that the Post Office is a high street presence that gives reassurance, with staff who can answer questions on all manner of official relations between citizen and state. Post Office staff are public servants, with a different relationship to people from the staff in Menzies': they exercise a special responsibility, based on government authority, whether dispensing social benefits, operating the postal delivery system or acting as the high street portal to licences, passports and so on. With the end of the Post Office and Royal Mail the state retreats.

Far away from the high street, caught by the tide, lost in the mist on the mountains, trapped by the rising river, it's no longer a Royal Navy or RAF helicopter that will – you hope – fly to the rescue and let down a safety harness. Since April 2015, search and rescue has been run by Bristow, a helicopter manufacturing company. If the pilot, in dangerous conditions, considers coming in for one last try at rescue, we have to hope he or she is motivated by more than the corporate bottom line. Don't fret, says Bristow's website, many of our pilots were trained by the RAF and the navy – without acknowledging how this company is profiting out of very expensive state-funded training services or wondering what will happen as training in the forces runs down.

Contracting, which its advocates said was going to clarify costs and responsibilities, only makes things more complicated. Search and rescue is commissioned by the state in the shape of the Maritime and Coastguard Agency (MCA) and this entails monitoring what Bristow is doing. Did it respond to the emergency call? What if the rescue was called off before the helicopter left base – was that counted as a trip, for the purposes of payment? The MCA has to verify the data it is presented with; should it periodically check the aircraft black boxes? Because Bristow is the only supplier of search and rescue, it can't compare the firm's performance with other private firms for checking, nor compare it with a state-provided alternative.

Bristow Group board may be stuffed with upright men who would not dream of filching from the UK public purse; but can the public wholeheartedly trust them? Bristow says the 'legacy, heritage and experience' of state search and rescue are 'being honored' (using the American spelling as befits a US-owned company). The truth is, the public probably does not realise search and rescue is no longer provided by the state – the Cameron government kept the transfer quiet. But at some point the penny will drop, perhaps because of some failure of service, or a revelation that corners are being cut for the sake of revenue. Then what happens to public confidence on the beaches, at sea or climbing the hills?

Breaking Up and Breaking Down

For nearly 30 years, the public sector has been in the throes of dismemberment. It has been a far from continuous process, with many stops and starts along the way.

Dwelling places have been provided by the state since the high Victorian Benjamin Disraeli conceded that leaving housing to the market produced disease and dysfunction. But between 1980 and 2015, 2.8 million publicly owned dwellings were sold off under the 'right to buy'. The intent was both partisan – the Thatcherites thought owner-occupiers were more likely to vote Tory – and ideological: they did not like state activity. Deep discounts, increased under Cameron, turned the sell-off into a random gift of a public asset to tenants who happened to be in the right place at the right time, as housing expert Professor Alan Murie puts it.[8]

Rolling back the state did not, as promised, encourage housing investment; the private sector failed to construct the new dwellings required to fill the gap. The Tory refusal to reinvest the proceeds or to allow councils to replace lost stock helps explain today's housing crisis. Four out of ten Right to Buy properties have been transferred back to private landlords, who charge far higher rents, sucking in housing benefit and adding to the Department for Work and Pensions' costs. In Tory terms it worked. By 2015 the number of secure council tenancies had been cut by two thirds compared to 1980. Alongside Right to Buy came the transfer of publicly owned dwellings to housing associations, their non-profit status changing as many aspire to become private developers and build what the market will bear, not what younger or lower-income tenants can afford.

The dismemberment and diminution of the state characterise the past 35 years. For all the ambiguity of public attitudes towards tax and their tabloid-inflected criticism of bureaucracy, British people never signed up to a process that has degraded our national life, jeopardised financial accountability and engendered new costs as the fragments compete, overlap with or duplicate one another. Public and private mix and mingle, potentially compromising accountability and befuddling the public – who have limited tolerance of administrative complexity.

Dismemberment did not stop in 1997 when Tony Blair swept Labour into power; in many respects it accelerated. In hindsight, social democracy shot itself. Labour did not just collude in but accelerated the fracturing of the NHS, the ultimate symbol of state-guaranteed solidarity.

Since 1948, the organisation of the NHS had been reviewed and revised, but it has never quite addressed the anomaly in its midst: GPs, many of which are small businesses but embedded in a public system. The Thatcherites rightly viewed the NHS as the state in action, delivering a kind of socialism. Knowing a direct assault on the principle of free NHS care – and her preferred option of replacing it with private insurance on American lines – would fail, Thatcher determined to make the

NHS into a market. Health secretaries such as Norman Fowler and later Kenneth Clarke may have believed that commercialisation would make the NHS more efficient. But one of us (David Walker) was a leader writer on *The Times* at that period and saw at close quarters the American gurus passing through Number 10 and the strong commitment of the Tory core to subvert the 'Soviet' NHS from within.

GPs became 'fund-holding practices', given a budget to purchase services. Hospitals became autonomous bodies within an 'internal market'. Labour ministers were devotees of the cult of competition. As the Blair government poured in urgently needed funds, promising to bring UK health spending up to the EU average, all providers of healthcare – acute hospitals, mental health and community services – were trustified. Some became freestanding foundation trusts and were told to behave like companies, owning their own property, which they could sell if they chose, and going head to head with other NHS bodies for available work.

Cameron's contribution was simultaneously to fund the NHS at a starveling 0.8 per cent increase in spending per year and attempt to realise the Thatcherite promise of marketisation. Since 2010, the NHS has suffered its toughest financial squeeze since it was founded, with budgets simply not matching growing costs, population and specifically more older people. But it was the 2012 Health and Social Care Act that sent the NHS into the downward spiral it is now in, combining extra competition with swathes of additional bureaucracy.

This act prioritised the concept of the NHS 'commissioning' its services. The NHS now revolves around unaccountable, management consultant-dependent groups, ostensibly run by GPs, which let contracts to 'any willing provider', be they private or NHS. Outrage forced Cameron to change the wording to 'any qualified provider', but that made little difference to the open invitation not only for NHS trusts to fight one another for contracts, but for the likes of Virgin Care, Circle, UnitedHealth and others to pick off anything they reckoned profitable, bidding low to get a foothold with the expectation of later raising their prices.

Talking about the latter-day NHS, we are aware of just how baffling the structure is, and how little known to the public. Confusion, unfortunately, serves a purpose. There's a menagerie of administrative beasts, intermingled with private firms and overlapping jurisdictions. Labour created a new quango called Monitor to enforce competition. It has been renamed NHS Improvement and exists in uneasy symmetry with NHS England, which notionally supervises the commissioners. The foundation trusts are ostensibly responsible to governors who come from electoral colleges formed by the public, staff and patients; in practice, the financial squeeze of recent years has all but eradicated the difference between trusts. All boards are subject to dissolution if they fail to make the required savings.

Ironically, austerity has repelled the private sector. Profitable sections are still being targeted (sexual health, prison care, community services) but losses made by Circle at Hinchingbrooke Hospital have made investors turn tail and run from A&E and acute care.

The NHS implosion has been so catastrophic that even with the Tories in power, efforts are being made to bind fragments together. Like a member of the politburo, the hapless Tory health secretary Andrew Lansley has become a non-person. NHS England chief executive Simon Stevens devised 'sustainability and transformation' plans that seek to unite trusts and commissioners in one area under one budget. It is an attempt to get back to the pre-Thatcher model. But the odds are not good. Unification needs to be lubricated and money is tight. The government is half-hearted, and binding the NHS up with local government would require ministers to believe in active, purposeful government. And they don't.

Meanwhile the people on whom healthcare depends – the cleaners, managers, clinicians and therapists – are stupefied. A survey by PricewaterhouseCoopers found 70 per cent saying they did not understand the role of the multiplicity of health-care bodies. Ironically the architect of Labour's contribution to the mess, Alan Milburn, blames 'confused and complex archi-tecture'.[9] Et tu, Brute?

Splintering the School System

As the public realm dislocates, the state is occluded. It wears too many confusing faces for people to recognise it. What are parents to make of academies and academy chains embossed with carpet manufacturers' names?

The story of English schools runs parallel to health. The Thatcherites were tempted to abandon public provision alto-gether, to follow free market dogma and give parents vouchers allowing them to 'purchase' schooling; this had the advantage of paying off Tory supporters in the private schools, which like a lunchtime sandwich shop would gladly accept vouchers. Backing away from disruption on such a scale, eighties Tories opted instead to move down the road of turning schools into mini-companies, which might eventually charge parents; this plan had the advantage of excluding the state in the shape of local authorities. Policymaking is never pat, however. The

Tories were also highly interventionist in schools, prescribing curriculum and teaching styles.

As with health, Labour carried the process on, creating 'academies' entirely divorced from council influence – but heavily dependent on private donors, such as Lord Harris, the flooring magnate. Under Cameron, it was decreed that all schools, everywhere, would be academised, whatever the wishes of parents and governors. In addition, scarce resources were to be reserved for quixotic groups to set up 'free schools', 'studio schools' and (a favourite of the Blair years, too) additional 'faith schools'. To break up the state was an attested ambition of the Tories, but their formula for schooling seems to embody an intent to further fragment society and reinforce divisions; hence under Theresa May a bid to revivify selective secondary schools, a prime consequence of which is inevitably the channelling of the majority into second-class education.

Recent years have seen chatter about making policies more evidence based. The drive to make schools autonomous has, however, shown reliance on faith and conviction rather than research and study. What the evidence tells schools is that they need to get, train and keep excellent teachers. In England some 10 per cent of trained teachers leave the profession each year; the challenge is to encourage more of them to stay. Schools and the teachers working in them do need a degree of independence to flourish, provided they are simultaneously nested inside local systems dealing with transport, meals, administration, pay, children with special needs, playing fields, sports facilities and – critically – the management of admissions, catchment areas and transition from one phase of school life to another.

What has happened to English schools is not formal privatisation or even contractualisation; they don't have shareholders.

Instead they have been broken apart from one another, alienated, atomised. But also, an additional Tory twist, many have been taken over by a new breed of non-public corporation called Multi-Academy Trusts, shadowy bodies that aren't charities but don't show up in registers of public bodies; they appoint their own boards, which rarely include parents.

In 2011–12, councils transferred to academies land and buildings with a book value of £6.5bn; the academies' accounts showed additions of land and buildings to be worth £12.3bn. Yet nobody, the Treasury sheepishly admitted, quite knows what the academies' balance sheets look like or how this discrepancy occurred – which helps explain why in successive years the Comptroller and Auditor General has refused to sign off the Department for Education's annual accounts.

The Durand Academy in South London, beloved of Michael Gove, became notorious and its funding was withdrawn by his successor Justine Greening in the face of deep concerns over conflicts of interest. It turned out that the land on which the school had been built, though owned by the Department for Education, had acquired some alienated status and could not be used to house another school. The chair of governors (the school's former head, who had been receiving £400,000 a year) refused to budge. He was 'unapologetic' about the £175,000 income he was receiving through the leisure centre operating on the school site, which he said was a just reward for commercial success.[10] But when there is no regulation, who is looking out for the pupils' best interests?

———

This is what education dismemberment feels like. Whatever glitz Blackpool might once have had, it faded long ago. The rain always blew in from the Irish Sea, but in recent years the town has become an increasingly bleak place for jobs and opportunities for adults and young people alike. But Blackpool's primary schools have struggled hard to pull themselves up, working together, so that now 90 per cent of them are rated good or outstanding.

We talked to Andy Mellor, the head teacher, just after his school, St Nicholas, proud bearer of OFSTED's highest accolade, had just been named Primary of the Year by the *Blackpool Gazette*. He's an energetic and funny man but he was bristling with indignation.

His catchment is deprived and largely white: there are only three Muslim children among his 400 pupils. He talks of his determination to help pull up neighbouring primaries, as six local schools have banded together: one of them is becoming a teaching school – a Department for Education (DfE) designation that brings extra money in exchange for focused attention on developing leadership and skills in an area.

But the selfsame department has just dropped a bombshell on them. It has approved an academy chain's plan to open a large new free school on their doorstep. The culprit is the Fylde Coast Academy Trust, which is being subsidised by the government to take over the dilapidated buildings of a former private school. It's pure empire building by a trust that doesn't even run particularly good schools, Mellor says, noting that one of them is rated as requiring improvement. Worst of all, the opening would disrupt the ecology of the area. 'There's no need for extra primary places here. We all have some empty spaces as it is and losing any pupils is financially disastrous.'

Blackpool's north shore needs new school places, he says, not here in the south of the borough. The favoured free school is getting £7m from the DfE to spend on renovating the premises, yet St Nicholas and the other already-existing schools are short of funds.

He calls in Rachel his business manager and they thumb through the accounts. 'Here!' he says as she hands him the right figures. 'We had £3,604 per pupil in 2011–12 but this year it was down £90 each to £3,514. That's a lot when you multiply it by 400 pupils and add in all the rising costs in those years.' What has he had to cut? 'I had to let four staff go this year, plus one temporary post. There's just nothing left to strip out.'

Why would the government make such a perverse decision? According to Mellor, 'It's pure ideology. It's what they believe, never mind any evidence. I think they like to break things up, break things down, put in anything that feels private.'

Does It Work?

You could take the 'what works' line and say it doesn't matter how academy schools are governed provided they offer children a better start in life. LSE researchers say that the status of primary schools has no effect on how well pupils perform.[11] Other evidence is dubious and the DfE itself said that at Key Stage 2, while 24 per cent of Multi-Academy Trust schools were performing significantly above the national average, 28.6 per cent are significantly below. International comparisons fail to register any academy effect. At the end of 2016, England stood where it did in 2012, middling among the 70 countries tested in the OECD ranking, well behind Finland, Estonia, Ireland and Germany. Average scores for all pupils in England in science and maths have been pretty steady since 2006; 15-year-olds score above average in science, and average for maths and English. Performance isn't the only criterion and the trouble is that other vital questions have become much harder to answer: whether academy schools employ good and happy teachers, offer value for money, treat admissions fairly and don't discriminate – and if not, who is responsible?

So Why Do They Do It?

While the amount spent on schools and healthcare and the size of the public realm of course matters, equally important are unity and coherence in what the state does and what it stands for. Cameron's chilled demeanour persuaded some commentators that he was never 'committed' in an ideological sense but in *Cameron's Coup* we offered contrary evidence. Cameron appointed his close ally, the Cabinet Office minister Oliver Letwin, to give his government ideological rigour. Letwin's credo had been given to him by his mother, politics professor Shirley Letwin, whose dictum said the only important political question since the 18th century had been how big government should be. For Letwin and other Tory leaders the best way to cut it back was to break things apart so that the centre cannot hold: disarray was part of the purpose.

Under Theresa May, things are further confused as promises about grammar schools and technical colleges have been added to the jumble and, with less fanfare, projections of declining per pupil spending. Let's assume she sincerely wants to improve young people's life chances through education. How much more likely she would be to succeed if she acknowledged that schooling is a pristine public function, which demands high levels of accountability, adequate funding and community involvement. Above all, it needs deep awareness that education has to be embedded in a system, in which schools, children's services, buses, meals and sports facilities mesh together in a planned, purposeful way.

Chapter 3

The State's Parlous State

Governing feels like it has been getting harder. Changes in technology, employment and the power of big companies are matched by shifts in behaviour, attitude and expectations, resulting in greater pressure on the decision-takers – though objective comparisons of one era against another are hard to make. As the government struggles to meet these disparate needs, there is a lot of inchoate resentment among the public, as the Brexit vote showed.

Increasingly, people live online; but as well as an escape, the internet can be a site of exploitation, bullying and despair. Meanwhile, population is increasing, with consequences for the number of households with nowhere affordable to live, pressure on school places and the NHS. Solving collective problems is all the harder when people are taught to be more individualist in attitude, to come to public services as if they were consumers, expecting instant, 24/7 click-of-a-mouse responses.

The recession stalled growth in incomes, which have struggled to return to pre-crash levels, even if its effects on employment were muted. Then followed the cuts, capricious and precipitate. Faced with a rising deficit, other paths could and should have been taken – but even within its self-imposed strait-jacket, a modest and stable Tory leadership could have adjusted taxes and spending fairly, rationally, careful not to exert extra pressure on those least able to bear it. Instead, lacking knowledge and modesty, the Cameron government struck out for grandiose schemes such as Universal Credit and HS2, while draining core services.

Governing has become harder because the state has been under assault. Tory ministers indulge in hoary jibes about red tape. They appoint business pals, party donors and ideological fellow travellers to boards, commissions and high places, undermining functions and alienating civil servants.

But such tinkering is much less damaging than insidious, decades-long delegitimation of public service itself. To call it a campaign or project sounds conspiratorial, a feeling backed up by the fact that these things rarely unfold as if according to plan. After all, wasn't Labour, traditionally the party of bigger government, in power for 13 recent years, when it mightily expanded public provision? But under Labour little was done to wage the battle of ideas – and the military metaphor fits. During the past 40 years munitions have been shipped across the Atlantic, while flanking fire has come from the UK media, both mainstream and social. Pick up an ostensibly serious title such as the *Sunday Times* and sample the bias. Journalists' and editors' natural bent is criticism; the state opens itself up to it, and regular National Audit Office and MPs' scrutinies advertise failings. Contrast this with privately owned companies, with legions of lawyers to protect their secrets, and the state is always going to come off worse. Our public service culture doesn't help, silencing officials for fear of transgressing codes of neutrality. They don't speak out, even when they themselves are denigrated and abused – which we discuss in Chapter 6.

The Cuts

The austerity decreed by George Osborne in 2010 cut spending savagely. Which is not to say all spending should have then continued to increase in every category. Imperfect science that it is, budgeting is about priorities, understanding who is affected, knowing where the pressure is being felt. To cut well, you need to be even smarter than in spending well. The Ministry of Defence, for example, has not been clever; the NAO says constraints on funding for its properties are leading it to make decisions that are poor value for money in the longer term as the forces' housing falls into expensive disrepair. Intelligent cutting should not create extra demands for government intervention further down the line. Stupid cutting results in acute shortages of expert staff, as the NAO reported the case to be in the environment department; to remedy the situation, consultants had to be recruited costing £61 million in 2015–16.

If Osborne had meant it when he said *we're all in it together* (words that became one of the decade's great clichés), he would have spread austerity fairly and proportionately. Necessary spending cuts would have been transparent and ordered. Instead, ministers tried to disguise them. They 'devolved the axe', pushing cuts on councils, forcing them to take the opprobrium. For example, councils caught the flak for cutting the number of meals on wheels delivered in England, which fell from 6.7 million to 3.5 million between 2010–11 and 2015–16, despite the fact that over this period the price charged for the service rose by a fifth on average.

The Tory-controlled Local Government Association could not or would not put the blame where it lay.

They cut according to what they could get away with, not what would cause least pain. Individuals, disconnected, powerless to protest, and regions far from London were easy meat – so it was the families on benefits, children, disabled people and old people at home lacking care who suffered. Ministers themselves have been surprised by how far they could go without provoking rebellion.

At the centre of UK government sits the Treasury, an institution that bears much responsibility for shrinkage and dismemberment. Its officials revel at being seen as parsimonious trimmers of candle ends. More accurate charges are that too often in recent decades senior officials surrendered to fashionable and erroneous economic theory, and that the Treasury failed to look at spending in the round or assess the wider and the long-term effects of cuts. It helped ministers cut whatever might make least noise and failed to rein in extravagant 'reform' projects.

How the State Shrank

Since 2010, public spending fell as a proportion of GDP from 45 per cent to 39 per cent in 2017. (Those figures are general government expenditure, on the International Monetary Fund's definition.) It is planned to fall to 36 per cent by 2021. In actual cash outlays, adjusted for inflation, this broadly means that current spending will have stayed about the same at around £680bn from 2010 on, despite growth in population and growth in GDP.

Government employment is falling by 1.1 million between 2010–11 and 2018–19, to about 4.5 million. At a fifth of total employment, the state is already a smaller presence than at any time since the early 1960s. This is at a time when the population is growing, up each year by some 0.8 per cent, rising from 58.2 million people when Labour took power in 1997 to 65.8 million in 2016.

Of course not all cuts have deleterious effects. Some service areas are in the throes of longer-running change, with which austerity has coincided. Spending by fire and rescue authorities in England fell significantly between 2010–11 and 2015–16, resulting in cuts in the number of fire crew sent to incidents. But before 2010, there was a downwards trend in the number of fires and casualties, which is partly due to fire authorities' repositioning to focus on smoke alarms and prevention.

Or take health. In 2010, NHS spending was to be 'protected'. What that meant was that for five years per capita health spending in England increased very slightly, by about £50. But we've been ageing as a population, and therefore need more attention; in fact if you take into account the extra needs of the ageing population the spend per head actually *fell* by £50 and over the decade from 2010 will have fallen by around 8 per cent. On OECD terms, public health spend will fall from just under 8 per cent of GDP in 2015 to 6 per cent in 2020.

The schools budget in 2015–16 was around £40bn, about a third of the NHS spend. Average spending per pupil was largely frozen between 2010 and 2015, despite the vaunted 'pupil premium'. The pupil–teacher ratio remained stable. But from 2015–2020 the IFS projects a real-terms cut in spending of 8 per cent per pupil. As it caustically notes, ministers' press secretaries trumpeted an increase in spending of over 7 per cent, conveniently omitting to mention the 174,000 extra primary and 284,000 extra secondary students. Cash spend is going up (from £5,447 to £5,519) but of course that has to be adjusted for cost increases. These cuts are more damaging, says the Commons Public Accounts Committee (PAC) because many schools have been cut adrift from council advice about workforce and procurement and are making poor decisions about how to cope. Academy schools have been cutting staff costs by 'replacing more experienced teachers with younger recruits and relying on more unqualified staff'.[1]

Wherever you look the figures tell the same story. Civilian staff in the Ministry of Defence fell from 85,000 full-time equivalents in 2011 to 55,000 in 2016, with a further 14,000 jobs to go by 2020. Armed forces' personnel have been falling in number, to 140,000 trained strength by 2016. Cameron took fright at the scale of the cuts and revised defence spending back towards the symbolic level of 2 per cent of GDP, which NATO members are supposed to sustain. This should, in theory, see military strength rise up to 144,000 by 2020, plus 7,000 extra reservists.

Devolving the Axe

Until 2020, today's spending horizon, wounds opened since 2010 in local authorities will fester. Local government spending per person in England fell by 23 per cent between 2010 and 2015. Full-time headcount for councils in England and Wales dropped by 350,000 employees.

But these averages cover up a distinct bias, engineered by Eric Pickles and his successors, in favour of their own constituencies. Real terms spending cuts have been close to zero in Surrey and Hants, but 45 per cent in Salford. (That hasn't turned the Home Counties into paradise; Tory Surrey has complained bitterly at Tory ministers' failure to recognise its need to spend on, for example, social care.) The tenth of councils most dependent on grants to get by (generally the poorest) experienced an average cut in spending of 33 per cent. The tenth least needy councils had their grants cut by only 9 per cent.

Mark Rogers, Birmingham City Council's chief executive, was no sensationalist so it was noteworthy when at the end of 2016 he went on record noting 'catastrophic consequences' for a number of the city's residents. Youth services had 'all but gone'; rough sleeping had quadrupled because of cuts to homelessness prevention; remaining children's centres were for the 'super deprived' only; only elderly people with 'substantial and critical' needs were getting help. The city council had cut staff by 11,500 since 2008, with a further reduction of 4,500 by 2020, leaving it with 8,000 staff compared to 24,500. The central government grant they received had been cut in half.

Similarly, in Manchester, spending on adult social care – a priority for most councils – is being cut by £27m between 2016 and 2019. This follows a general reduction in spending from £682m a year in 2010–11 to £528m a year in 2016, which meant Manchester had to cut its workforce by a huge 40 per cent.

Contrary to claims about 'Big Society', volunteers won't pick up those pieces. Grants to voluntary bodies have also been cut by two thirds. Utopians suggested councils should pass leisure and community centres to volunteers. In a comment on the *Municipal Journal* website, Richard Styles, a local government employee, responded: 'Without a revenue stream for care and maintenance, the asset will become a liability. I have seen this countless times. An asset gets grant funding as it is handed over and then over a period not exceeding 10 years it becomes derelict. It's the Women's Institute school of local government finance (nothing wrong with the WI), that holds to the notion that voluntary groups can buy, run and maintain complex assets and services on a diet of charity shops and whist drives.'[2]

Spending on planning and development in English local authorities has been cut by 46 per cent since 2010. Maintenance budgets have been sliced and diced. The Asphalt Industry Alliance – yes, it is an interested party but its sums are corroborated – valued outstanding road repairs in England at £12bn and stated it would take 14 years to fill all potholes, up from 11 years in 2006. Among the many knock-on effects, the Ramblers Association have found that more than a third of local paths have problems with unsafe gates, potholes and heavy undergrowth.[3]

Meanwhile, spending on children's social work rose, 11 per cent in real terms between 2012 and 2015. But, as always, averages conceal much. In 2014–15, spending ranged from £340 per child in need in one council area to £4,970 per child in another. Projections show funding for early intervention will be cut by 71 per cent over the course of this decade – which means many fewer mothers and babies given help, perpetuating disadvantage and wasting human potential.

Dysfunction and Destruction

Unison, the local government union, an interested but not unreliable source, calculates that some 600 youth centres have been shut since 2010 and 139,000 places on schemes for young people have gone as a result of £387 million being cut by councils from youth budgets. There is a plausible if not provable link between youth work and reducing mental illness and crime. So this is a cut difficult to reconcile with support for Cameron's vanity project, the National Citizen Service, also promoted by his successor. The scheme, based on three-week courses for 300,000 16- and 17-year-olds, is popular with those who do it but will cost £1.1bn by 2020.

The money might be better spent earlier. One in five babies in England has not been seen by health visitors by the time the infant reaches 15 months.[4] Only 2,600 school nurses look after 8.4 million school-age children in England. No wonder they report they have limited time to help children with long-term health needs.

Need isn't static. More children need help from mental health professionals, yet large numbers are now turned away and schools are becoming desperate for support. Four fifths of Child and Adolescent Mental Health Services say that cases now have to be 'severe' before they qualify for any help, and even then waiting times can be up to 200 days. 'I think that is possibly the biggest single area of weakness in NHS provision at the moment,' Jeremy Hunt said. 'There are too many tragedies because children develop eating disorders or psychosis or chronic depression, which is then very difficult to put right as they get older.' The government promised 'parity of esteem' between physical and mental health, but A&E headlines dominate spending patterns. Due to a severe lack of beds, NHS England is sending seriously ill patients with eating disorders to Scotland, many of them teenagers being taken hundreds of miles from home for residential care.[5]

Criminal Justice Criminal

Staffing is a matter of great concern in jails. The ills of the criminal justice system cannot all be blamed on contracting but equally the extraction of profit has contributed nothing to improvement.

Though Labour home secretaries allowed the prison population to rise, they also increased spending so that by 2010 the jails were overcrowded but stable, with fewer suicides and improvement in reoffending. The situation has since declined; the budget has been cut but no effort made to reduce inmate numbers. In five years, the prison service had to contend with major administrative upheavals, contracting out, severe cuts to budgets and staffing and an adamant refusal to reduce offender numbers, which increased to a record 85,583 in England by winter 2016. Staff numbers, meanwhile, dropped from 34,000 to 24,000.

Justice Secretary Elizabeth Truss accepts that there is a causal link to increases in the number of assaults and suicides, which are now up at their highest recorded level. Locked in cells for excessively long hours, one in ten prisoners were self-harming. As the rate of attrition for prison staff is so high, the Ministry of Justice says it will have to target the recruitment of 8,000 employees by 2018 so that the service can hope to have 2,500 extra staff.

Alongside the significant rise in prison suicides, the cuts have resulted in an epidemic of drug misuse behind bars as well as periodic riots. At Birmingham Prison in December 2016, G4S staff ran as trouble brewed, leaving it up to the state in the form of squads of prison staff to restore order; the incident was one among several at other jails. Doubtless intending well, the charity Unlocked, promoted by ex Liberal Democrat minister David Laws, said it wanted to help recruit top graduates to bolster management. 'We need people with a strong sense of social responsibility,' Unlocked said.[6] But they did not add, as they should have done, that social responsibility can only be realised by and through the state. Laws, it might be added, was one of the Liberal Democrats most enamoured of austerity and state reduction when he was a minister in the Cameron coalition.

Magistrates' courts have shut, affecting the speed and fairness with which cases are handled. The Forensic Science Service was abolished in 2012 and since then, says the regulator, spending cuts have damaged the quality of evidence supplied to the courts.[7] Cuts to legal aid mean that getting advice regarding housing or benefits has become difficult or impossible. Since 2010, eligibility for legal aid in divorce and family cases has been removed, with the effect of reducing by 600,000 a year the number of people entitled to civil legal aid, according to the Law Society. Backlogs have increased and the waiting time for a Crown Court hearing increased to 134 days by 2015.

Increased fees have choked off applications to industrial tribunals. As a result, unfair dismissal and discrimination cases have fallen sharply since the £1,200 fees were introduced in 2012, a cost beyond the means of the growing army of low-paid workers in the perilous jobs who require such protection. Since then claims have fallen by nearly 70 per cent, which may have been the intention.[8]

Quality of Life

Arts Council England's grants have been cut by 30 per cent in the five years since 2010. The counter argument runs that the theatre and galleries are booming: people are queuing for returns in Shaftesbury Avenue. But this argument mistakes both the ecology of the theatre (the mainstream stage in London and Stratford relies on thriving companies around England) and the lagged nature of artistic development. Even if students dare take on the debt for an uncertain arts career ahead, the opportunities to grow their skills and gain experience in regional arts networks, sponsored by local authorities and the Arts Council, are vanishing.

Newcastle upon Tyne City Council proposed ending all support to arts groups. Erica Whyman, who for eight years ran Newcastle's Northern Stage Company, does not blame the council leader, Nick Forbes. 'He's caught in an impossible situation', she says, having to balance child protection and social care against street maintenance and support for the array of arts that blossomed in the millennium years along the Tyne, the Baltic and the Sage. They cling on, just. The Live Theatre, Newcastle, the first home of Lee Hall's *The Pitmen Painters*, which went on to tour the world, can now only produce one play a year when it used to stage seven.

Failing to Keep Up

Cuts stall or halt previous progress. Road traffic deaths have been falling over many years, both in number and as a proportion of all accidental deaths. But the decline has stopped and deaths in 2015 were 6 per cent up on 2010.[9] Decreases in police staffing, and particularly the number of dedicated traffic officers, may be a factor here along with over-reliance on enforcement cameras.

Cuts also make an already bad situation worse. Imbalances in UK housing are not new, in particular in the south east of England and hot spots such as Cambridge and Edinburgh. Housing is not fairly taxed; house-builders hoard land; 'planning' is passive and restrictive instead of proactive, imaginative and developmental; and dogma prevents the state –

local and national – building and letting dwellings. The result is widespread hardship and downright waste of human potential.

In the days when the state took responsibility for remedying the permanent failure of markets to supply affordable homes, Emma and Rob Percy could have lived comfortably enough on their income. The Folkestone couple's earnings would once have been adequate for a family with three children to pay the rent on a council or housing association dwelling. Now they have no choice but to pay ever rising sums to serial landlords.

They just about manage, to use Theresa May's notorious phrase, but only because Emma is ingenious. If she dropped her guard for a moment, the family would fail. They have a 1950s three-bedroom house that is warm and comfortable enough. But the rent, at £750 a month, takes up half of Rob's post-tax earnings as a site manager at a local school. They don't qualify for housing benefit. Emma looks enviously at the rent for one of the rare council houses in the area, just £450. 'Paying that much less would make a very big difference to us,' she says, 'but the council told us we didn't stand a chance, not to bother going on the waiting list because we'd never get one.'

For the Percy family, affordability means permanence, security and knowing they won't be moved on yet again from one short-term rental to another. It means never again being forced to move their children out of school and away from friends to start their lives over in a new area.

The story of their married life is now typical of millions. They have never been homeless, never destitute, never reliant on benefits. Their children have never been among the 120,000

Shelter finds homeless at Christmas. But they have often been forced to move, never certain of the roof over their heads.

When their first child was born 14 years ago, they lived above a pub where Rob worked as a chef, but had to move because children weren't allowed in staff quarters. Bromley council offered them a place in a bed-and-breakfast hotel but it was too far from Rob's work. They found somewhere in Ashford where he got a new job, but it was just a six-month let, and the owner ended the tenancy in order to cash in on the house price boom.

They moved in with Emma's parents in Folkestone. When their second child was born, living in one room at her parents was too cramped. The borough council offered them emergency accommodation in a former Salvation Army hostel by the harbour, 'but the toilet in the flat above leaked straight down onto us. It wasn't even cheap, as we had to pay £800 a month.' They found a private let at £700 a month, she went to work part-time at Sainsbury's and they managed. But after the first six months, the landlord put the rent up by £50 – with a warning it would rise another £50 in six months' time.

They had to take the children out of the school they were attending to move to a cheaper home. But here they faced further rent rises. Moving again at the end of the lease, 'the next one was a nightmare, filthy … and for five months in the winter we had a broken boiler, so no hot water or heating, costing £750.'

Rob earns £24,000, and after tax all of it goes on rent, heating, phone, council tax and the car he needs for work. That leaves Emma with £500 a month in tax credits and £190 a month in child benefit to pay for everything else. That's about £150 a week for food, clothes, school meals (£4.20 a day), travel, toiletries and everything else a family of five needs to get by. They haven't had a holiday in years.

'I try to set aside £50 a month for birthdays and Christmas, but that's not easy. All our clothes are second-hand. I switch energy provider every year and that's usually a £20 bonus.'

They have now been in the same house for 18 months. 'We've always paid our rent promptly. We are very careful tenants.' They have plans. Emma is taking an Open University course and hopes to become a teacher, so that once she is earning they will be able to save for a deposit on a house. But 'that's only if house prices don't rise and if interest rates don't rise and if food prices don't go on rising a lot more than our pay over the next years. That's a lot of ifs, isn't it?' As home ownership falls, their generation are the first to be less well off than their parents, and less likely to own a home.

————

There is nothing inherently virtuous in state ownership of large numbers of dwellings. Municipal involvement was and remains an entirely practical matter of remedying gaping deficiencies in supply. The problem with Right to Buy, enforced by Thatcher and her successors, has been the random subsidies it gives a few new homeowners, while wreaking havoc on the public financing of social homes for others.

Who's Responsible for What?

Cuts to resources are only part of the story. The state has long been subject to destructive rearrangement dressed up as 'reform', consuming vast amounts of time and energy. We've already looked in Chapter 2 at the breakdown and complexification of education, and the increasingly convuluted NHS, where the patient pathway now threads incoherently through a jungle of different, often competing bits of the system. The resulting confusion is insidious. When people can no longer map boundaries they detach and may become less willing to pay any tax, let alone pay more.

An example of needless complication is flood insurance. The market won't provide in this area, but Tory ministers, instead of straightforwardly making it a state responsibility, invented a new not-for-profit company. In theory this ambiguous entity (is it or isn't it government?) will step in when Churchill, Aviva or Liverpool Victoria won't cover properties in flood-prone areas, though the scheme still doesn't cover dwellings built after 2009 or any businesses.

Prison governors are to be 'autonomised', so the 2017 prison and courts bill announced. This could be a device to slough off accountability for the effects of spending cuts on jails, handing their managers the blame. Or if governors put the interests of their prison's bottom line first, they may be less willing to collaborate with probation, which itself has been dismembered and contracted out, thwarting efforts to stop reoffending.

We saw how the Cameron coalition built conflicts of interest into how academy schools are run. The same problem afflicts local enterprise partnerships (LEPs). These are wonderful specimens of the administrative exotica created by ministers who would rather do nothing but can't get away with it. In 2010 they summarily abolished the regional economic development agencies: clearing the ground for a market solution. But business in the regions demanded a replacement, hence LEPs, which are committees of local businesspeople who give grants to … local businesspeople. How they are run and financed is opaque.

―――――――

Tracking down, for example, the LEP for Devon and Somerset takes you through the sheds of the Lufton business park to Yeovil Innovation Centre; but it turns out just to be a phone forwarding system. The Heart of the South West LEP has a chief executive but no office – it is hosted by South Somerset District Council.

Among its leading lights is an ex-PricewaterhouseCoopers accountant who used to work for outsourcers Serco and who is now managing director of Supacat, an engineering company that makes most of its money from defence contracting (you could say he personifies the interpenetration of state and markets). Another is the managing director of South West Water, which belongs to Pennon Group, a company that has largely developed on the back of the sale of public assets and contracting out of waste management … one of its acquisitions bears the indicative name of Churngold Holdings.

What's striking about these affiliations isn't that public and private interests align but that people like these and the political milieu they inhabit should cleave to the right, being antagonistic towards government. It's a marked cultural inconsistency, though one that runs through the south west of England. A considerable degree of dependency on government including the European Union is accompanied by ideological attachments to small statism and Leave.

The Heart of the South West LEP has a roster of projects: widening the A382 at Newton Abbot, developing a listed factory building within the Royal William Yard in Plymouth, providing advice to small and medium-sized manufacturing companies … Oops, the last of those is actually paid for by EU Structural Funds. What's puzzling about the list is that the road schemes would have gone ahead anyway, dependent on the Department of Transport's timetable. As for property development, it's far from clear why the LEP should do this when the markets won't.

The LEPs have very thin administrative backup, which is another example of a generic problem. Various Devon and Somerset projects appear to be funded from pre-existing grants, such as the City Deal through which the Department of Communities and Local Government hands money to favoured schemes. The LEPs themselves are disbursing £12bn over the five years to 2020, but under minimal scrutiny. It is hard to tell if they offer value for money. When the NAO investigated, it found they had no obvious aims and objectives so it was difficult 'to assess the extent to which spending money on them contributed to economic growth'.[10] Even the LEPs themselves had 'serious reservations about the increasing complexity of the local landscape'.

Rail privatisation is another such tale of hybrid confusion, to be inscribed on John Major's political tombstone. Like the Bourbons, Cameron and May forgot nothing and learned nothing, and wanted to break up one of the few unifying elements in Network Rail and hand the track to the train companies. 'I want the routes competing with one another,' said Transport Secretary Chris Grayling, fresh from his dismemberment of probation. 'I also want them collaborating with one another.'[11] A proposed line reconnecting Oxford and Cambridge – growth nodes that are crying out for robust, long-term planning of land use and development – is to be excluded from Network Rail altogether, said Grayling. This of course would jeopardise connections with the rest of the railway.

This blindness is not some passing ailment of an individual secretary of state but a congenital condition. The pathology stems from a deep but inarticulate belief that markets will, eventually, sort things out. The invisible hand will fix it, so we need not worry about blurring the line between public and private: in fact the more obscure the demarcation the better.

This explains the insouciance with which ministers (and this was true under Labour too) wink at the rapid movement of consultants from the status of profit-avid private companies one minute to servants of the public interest the next. Through one eye, PricewaterhouseCoopers, Deloitte, KPMG and the other big firms (especially McKinsey) are part of the state; their people have passes that let them into government offices as if they were staff; their partners are intimate with ministers and have permanent secretaries' mobile numbers. Conflict of interest between state and business dissolves and the management consultancies, for example, simultaneously advise policymakers on contracting out and then advise and audit the contractors, playing both sides of the net.

University Bonanza – Public or Private?

Stand on Waterloo Bridge and gaze at the sweep of Somerset House on the north bank of the River Thames. It looks all of a piece, but in fact you are looking at two buildings, on the site of Lord Protector Somerset's mansion: a Georgian original and a 19th-century add-on built to accommodate King's College, the core of London University.

One part used to be occupied by the Inland Revenue; its commissioners used to meet in solemn session in the board-room. It is now run by a trust as a museum and cultural centre. The other part belongs to King's College, but which sector, public or private, does this fall into? The former principal, Rick

Trainor, who went on to become President of Universities UK, said vehemently that 'universities are not part of the public sector and should not be treated as if they were'.[12]

So Somerset House, part of the national patrimony, is divvied up between a board sort of answerable to the Department of Culture, Media and Sport and a university that may once have been but is no longer part of the public sector. Yet it gets its income from fees charged to students for tuition, which they pay by borrowing from the state. In recent years the fee stream has become a mighty river, which pays for the cranes swinging above the King's site; like so many others, this university has embarked on a building spree.

Universities have always had a special, arm's-length relationship with the state, shielded by grants committees, councils and academics' prickly alertness to infringement of their prized autonomy. Until recently there was no doubt they belonged to the broad public realm, like museums, galleries and arts companies, occupying a privileged space in which the state underwrote intellectual freedom. These existing universities are currently fighting against proposals carried over from Cameron to May to allow more (genuinely) private sector universities to set up.

Universities issue bonds, in order to build student accommodation and boost their income. The National Accounts say they are private sector 'non-profit institutions' so these bonds will not add to public sector net debt. But purchasers assume that the state will guarantee them and they are right. 'Given the public service nature of universities' roles,' says the OBR, 'it is possible that if one or more were to default on their bonds, the liabilities could ultimately be transferred to government.' That financial ambiguity is mirrored in the corporate behaviour of universities, which is often extravagant, and also among academics, many of whom resent having to demonstrate any public 'impact' for their work. This, too, is a form of privatisation.

Universities have aped the private sector in worsening conditions for many of their staff. The Russell Group of top universities relies on precarious work contracts. More than half – 53 per cent – of staff are employed on temporary or non-permanent short-term contracts. At the other end of the scale, vice chancellors' average salaries have risen 14 per cent during austerity years – to £272,432 – and some are now paid hugely inflated sums.

The bonanza comes from the £9,000-plus now paid by all students in yearly tuition fees. They borrow from the state-owned Student Loans Company, so universities take on none of the risk of bad debts. The IFS says 70 per cent of today's students will never repay in full. Their aggregate debt will reach £100bn in 2018 and increase to £330bn (in 2014–15 prices) by the 2030s. It's a transaction between generations from which the state has been edged out, resulting in young people burdening themselves to pay interest on the glitzy buildings in which they were once taught.

A Bridge Too Far?

The blurring of the private and public sectors extends across many spheres. From King's College's new terraces overhanging the river, you can see the line of what Joanna Lumley envisions as the 'garden bridge'. It's a brilliant example of (deliberate) obfuscation about what is and isn't public. Promoted as a purely private enterprise, needing not a penny from taxpayers, from the outset the bridge siphoned off public money, starting with £30m from the Department of Transport to pay consultants to draw up a plan.

Some people found the very idea of colonising the River Thames objectionable. No, said the promoters, the people will be able to cross our bridge, except for when we will be holding money-making parties and dinners and, by the way, we won't let buskers and cyclists over either.

Subsidies were paid from the promoters' friends in government and, during Boris Johnson's term as mayor, in City Hall. George Osborne – otherwise such an avid saver of public spending – ordained the support, despite huge uncertainty as to whether the promised £150m of private donations would ever materialise.

The bridge illustrates this casual transfer of public areas into private use and ownership. Canary Wharf and shopping malls up and down the country also illustrate the phenomenon. What looks and feels like a place open to – belonging to – the public is policed by private uniformed patrols; at 6 or 8 p.m. the shutters come down and it's closed off. Security guards are instructed to remove anyone behaving in an unseemly fashion, such as mounting a protest.

The *Guardian* mapped the phenomenon through crowd-sourced data.[13] 'Streets and open spaces are being defined as private land after redevelopment. It is now a standard feature of urban regeneration. One of the biggest public squares in Europe – Granary Square, in the new development around King's Cross – is privately owned. There are privatised public zones across Britain, from Brindley Place in Birmingham to Liverpool One.'

City Hall near Tower Bridge is home to London's mayor and assembly and the area around it throngs with tourists. But the 13-acre More London estate is owned by a Kuwaiti property company. The estate managers impose conditions on access and use, and even for some years restricted filming, including TV interviews with the politicians inhabiting the building.

Whose Sewage Is This?

Willed ambiguity is not just apparent above ground, either. The Cameron government created a special purpose company, called Tideway, underpinned by Treasury guarantees, to work on behalf of privately owned Thames Water and construct a £4.2bn tunnel to carry sewage in parallel with the river. Thames Water belongs to a shifting cast of international investors, including Canadian teachers' pension funds and shadowy Chinese corporations that, automatically, are supervised by the Communist Party. So here we have the UK state entering into occluded, ambiguous contracts with a private company whose profitability ultimately benefits the Chinese state. Odd, to say the least, when cheaper finance could be raised directly by the British state. Odder still, if it turns out there was no genuine need for this mammoth project, beyond profits to the companies involved. The nature of the public financial guarantees has been examined more than once and the National Audit Office is rightly anxious about the huge contingent liabilities being foisted on the taxpayer.

We talked to Sir Ian Byatt, the former Treasury official who became the first head of the Office of Water Services, Ofwat, regulator of the privatised water industry. He was in favour of the new regime for water and sewerage but now feels things have gone too far. Neither the fish in the Thames nor households will benefit, he says. 'Governments get hooked on big projects, like HS2 or Hinckley Point, when usually a series of smaller ones would do the job better and cheaper.'

He won't say whether this is really the government's *folie de grandeur* or financiers spotting an opportunity to make huge gains. In 2005, Labour appointed Chris Binnie, a leading water engineer, to examine pollution levels in the Thames. He proposed the super sewer, but has now recanted. Water in the Thames already meets EU standards, but Tideway managed to alarm ministers with unwarranted warnings of untreated sewage pouring into the river. However precedent suggests that simpler, local projects could take care of the problem of run-off after heavy rainfall. Byatt notes, for example, that treatment plants at Beckton and Lee Tunnel have been extensively modernised, as opposed to whole new systems being built.

Even Byatt, a cautious civil servant, gives a straightforward answer to the question of who gains. 'Thames Water is an incredibly complicated company. There will be an array of extra dividends sliced and diced into the pockets of all these different interests along the way.' Paying needlessly higher interest rates, the cost of the super sewer will be added to all Thames Water customers' bills. Those customers have no choice but to pay, despite the fact that those in Oxfordshire – or anywhere except central London – will not see any of the benefits of it.

The Dogma Behind Dismemberment

There's more to dismemberment than securing financial gains for friends and political allies. Cuts, privatisation, the willed disorganisation of government, all relate to a body of beliefs. In *Cameron's Coup* we took issue with the notion of the Tory prime minister as a mere pragmatist, citing the densely Thatcherite climate in which he assumed political identity. Unlike her, he was never likely to reach for a dog-eared copy of Friedrich von Hayek's *The Road to Serfdom*, yet his instincts were no less ideological. Cameron's *summa theologica* was the 2011 Open Public Services white paper. It was a tract for the 'public bad, private good' gospel. Public services cause 'damage'. They 'grip'. They are 'monopolistic'. Bureaucracy 'overrules'. 'Our mission', he said plainly, 'is to dismantle Big Government'. A key phrase was 'any qualified provider': when public sector work was up for grabs, private companies should be first in line to bid and win.

Writers tracing the genealogy of anti-statist ideas quibble over labels such as neo-liberal, neo-conservative or classical liberal. They are wrong if they think it's merely an intellectual contest, in which fine distinctions matter. Ideas don't dominate because they are good or workable; intellectual history is not Darwinian natural selection. The winners, in politics at least, are the mounts with the richest owners, the thinking propagated with the most energy and money behind it.

It's also a disadvantage that ideas in and around government tend towards abstraction and complexity. Take 'the state' itself, or 'accountability'. How much easier to say it should all be as easy as buying a track from iTunes, and anything more difficult than that is 'bureaucratic'. An audience that's bored or stupefied will favour black and white, declarative arguments.

Brexit was ostensibly simple: a binary choice. You heard from both right and left – 'don't tell me it's complicated'. Simple ideas are wanted here and few ideas are clearer than markets (shopping for groceries is the commonest citation) versus the taxing, money-wasting, complicated and oppressive state.

It won't do, however, to exaggerate the consistency or rigour of marketeers. A Tory who carries the Thatcherite flame aloft is Liam Fox, a leader of the Leave campaign and keen anti-statist. No sooner was he in the non-job of secretary for international trade than he started telling business executives it was their 'duty' to export. Duty? Markets recognise no such thing, only profit and loss. The duty of business is moneymaking and how that is done, at home or abroad, is merely contingent.

Right Thinking

The supremacy of anti-public sector ideas in recent times relies on transmission mechanisms. One of most subtle has been the management consultancies, notably McKinsey, another the nominally independent but actually deeply partisan think-tanks. The founders of the Adam Smith Institute, Madsen Pirie and Eamonn Butler, infiltrated the Tory government in the 1980s through stealth and American money, and wrote a book extolling their success; they were followed later by business-funded groups such as the Taxpayers' Alliance. Margaret Thatcher seized on the pro-privatisation, anti-government slogans that the Smithites – able publicists – supplied.

Another group of pals – Nick Boles, Francis Maude and Michael Gove – launched the thinktank Policy Exchange in 2002. It styled itself as 'modernising', but the ideas were mostly reactionary – reinstate grammar schools (now enthusiastically endorsed by Theresa May), cut taxes and sack town and country planners. Policy Exchange enjoyed some influence when Cameron was prime minister; you can connect up the dots between it and his government's cuts in housing benefit and welfare changes.

Anti-statist ideas 'made the weather', particularly through economics. Practitioners of the discipline deny their subject is ideological, preferring to clothe themselves in the mantle of science. Yet economic models, no matter how sophisticated the mathematics they employ, rest on a priori assumptions. What gets taken for granted in much economic reasoning is the predominance of transactions, exchange, buying, selling and explicit individual choices based on a pared-down notion of self-interest. Prizes are awarded to thinkers who blame government for getting in the way of market perfection – academics such as Ronald Coase, the British-born American economist who said lighthouses should be run by private companies, opposed regulating taxis and thought pollution was a price worth paying for profit.

If, over a long career, such a 'scientist' never once addressed the facts of income and wealth inequality or, in markets, the everyday imbalance of bargaining power between employers and employees, you might think his qualification for a Nobel Prize was debatable. But Coase (and there are many others like him) illustrates the potency of a line of thinking about the world that not only helps explain the 2008 crash ('markets are always efficient') but also explains why antagonism to the state has become so prevalent.

If markets are always efficient, then no wonder management consultants and gurus get away with preaching the testament of competition, preferably involving opportunities for private contractors. They assume a natural order of things; wellbeing will be maximised, as long as people are free to pursue profit. Touched by the magic, market theorists look at a school or hospital – even a police force – and glibly say that if they fail tests of competitiveness or effectiveness they will be swept away, and new ones will spring up in their stead, just like that.

This mentality was displayed most starkly first in western responses to the collapse of Communism in the Soviet Union and Eastern Europe, then in the invasion of Iraq. The pat American assumption that after invasion, society and markets would just spring up – a belief that Tony Blair bought into – was exposed as false, but it lingered on in approaches to the Arab spring, the toppling of Gaddafi in Libya and the crisis in Syria. In *Age of Fracture*, Princeton history professor Daniel Rodgers talks about 'the era's sense of foreshortened time' that mirrored its 'new image of the global markets' instant capacities for adjustment [and] the new managerial rhetoric of quick response and flexible production'.[14] In reality, history shapes institutions over the long haul, taking time to fashion and consolidate. And, like limbs, many organisations, once severed, don't grow back.

When the state did not wither away naturally, anti-statists turned to subversion. It's no surprise that the bundle of ideas called New Public Management (NPM) won favourable attention in the US, where distrust of government and dislike of taxation is hardwired into both the constitution and political practice. What is puzzling, however, is the unquestioning adoption of the recipe in the United Kingdom, where principles of a welfare state remain strongly implanted.

The key text for anti-statist preachers is the book by David Osborne and Ted Gaebler, *Reinventing Government*. Public bodies should embrace the market and outsource functions; managers should become risk-takers and entrepreneurs ... just like (an idealised version of) the directors of private companies. The book extolled 'the most revolutionary idea of our time – an idea whose time has come. Government does not have to be a gigantic and inefficient bureaucracy. Instead, it can govern by tapping the tremendous power of the entrepreneurial process and the force of the free market.' They must have known, and experience since has confirmed, that 'tapping' is a weasel word: the force of the free market destroys government capacity and entrepreneurs are usually unsuited by temperament and skills to conduct the business of government.

New Public Management

NPM hit the UK just as Margaret Thatcher consolidated her command of the Tory party in the 1980s and lieutenants such as Nigel Lawson pushed the freeing of financial markets and housing from regulation – leading to, among other things, the crash and dangerous price inflation. In 1989, a year after Lawson's big bang, the Tories published the white paper 'Working for Patients', which outlined the introduction of an internal market in the NHS and became law as the NHS and Community Care Act 1990. The Health and Social Care Act 22 years later was yet another attempt to impose the doctrine of the internal market, which had been applied across services. During those years, the mantras that *markets are competitive* and that *competition drives progress* were drummed into public managers' brains. Even (especially) during the great public services boom of 2001 to 2009, management consultants were raking in fees from telling the public sector to be more like companies. They are still at it in the NHS and local government today.

New Labour ministers were enthusiastic adepts. Blair's mantra was 'reform': what he meant was bringing in private companies. To save the patient the doctor must first kill her: deconstructing public services was a necessary precondition for generating public support to spend on them. During Blair's second term Alan Milburn made a canonical speech. Initially he ruled out the marketisation of criminal justice (subsequently, Labour home secretaries pushed to bring private firms into managing prisons), but stated that 'when it comes to the provision of other services, such as health or education, they do not need to be exclusively provided by the state. Indeed as the state's role evolves from one of exclusive provider to becoming more of a purchaser, schools and hospitals, alongside councils and surgeries, should be able to enjoy more autonomy within the public sector. And new providers will be able to join them from outside.'[15]

In the face of such a confident expression of the Zeitgeist, public sector boards and executives surrendered, unable or unwilling to push back. However, New Public Management did not triumph everywhere. In Scotland, even before devolution, it gained less ground and after the Scottish parliament was established the 'internal market' in health was scrapped. Scotland also has no academy schools (which come straight from the Osborne and Gaebler playbook).

In England, however, the doctrine prospered – despite the absence of empirical confirmation that it worked, indeed in the presence of mounds of evidence contesting both its premises and its claims of success. The Cameron 2012 Health Act, shamefully supported by the Liberal Democrats, showed the theory in all its malign simplicity. The more autonomous and 'entrepreneurial' the prison governor, school head or GP consortium, the less likely they are to coordinate with what remains of the probation or education or health service, let alone work with council housing departments, which don't have accommodation to offer anyway, or work and pensions offices, which have less and less time for needy ex-offenders.

And it goes on. One bit of the public sector 'commissions' another to provide a service but the provider may then 'contract' with a private company for all or part of the service. In practice the words mean the same and in the resulting confusion, people lose confidence. Yet the doctrine keeps its grip. MPs, rightly concerned about flooding, could have focused on spending money where it was immediately needed, and on flood prevention for the future. Instead they recommended a new grand-sounding National Flood Commissioner who would secure services from a new English Rivers and Coastal Authority.[16] This is classic NPM: fragment and conquer. Creating subordinate units is often the first stage on the path to contracting the service out.

The Rise of Individualism

NPM says that citizens are customers. Forget duties and civic identity. Collective decision-making in the common interest is old-fashioned: as customers we will pick and choose. Customers … of the police, courts, prisons, HMRC, parking attendants. Too many public bodies condoned this nonsense on stilts. Yet in NHS trusts up and down England you see this phrase repeated: 'The patient is at the core and centre of everything we do.' Of course staff should focus on care but patients are more than individuals; they belong to families, to places, to classes and localities. The Care Quality Commission demands that hospitals and in-community providers continually ask only one thing: how was it for you; give us your personal response.

In local government as well, the preferred style has become individualistic. People are rarely asked about their sense of the fairness of arrangements or how services broadly serve an area or community.

The truth is that public services can never just be about 'you'. They are about distributing benefits on the basis of need. Need, stemming from disadvantage and an unequal distribution of life chances, is asymmetrical. If patients knew as much as clinicians, they would not have to attend clinics. The NHS must be about attempting, within constrained budgets, to address need for treatment as mediated by professional judgment, which again is asymmetrical. Of course relationships are personal and individual, between patient and clinician, service user and therapist. But those relationships take place within a collective context, and that is what has been degraded and ignored.

Now, as the chill winds blow, it's the right time to talk a different language, and start emphasising the collective and common benefits of services. Not 'me' but 'us'.

Chapter 4

Contracting Out

Marketeers have long pushed the line that the state is burdensome and should get off our backs. They have also been saying that firms can do what government does and do it better. Begun for a variety of reasons – ideology, desperation, genuine practical evaluation of alternatives and fashion – contracting has triumphed, hollowing public services out.

Walk down the street on bin day and that refuse lorry belongs to – or more usually is leased by – Veolia, SITA, Biffa or Serco. That bus is run by Stagecoach or Arriva or some other franchisee, the driver's terms and conditions determined by its pursuit of profit. Here's a government office. The front desk staff have G4S or similar as their insignia: what connection do they have to the functions and identity of the department they are gatekeeping for? At the reception in a big department on Whitehall we ask for Vicky Smith. 'Don't know her, not on the phone list,' says the receptionist. Ten minutes later Vicky Smith comes looking for her visitor. 'Oh, she's listed as *Victoria* Smith,' explains the receptionist. A slight apology follows, but why should she know or care about the department's staff?

Over the past two decades private companies have taken over a multiplicity of services formerly regarded as intrinsically 'public'. Unless they are keen students of badges, NHS patients will usually have no clue who is looking after them; even the obvious signpost of the NHS logo can mislead, as firms try to appropriate it. NHS contracting is worth some £54bn a year, paying for beds, procedures, diagnostics and ambulances.

In 2014–15, the public sector spent £242bn a year with private and voluntary sector suppliers, considerably more than it did on its own staff (£194bn). Contracting accounts for one pound in every three of total government spending.[1] This makes for a tangled web between the two sectors. For example, the National Savings and Investment brand that backs premium bonds remains public, but the people who process them work for Atos, a French public services company. The contract used to be held by Siemens – no longer an engineering company, but still largely German-owned. The roster of public work done privately runs through rail franchisees, the ubiquitous Virgin, to air search and rescue, maintaining nuclear submarines, training military pilots and assessing people's disability and their right to support from the state.

During Labour's love affair with marketisation, the business secretary John Hutton welcomed a report from the American economist DeAnne Julius who went as far as saying 100 per cent of services could theoretically be contracted. Though such a proposition is both theoretical and practical nonsense, the contracting boom is far from over. In its 2017 plan, NHS Improvement states that the NHS has underutilised the private sector, and it wants to see more independent sector providers. Justin Crowther, head of healthcare at Catalyst corporate finance, says confidently, 'Despite the political rhetoric, the trend to outsourcing with the private sector continues.'[2] For companies such as GenesisCare, offering cancer diagnosis (using NHS-trained personnel), it's a two-way bet. Even if the NHS can't afford to use their units – *especially* if the NHS can't afford it – then longer waiting lists will lead more patients to seek out the private sector.

Contracting is also still increasing among local councils. The value of outsourcing contracts signed by UK local authorities in the first half of 2016 increased by 84 per cent; outsourcing contracts signed by councils in the first six months of 2016 increased to £684.9m. While IT is the biggest spend, other areas where private firms are now common are facilities management, defence work, professional services and construction. And as we have discussed in the previous chapter, private providers have expanded in the social care, probation, prisons and custody services.

More Than a Technical Exercise

It has suited contractors to pass this revolution off as merely technical, an exercise in practical public administration – no need to worry about what it might mean for politics or civic identity, let alone perceptions of the state. Look, they say, it's a continuum. Local authorities spend around a quarter of their annual expenditure – worth £45bn – on procuring goods and services from third parties. Even in the heyday of council house building, local authorities and development corporations used firms and did not lay bricks themselves. Tradespeople competed to supply the Royal Navy with rum and sailors in the 18th century. The state has always been involved with suppliers, so there is no real difference between buying software, hiring in lawyers and signing a contract with Amey to maintain the traffic lights.

A small NHS trust or council can't afford to employ its own lawyers or property experts so contracting gives access to specialised services. Similarly, the state has been bereft of IT specialists for a long time and has little choice but to buy them in from contractors. They can, in principle, introduce new, better ways of working; consultants and interims can fill a short-run demand for extra bodies. You have to ask, however, if the £1.3bn spent on consultants in 2014–15 by central government was excessive and an indicator the state had simply lost too many bodies and too much brainpower. Under the Labour government independent treatment centres for routine cataract and hip surgeries were a useful expedient for driving down waiting lists while the NHS retooled.

It's practical, there's no ideology driving it, say its defenders: if IT or customer servicing can be done more cheaply or effectively on a contract, why not? This tone of common sense has been heard in various official reviews under both Labour and the Tories, for example Sir Peter Gershon's efficiency review in 2004: 'It's obvious, isn't it?'

But underneath these pragmatic propositions are questions of principle, about boundaries and proportions. Contracting on today's scale involves profound changes in the nature of the public realm. Contrary to claims that it is merely a practical solution, contracting has been pushed by dogmatists who insist that government is inherently incapable and costly, and that private firms are necessarily more efficient. The full history of the crusade to advance the doctrine has yet to be written: in it, the Big Four consultancies, IBM and company-supported thinktanks would be in the front ranks. Not to put too fine a point on it, people outside and inside government saw a chance to make money. The 'right to contract' – asserted by Tory ministers and the Confederation of British Industry (CBI) – runs parallel to the right to buy council houses: it too is a means of shifting state assets and revenue into private hands.

Friends and Allies

Contractors become friends and allies. Ruby McGregor-Smith, until 2016 chief executive of Mitie, which cleans government offices and runs immigration removal centres, sits in the House of Lords as a Tory peer and is on the board of the Department for Education.

It would be conspiratorial to say Andrew Lansley or Alan Milburn before him plotted to marketise the entire NHS. Equally it would be naïve not to hear the relentless throb of management consultants, lobbyists, ministers and regulators constantly telling the NHS that there has to be more competition, that private firms do better and that 'world-class commissioning' (a stupid, Labour-era phrase) would justify splitting public healthcare into uncoordinated pieces.

Not all free-market advocates are keen on dissolving boundaries between public and private, however. In his book *Capitalism and Freedom*, Milton Friedman strongly commends clear separation of political and economic power. One practical reason for caution is that the closer the relationship between government and suppliers, the stronger the temptation to corruption. Joint ventures and arm's-length bodies create opportunities for companies to dangle persuaders such as future jobs or board positions before government ministers, and for councillors and senior officers to seek a payoff.

Poacher can turn gamekeeper with dizzying speed; contract-writer becomes contractor in the blink of an eye. Health has lately become a regular swap shop. Simon Stevens promoted contracting out when he was inside government as a Number 10 adviser and at the Department of Health, then went over to the private side to deliver contracts as chairman of United Healthcare Europe, a branch of the American giant – and now he is in charge of NHS England. Officials and ministers, Labour as often as Tory, move seamlessly from the top floors of departments to contractors' C-suites.

Call the Commissioner

Behind contracting lies New Public Management doctrine. It takes a green baize view of the world: organisations are like billiard balls. The state is broken up into disconnected units, which bounce off one another. This one 'provides', the other commissions. Through contracts – so the theory runs – rival providers will compete to drive down price. (Quality is another story.) In practice, commissioning foments distrust, befuddles the public and absorbs time, money and energy.

The doctrine was applied by John Birt when he was director general of the BBC in the 1990s. In its internal market, a radio producer wanting a book from the BBC library was charged. If she didn't like the price she could buy it from Waterstone's, which in the billiard ball world would encourage the library to become more efficient and win back the business. The result was confusion, a threat to the library's existence and a mountain of chitties. We spoke to council chiefs bemoaning the 'paper chase of invoices' as one organisation sells to another. Indeed the weakest link in the doctrine is that it creates many more transactions. Academy schools spend huge amounts of time writing invoices for grass cutting and playing field maintenance, as well as for safe-guarding training and teacher assessment, all of which used to be automatically provided by the council.

The bane of the NHS is now the diversion of millions of pounds into contract writing and bidding, with lawyers engaged by one NHS trust to threaten litigation against another and even, absurdly, talk of sending bailiffs in to redeem outstanding debt.

Private contractors have moved into the clinical commissioning groups to deal with payments to, and assessment of results from, hospitals and surgeries. Yes, that's two lots of commissioning, one on top of another. The NHS relied on contractors to help manage the contract with Capita for processing data from GPs for wider use within the NHS: perhaps it's no wonder the contract collapsed in acrimony. Having two lots of private companies providing services in between the accountable public body and the public obscures accountability and opens the door to waste, as both companies are profiting every step of the way.

The Contradiction of Contracting

The contracting boom is based on a contradiction. Contractors step in because the state is deemed not cheap or efficient enough. But contracting only works if the state is efficient and economical in writing contracts and supervising how private firms carry them out. Unless contracts are specified in the greatest detail, and cover every contingency, unless they are monitored, checked and supervised, the model breaks down. Contracts have to be complex not because firms are malevolent or greedy, but because competitive free enterprise literally has no place for trust, let alone for an ethos of public service. The driver on the Stagecoach bus is not a public servant: she takes her orders from a depot manager who has a profit target to reach. Stay at the bus stop too long (to give an old dear a few more minutes to get on board) and the firm's supply model breaks down. And the contract also has to be monitored from the public side: the council, Transport for London or the passenger transport authority has not only to check the company is doing what it promised, but all the time they must also be making mental notes about replacing the incumbent firm with a rival; without that caveat the model doesn't function.

Not that companies accept the model. We know a public body that lost patience with failures on a facilities management contract, including having to put plastic buckets in meeting rooms to collect drips from a leaking pipe, and tried to cancel the contract. But the company involved wouldn't accept the recommissioning and brought in highly paid QCs and tried to claim it had a 'right' to a contract extension.

Proponents of contracting are wont to blame failures on inadequate commissioning, rather than the model itself. That's as correct as the proposition that in a shunt, the vehicle behind is always at fault for failing to maintain a braking distance. But managing contracts, let alone writing them, is fiendishly complicated because a wise organisation should never assume suppliers are going to be reliable over the contract's life. That means they must specify everything in brain-aching detail.

For the model to work, suppliers have to jostle in a competitive market, driving down the cost in order to secure the contract. This is often fanciful. The Institute for Government notes that 'markets', as they are confidently described, are in fact often rigged into cartels and even monopolies. At best, in fields such as IT, 'what happens is we tend to get the oligopoly – the same suppliers bidding', said a Cabinet Office official. Very few civil servants feel they have access to a wide enough range of suppliers. By their nature and background, public sector staff can never know enough to anticipate markets, or to form judgments about what a company could or could not do – which puts them at a permanent disadvantage. How can they know in advance about, say, companies' tax affairs? Surely one requirement from any company bidding for public funds should be absolute tax honesty and transparency, since taxes are paying for that contract.

The Great PFI Debacle

In essence, the Private Finance Initiative (PFI) is a form of contracting that relieves a firm of competition. A contractor builds a school, say, or a refuse disposal plant, by borrowing the money, and gets a very long contract for maintaining the building. In the PFI contract the council or NHS trust agree to cover the (high) borrowing charges plus the ongoing maintenance. The contractor promptly refinances the deal, opening up an attractive gap between what they get and what the public body is locked into paying.

Given that the state can always borrow more cheaply itself, PFI deals are almost by definition worse value. But advocates claimed that the private sector could not only build but manage better than the state, and the Treasury sanctioned deals because they concealed capital spending.

One of the first was the road bridge to Skye opened under John Major in 1992; it was late, ran £10m over budget and caused instant outrage because the consortium that built it sought to profit by charging an £11.40 return toll, fourteen times the price of crossing the Forth Road Bridge (which was twice the length). By the time local protests forced the Scottish government to buy it back at a cost of £27m in 2004, the PFI had gathered £33.3m in tolls against operating costs of just £3.5m.

The head of an Enfield school complained to us about having to negotiate every new toilet roll holder from the school's PFI contractor. In some schools, parents' evenings had to be abandoned because the contractors insisted on exorbitant out-of-hours fees. Hospitals found they couldn't change the use of wards or operating theatres. In some deals, the cleaners, porters, repairs and facilities operators were employed by the contractor and not the institute itself: tiny changes to contracted terms brought steep penalty charges and a ward sister had no power to ask a porter or a cleaner for anything.

PFI boomed under Labour, which rushed ahead for the best of reasons. Chancellor Gordon Brown declared that in reconstruction it was PFI or bust and thanks to the devious device hundreds of thousands of pupils are now being educated in new and modernised schools. The NHS estate still relies on pre-1948 buildings, but much less so than before the boom in construction from 2000 – and similarly with prisons.

Rising above the bustle of Commercial Road in London's East End with all its dense urbanness and ethnic diversity is the PFI's Royal London Hospital. In a very different part of the city, near Euston, soars the tower block housing the rebuilt University College Hospital. Thanks to PFI, both emerged with fine new facilities – plus colossal debts and an ultra-complex web of contracts and maintenance arrangements. A £200m deal rebuilt the Norfolk and Norwich University Hospital in

2006; after completion, borrowings increased to £300m, to give the original investors a £100m dividend. However, to meet the finance charges, 450 jobs were threatened, prompting the Tory chair of the Public Accounts Committee, Edward Leigh, to echo Ted Heath in saying this was the 'unacceptable face' of capitalism.

Unaffordable PFI debt engendered at the Queen Elizabeth Hospital in Woolwich upended the whole local health economy and only vigorous local protest stopped the closure of the successful Lewisham Hospital to try to pay for it. Critics complained that PFI builders had every incentive to inflate the cost and grandiosity of the schemes: the M25 could have been widened by using the hard shoulder at a cost of £478m instead of the PFI scheme that involved building new lanes costing £5bn. Some deals became bywords for excess.

After the crash, PFIs dried up as bank lending to consortia ceased. Rightly eager to keep the economy going with capital projects, Labour absurdly lent £2bn to PFI schemes to build schools, which ended up costing far more than if the state had borrowed and spent the money itself. In opposition, George Osborne promised 'to remove the perverse incentives that result in PFI simply being used to keep liabilities off the balance sheet ... The current system – heads the contractor wins, tails the taxpayer loses – will end.' Once in power, however, he succumbed to the Treasury equivalent of loan sharking. Some 61 schemes worth a total of £6.9bn began in his first year as chancellor. He also changed the inflation up-rating in PFIs so public bodies got a lower rate than PFI contractors.

PFI deals continue being made – there are some 600 in operation. The later deals are supposed to be better structured than the earlier PFI splurge between the early 1990s and mid 2000s.

But according to the Whole of Government Accounts, in March 2015 £150bn was outstanding in PFI payments, with many payments stretching far into the future. For example, payments will be due every year on Manchester's waste disposal plant until 2034. Accommodation for service families at Aldershot barracks and elsewhere will still be paid for until 2041.

Contracting and Doctrine

PFI became a byword for complexity: the less officials and the public understood, the more generous the terms of the contract. Yet contracting was meant to simplify things. A Whitehall department gets rid of its cleaners and Mitie comes in. Cheaper, and no one has to worry till the contract is up.

But what does 'clean' mean; how often should waste bins under desks be emptied; who is to assess the sheen of the polish? A council contracts out environmental services, but what is the specification for grass cutting – how often, with what regard to sustainability? A profit-seeking firm will be motivated, according to the logic of markets, to minimise costs, cut corners, fulfil only the minimum contract terms. The antidote is detail: cleaning means using x disinfectant, spending y minutes per ward – and under the beds, but someone forgot to write down behind cupboards. How do you enforce such terms, without making contract management itself exorbitant?

The answer should of course be trust. But, as we see in the case study below, why should the state trust Mitie or G4S? Besides, what has trust got to do with competition and creative destruction, as prophesied by the anarcho-capitalists?

As it has turned out, contracting has made the provision of public services more not less complex.

Complexification Behind Bars

Unlike Pentonville or Lewes or Victorian jails that look like urban fortresses, Bronzefield Prison is a group of low-rise buildings set in a grassy park in suburban Ashford in Surrey. It is still a prison: fencing, doubled in parts, is high. Entry to the most secure wings is through multiple gates. As in every prison, staff wear heavy belts sagging under the weight of the many keys. Still, with its vegetable garden, landscaping and low-rise brick blocks, it looks the model of a modern jail.

The staff on reception and in the wings are not public employees. They work for Sodexo Justice Services, which also runs prisons in Peterborough and Northumberland. It is one division of a French company that does 'quality of life services' and employs 35,000 staff in the UK. They run military bases, maintain buildings and grounds, operate school and hospital kitchens; Sodexo staff are cleaners and porters. And this is a far from exhaustive list: Sodexo also sterilises NHS equipment, runs car parking and provides staff for reception desks, and many other jobs besides.

Some might object to a private firm locking up the women offenders at Bronzefield on the grounds that deprivation of liberty should be a matter for the state alone: it's too sensitive a public function to be alienated to a profit-seeking company, British or French. Others, cynical or realist, might ask whether Bronzefield's inmates care who turns the key; they are there for the duration and whether the beefy (male) officer is employed by Sodexo or the Ministry of Justice via HM Prison and Probation Service is immaterial.

Actually it does matter – to offenders, their relatives and the public – for good reasons, especially its effect on the idea and practice of 'the public'. At Bronzefield, as elsewhere in contracted-out services, lines of accountability become tangled skeins. To promote rehabilitation, prison staff would need to work more closely with probation officers, families, addictions services, the Department of Work and Pensions (DWP); unfortunately, contracting inhibits collaboration. Try and write 'cooperation' into a commercial contract and see how far you get.

If an inmate gets ill at Bronzefield – drug problems are rife throughout the prison estate – she will be referred to a sickbay run on a separate contract by a primary healthcare provider, commissioned by NHS England. Which turns out to be Sodexo, who also do health. The manager of the primary care unit – herself an NHS-trained nurse – is beholden to the company's bottom line.

But if a woman at Bronzefield is depressed or has mental health issues, she is referred to another provider within the prison, which is an NHS mental health trust.

Already one of the major attributes of contracting is evident – its contribution to complexification. Contracting makes the public sector harder to read and accountability becomes tougher to pin down, despite a proliferation of regulators. In the case of prisons, there is HM Inspectorate of Prisons and the Independent Monitoring Board, as well as the Care Quality Commission for health. More time has to be spent on liasion, linkage and transactions, either between the various contractors or between commissioners and contractors – time that might be more profitably spent on rehabilitation. Trust between staff – a vital prerequisite of the jail running effectively or even at all – takes longer to build when cost and profitability are so prevalent.

Contracting – the Solution to What?

Contractors have no magic formula for costs. Savings come either by paying staff less, by cutting their pension entitlements or by employing fewer of them and, if you can, derecognising their trade unions. But in prisons, as even Tory justice secretaries now admit, fewer staff means increasing problems with drugs, suicides, discipline and rehabilitation. This iron law linking staff numbers to quality of service applies across the public sector.

Extraordinarily little evidence underpins the contracting boom: anecdote and assertion, yes; objective data, no. Decisions have been made casually, even mindlessly.

When in 2004 Labour health secretary John Reid said he did not want private provision in NHS hospitals to exceed 15 per cent of today's NHS total, he might as well have wet his finger and held it in the wind. His predecessor Patricia Hewitt had mentioned 12 per cent, again with no rhyme or reason. It was a political calculation, about pleasing Prime Minister Tony Blair without riling Labour supporters.

The Institute for Government's Tom Gash – who is as clued up as anyone – had to reach back to the 1980s for credible figures on savings, and those came from the first round of local authority cleansing and bin-emptying contracts, which were very much of their time and place and offered no general lessons.[3] There is no reliable evidence that billions spent on outsourced IT contracts led to greater efficiency.

Contracting generally registers a quick hit on costs. Companies may bid low, hoping to recoup their revenues by later claims and price rises. Soon, companies – so the NAO reports – find ways to charge public bodies for extras or changes in the contract. This seems to be the story of the collapse of the UnitingCare Partnership, which made a significantly lower bid for Cambridgeshire and Peterborough community health than the local NHS service put in. The companies were expecting, after it was signed, to negotiate a 20 per cent increase; when the NHS commissioners would not pay, the companies walked away leaving the NHS to pick up the pieces.[4]

Deals have to be assessed in the round, over the long haul, and in the light of hidden costs of contracting. For example, Arvato (which is German) and Sopra Steria (which is French) are big players in Whitehall contracts for office services. Their formula for cutting costs involves offshoring – transferring business to firms based in India that, of course, pay much lower rates. So the model becomes cutting UK civil servant jobs to create employment in call centres abroad with the effect, in the short to medium run at least, of cutting the tax take and affordability of services.

But contracts don't exist in isolation: they affect the public's sense of what public services are, who is accountable and, of course, the morale and motivation of staff who are sacked, transferred or left wondering if they are next for the chop. While cost is vitally important, it can never be the only consideration: quality, public confidence and long-term consequences also have to be weighed up. Besides, the repeated claim that private contractors are cheaper is in fact dubious. Empirical and historical studies comparing performance are lacking, and as we've seen, assertions about contracting are much more common than good evidence. Once a state organisation has long lost the ability to take back the service, who knows if outside contractors are really cheaper over time?

It's only fair to compare like with like. The outputs of, for example, an NHS trust are broader and infinitely more complicated than Virgin Healthcare's selected, cherry-picked services: an NHS trust runs an A&E service, takes in frail people with multiple ailments, trains staff, participates in the Prevent anti-terrorism programmes while it works under Freedom of Information and so on. Virgin can walk away if a contract gets too difficult; state-run services must always be there. Public bodies are accountable, upwards and downwards, to regulators and inspectors. The strain on them is far more insistent and varied than simply meeting periodic profits targets. And on top of all this, the value for money calculus for a public body now has to include setting up the contracts with private providers, then monitoring them and paying for backup so that the public body can intervene in the event of failure.

The Big Four's Big Failures

There has also been failure, with some of the biggest examples laid at the door of a peculiar group of companies. The contracting boom produced a strange phenomenon: big companies, whose main business lies within the public sector. Capita, collector of the London congestion charge and BBC licence fee, is entirely a creature of state dismemberment. Serco, G4S and Atos are similarly dependent.

Curiously, these companies are inexpert. What they are good at is brigading staff and writing bids. None of the companies snapping up the new contracts for probation had any prior experience of criminal justice. Jackie Doyle-Price, a Tory member of the PAC, talked of 'companies that are good at bidding for contracts, and that know exactly how to tick boxes, but that are not necessarily delivering value for money'.[5]

The Cameron government outsourced accommodation for asylum seekers. This is a textbook example of how contracting fragments everything. Asylum seekers are going to need services provided by local authorities, the NHS and other public bodies; the closest coordination is needed over where and how they live. The problem, so the National Audit Office said, was that, new to the sector, Serco and G4S 'struggled to establish supply chains', ending up with a ragtag housing stock, elements of which were unsuitable, 'resulting in poor performance and additional costs for the Home Office'.[6]

During the Cameron coalition, those companies, together with Capita and Atos, regularly scooped up nearly every central government contract going. The trouble was, they often then failed to deliver.

G4S became notorious in 2012 for not delivering enough Olympic security on agreed terms, and leaving bussed-in staff cowering in the rain under a bridge all night. After serious lapses on its contract for tagging offenders, the Cabinet Office appointed a high-level 'crown representative' to assure the firm's conduct.

G4S took over the Lincolnshire police control room on a £200m contract. Dial 999 in Skegness or Louth and you no longer connect with a public official but a contractor. It turned out, however, that you didn't have to dial 999 to clock up a contract payment. In 2016, five staff including a manager were suspended after allegations that they had made hundreds of bogus calls to themselves during quiet times, in order to hit their target of answering 92 per cent of calls inside ten seconds. The staff were not malign, but rational. Public service depends on trust and often unseen performance above and beyond duty; private companies only pay for exactly what is specified.

Sometimes, however, the private companies do not even meet the specified terms. Serco, a firm with little previous medical experience, was given a contract to run out-of-hours GP services in Cornwall. Whistles were blown and in 2012 the NAO investigated. Members of Serco staff had been altering performance data, because Serco was not fulfilling the terms of the contract. The Care Quality Commission concluded that the out-of-hours service did not have enough qualified, skilled and experienced staff to meet people's needs. Serco later walked away from Cornwall.[7] But reputational damage from these disasters doesn't seem to stick, as the same companies continue to win contracts again and again.

The Big Four contractors have a total turnover of £23bn, of which the UK taxpayer contributes a quarter. Their share of certain sectors ought to have triggered investigation by the competition authorities long ago – for example when Atos gobbled up a large supplier of medical assessment services, giving it a whip hand in negotiations with the DWP. Some contractors now depend on the state for up to 75 per cent of their income. Tony Travers of the London School of Economics calls them 'para-statal', not so different from arm's-length bodies or quangos. But they do not have to conform to public sector norms of accountability, nor conditions and pay for their staff.

The relationships between contractor and state are asymmetric. BT provides services inside many town and county halls and gets to know a lot about their working. But conversely they have no idea what is happening inside BT. Public bodies are subject to freedom of information requests for data about their contracting and finances – information that it is vital for contractors to know in advance. The Information Commissioner says that 'private bodies that are basically doing work on behalf of the public' should be subject to freedom of information.[8] It has yet to happen, as the private bodies resist it strongly. What might be uncovered?

Contracting Can Work, But What Else is Lost?

Of course many contracts work. Bins are emptied, streets cleaned, school meals served, clinic floors disinfected and so on. Capita won a 10-year contract to run HR, finance, IT, estates and customer services for Tory Barnet, which at one stage had vowed to contract out all its functions. The deal was declared to have saved money and residents were reportedly satisfied.

Certain services do look as if they can safely be bundled up and outsourced: the same system and software ensuring staff get paid on time can be used for multiple organisations, for example. In principle, the more standardisation (everyone gets paid on the same day of the month, say) the cheaper the back office costs. But circumstances have to be right; much hinges on trust and mutuality between different organisations, and competition, as demanded by successive governments, is the antithesis of sharing. The jury is still out on NHS Shared Business Services, jointly owned by the Department of Health and Sopra Steria; in principle this could help reintegrate a fragmented health service. Corporate services don't have to be provided by a private company: the NHS in Wales owns and operates a central hub for auditing and other corporate services for health boards; in England, entrepreneurial trusts do back office work for others. Reading council prides itself on selling its pothole and housing repairs teams to neighbouring councils. Barnet and Harrow councils, though of different political colourings, run a common legal team, cutting spend on external lawyers and management. These seem to work.

But contracting has been controversial in human services: prisons, probation, welfare and employment advice. In these areas, trust and discretion are at a premium; they are qualities impossible to pin down in a contract. And so we see, for example, a benefits claimant shoe-horned into an unsustainable job; why should contractors care about family, training, health or the wider environment of the person when their objective is to get the box ticked and qualify for payment? The Cameron government insisted, without evidence, that contracting out probation to private firms would both reduce reoffending and cut costs. All but one of the 21 contracts – worth a total of £3.7bn a year – went to firms such as Ingeus, Working Links and Sodexo. Within two years, the NAO said bluntly that the deal had not worked. Meeting with an offender coming out of jail triggered a contracted payment, but no progress was made on actually cutting reoffending. Chris Grayling, the justice secretary, had tried to make it easier for the companies to profit by hiving off the difficult offenders into a smaller residual public probation service; as predicted, its caseload was high. The NAO found the 'supply chain' had narrowed, along with the number of private firms involved … in other words competition was in fact reduced.

A scathing report in December 2016 from HM Inspectorate of Probation found MTC Novo's privately run probation service in London had 20 per cent staff vacancies (cutting staff is the secret of contractor profit), leaving some staff with caseloads of 900 offenders. Some offenders had not been seen for months and the public was being put at undue risk.[9]

Dealing with people, especially those in need, is inherently difficult and will always involve a large area of discretionary judgment in fraught face-to-face situations. First Labour then coalition ministers bought the unevidenced argument that private firms could do better at chivvying people on benefits into jobs, and their role was greatly expanded in the Work Programme launched in 2011. But the NAO found that the Work Programme accomplished no more than its state-run predecessors; it found jobs for just one in six and was twice as successful in the south as the north, showing that the state of the labour market, not the programme, was key. Contractors spent less time and money on more difficult cases, often just parking them, and focusing instead on cheaper cases where they could quickly register a win. The Work Programme found jobs for just one in 20 disabled people. By mid-2014 the number of people claiming Employment Support Allowance (ESA) was starting to rise, because of problems with assessment. Atos feared profits were endangered and walked away from its contract to assess ESA claims.

The Contracting Con

Contracting can never be fully trusted if contractors can go bust, as Jarvis, a major rail maintenance firm, did in March 2010. Public services, on the other hand, are universal and baseline: schools, hospitals, security have to be provided. This means the state has to have backup. If a facilities management firm starts to try to charge extra for small jobs – hanging things on walls, repairing a broken loo – and the NHS trust involved won't pay, then the contractor walks, free as air from all responsibility. And the state is left to resolve the situation. Examining the Work Programme, the NAO found that theoretically failure by a firm would see competitors being able to step in, but 'in practice the contractual performance structure made it more expensive to terminate poor performing suppliers'.[10] Some councils have got the message.

From the top of Thurrock's civic offices you can look over to the great industrial Thamescape of Grays, with its striding pylons and smokestacks and Tilbury docks. (People who talk about the north as the seat of industry and manufacturing have never been downriver.) In Thurrock, as in a growing number of councils, there's a quiet counter-revolution going on. Thurrock is turning back the tide of outsourcing.

The Thameside local authority is not some leftist haven; a minority Tory group runs the council with 17 members, UKIP also holds 17 seats, with Labour in third place. Yet all parties agree that abandoning a contract with Serco and bringing services back has had a wholly beneficial effect. At the end of 2015 they bought out the Serco back-office contract and restored their own services for human resources, recruitment, procurement, IT and customer care. This followed lessons learned during an earlier decision to contract in waste collection services.

Chief executive Lyn Carpenter is blunt. 'It was a disaster. We had no idea if procurement was good, or if there were suspicious deals. We had no ownership of any of it. Serco did nothing online, so recruitment took forever, weeks to appoint people and check their references. Now we do it fast.

'Nothing was flexible, everything set in stone. If you wanted something done differently, they said, "That'll cost you."' She says local authorities have many skills, 'but often they are not good contract writers. This one was very badly written.'

It was an inflexible 15-year contract, giving Serco no incentive to change or modernise anything: many functions were still done on paper that had long ago been computerised elsewhere.

Carpenter pushed for escape. 'The contract was costing us £19m a year. They were taking £3.6m out as profit – through labelled overheads sent to their head office. That's £3.6m not being spent in Thurrock, and money we can now keep as an immediate saving.' Negotiations with the firm were hard, 'quite a fight'. Thurrock paid £9.9m to escape but will recoup that quickly, saving the annual £3.6m of Serco's profits, and even more on running those services more effectively. They can now get staff to work collaboratively, not in silos, each doing multiple tasks.

We talked to some of the 300 staff who were brought back in-house, discussing how things had functioned under Serco. 'It was awkward for us as Serco staff. We'd all been council staff, and now we were sitting next to old colleagues who were still council staff,' says one, working in customer services. 'They'd ask us to take their calls if they were pressed, and we'd want to do them a favour, but we had our key performance indicators and we couldn't.'

'It was so disjointed,' said another, 'with a Serco manager and a council manager. We could never suggest things should be done differently: it had to be done as the contract said.' And another spoke of the damage to staff morale: 'There was always a bit of tension between the two sets of staff, not able to work together as we should.'

Above all they spoke about how it felt to be back in the Thurrock fold, as one member of staff put it. 'It's a sense of belonging,' said another. Carpenter puts it this way: 'Here 80 per cent of our staff live in Thurrock, so they are providing services for their family, friends and community. We are the biggest employer and a lot of them have worked here for years. They know the service, and the area, they are our eyes and ears for what's going on, and we need them to feel valued by us. They often know best where there are inefficiencies. They see and know about the parking, the fly-tipping, the gullies that need clearing to stop creating potholes. I want them all, the street sweepers, everyone, to be the friendly face of the council wherever they go.' But has it cost her more? 'Yes, we have to do their payroll, appraisals and so on, but we're doing that for everyone else. Like every council, we've faced heavy cuts, with up to 20 per cent more to come. I was forced to cut my staff and change how they work, yet I couldn't touch the way anything or anyone in the contract worked.'

There are still some outsourced services that Thurrock staff want to be brought back in: we spoke to a council estate concierge who said how easy it had been to work with maintenance and repairs service when they belonged to the council, but the red tape and obstruction of calling in a plumber or a roofer from their contractor delayed everything. Red tape is the phrase used by them all to describe coping with fixed contracts – and yet that's an epithet more usually hurled at state services by those who think the market will always do better.

―――――

The state needs to keep in-house expertise, or be forever at the mercy of its contractors in a broadly uncompetitive market. And if it does keep some services, then it has a baseline for comparing cost and quality of the service that was contracted out. That means there must always be at least the prospect of contracting back in again. Ironically, austerity has made councils dig deeper and look harder at the value of their outsourced contracts, and when these contracts are frequently found wanting, councils are bringing their services back in-house at better value. This is hardly what Tory chancellors expected in their more-for-less budgeting.

Chapter 5

The State of Business

To go by the formal utterances of the Confederation of British Industry (CBI), the Institute of Directors or the chambers of commerce, all business wants is freedom, to employ those they like when they like at the lowest payable wages. The state stands in the way, regulating, impeding, taxing. The rhetoric of business is binary. We make money; they take it.

But both history and theory say that business and government always have been and always will be locked in embrace. In this symbiotic relationship markets need governance if they are to flourish. The company was created by the state: most firms in the FTSE 250 are descendants of the joint stock arrangement, through which the Victorian state gave directors an exemption from contract law, so they did not have to pay up when they lost their shareholders money. Without the Financial Conduct Authority or some such regulator, who's to monitor and prosecute insider trading – and if you let such safeguards go, corporate capitalism will stop working.

Look at the 'market' within which the retailer BHS was thrown around and pensions owed to staff disappeared, or the acquisition and sale of football clubs or the strength of oligopoly in retailing, aviation or pharmaceuticals. Scandals over non-payment saw the creation in 2004 of the statutory Pension Protection Fund, but it struggles to prevent staff interests falling to the bottom of the heap when companies are sold and assets stripped. The DWP is paying £7bn to members of occupational pension schemes that were underfunded or abandoned before the new arrangements kicked in.

Disequilibrium and Disorder

Private enterprise is not self-policing. Economists fantasise about equilibrium, but economic reality is drunk and disorderly. J. M. Keynes showed how the state could maintain demand. You don't need to know exactly where to balance fiscal and monetary policy to agree that both have to be propelled by government. It has to intervene in the labour market, both for equity and for efficiency. The National Minimum Wage, despite the resistance of business, turns out to push up productivity as well as sustain demand.

When under-regulated, companies create cartels. Monopoly is preferred by the Istanbul kebab shop in the high street as much as by Rupert Murdoch. His leader writers may propagate the doctrine of open markets but he is out to amass market share so News Corporation can bid up prices and increase profits.

Pin-ups of the right, such as Friedrich von Hayek, said that all business needs is the law, as if judges and justice were things that grow up spontaneously, separate from states. In reality, law and regulation, close cousins, depend on the strength of the state that builds the courts and creates the financial authorities and enforces their judgments. Business depends on the public sector at every turn. Not just for infrastructure, wavelength and policing, but for skills and workforce and, even more vitally, to sustain and underpin the social context in which to operate.

Markets and states also interact to secure freedom. Markets can disperse power and business enterprises act as a countervailing force against over-mighty states. Soviet society was grim partly for lack of the spice, liveliness, innovation, energy and exuberance of commerce.

Markets can correspondingly concentrate power and grab corrupt monopolies, as oligarchs seized unbridled control in post-soviet society. Against that, public ownership and public regulation can stand as bulwarks to protect freedoms, guarding staff against exploitation and consumers against fraud and poison. What is needed is always a balance between the state and the market.

The Fallout of a Financial Crisis

The state has to be solid when markets fail. Savers besieging Northern Rock's branches during the financial crisis told reporters they distrusted the chancellor, Alistair Darling, but no sooner had he issued a state guarantee for their money than the crowds dispersed, like mist in a May dawn. At some deep level of consciousness, depositors needed and drew assurance from government.

When markets fail, there is only the state and its credit. The Treasury disbursed around £133bn during and following the financial crisis of 2008, assumed the liabilities of Bradford & Bingley and extended over £1,000bn in guarantees. In the years since, this exposure lessened so that by March 2016 the state had gained back £56bn but the market values of RBS and Lloyds were still worth £22bn less than had been paid out to buy their shares. It's worth repeating the conclusion of the Office for Budget Responsibility, Mark Carney and his predecessor Mervyn King: the fiscal crisis of 2009–10 that served as the pretext for George Osborne's austerity was not caused by Labour overspending but by the bank bailout.

The collapse of the banks showed that the way companies are run is often seriously deficient and antagonistic to the broad public interest, not to mention the more selfish viewpoint of shareholders and staff. Some have tried to defend the directors of HBOS, Lloyds and RBS by saying that they weren't really responsible, their fat honoraria and bankers' bonuses aside: it was the fault of the Financial Services Authority, which should have stopped them behaving irresponsibly. And yet the record shows that before the crisis bankers lobbied hard to belittle and downgrade regulation and supervision of the banks by the state – the very institution that they later relied upon to rescue their enterprises.

Inquiries and parliamentary reports on RBS give the lie to the idea company boards can be trusted to be left alone. Be it governance, strategy, financial oversight or the quality of executive management, this fine, upstanding company was a disaster waiting to happen, and it did. RBS was not atypical within banking: there is no good reason to believe boards and management were particularly different in other sectors. The issue was not the avarice of Fred Goodwin but the phenomenon of Fred Goodwin – that such a creation should be permitted by the RBS board and market circumstances.

After their wild partying, the banks felt no regret. No sooner bailed out than they wanted to restore the status quo ante. The banks had gambled that in the event of a collapse the state would see them right – and they were correct: the taxpayers absorbed their risk.

Free Riders

Fans of unfettered free markets never quite get round to the problem of externalities: why should a company bother with costs that don't hit its balance sheet – pollution, say, or the social consequences of closing down a plant that formed the livelihood of a community, or running away from paying staff their promised pensions? A rational company seeks a free ride: why spend money on training an employee when she might take off to work for a rival and you in turn can snap up someone trained elsewhere?

No wonder vocational training in Britain is so contested, disrupted and inadequate, as shown by the figures for productivity. On an hourly output basis British workers are less productive than those doing similar work in France or Germany. For every hour worked, a German employee produces 35 per cent more. The congenital problem is that British employers prefer cheap labour they don't want to train. They resist levies for common skills programmes and denounce as 'corporatism' government efforts over the years to brigade them into sectors, in order to pool training costs. 'The basic problem,' says Barckley Sumner from UCATT, the building union, 'is that employers don't want to train anyone.'[1] Construction booms, but bricklayers are scarce. Skills don't match opportunities. Young people at school don't know which subject choices may lead where. It's only government that is ever going to forecast demand, plan ahead and subsidise vocational training.

In 2016, road haulage in the UK lacked between 45,000 and 60,000 drivers; nine out of ten companies surveyed by the Freight Transport Association reported difficulties in recruiting drivers[2] in an economy that relies on moving mountains of heavy goods. Operators are turning business away for lack of drivers. Yet at the same time there are large numbers of the unskilled, especially the young, who need training to get a job, or an upgrade from zero hours, low-paid work to something better. Easy, you might think, to connect the two – but it's not happening.

―――――――

Employers want ready-made, fully trained drivers with several years' experience. Many turn abroad, hiring eastern Europeans, but even this is still not plugging the gap. Few companies run their own training schemes, complaining that other companies just poach their trained employees.

From April 2017 the government is imposing a levy on large employers to pay for apprenticeships but there will be none for road haulage. Drivers are to pay to get their own licences, though courses cost £3,000, plus a £230 fee for a stiff test, which applicants often require several attempts to pass. They also face long waits to do so, due to lack of official examiners.

Textbook economics says a labour shortage should lead to a pay rise but this industry manages to keep pay low, despite the shortages. Lorry drivers get an average of £26,000 – the median wage – but pay rates have not risen in years. Employers fill gaps with agency staff and firms subcontract work down a chain, until the job is done by a low-paying, fly-by-night operator employing Latvians on rates as low as €1.20 an hour.

Lorry drivers' terms are harsh. Away from home for long stretches, they are only paid for driving hours: there is no pay for waiting while loading or for compulsory rest breaks, nor for over-night stops, with most sleeping in a bunk in the cab as unpaid security guards. Some literally live in their cabs for periods of up to three months. Lucky ones get £20 for overnight expenses to park in a truck stop, but, unpaid for night time, they usually save it and park in a lay-by. A House of Commons committee report describes the squalor of truck stops.[3]

We talked to Mick Johnson, a driver from Grimsby, who describes disgusting toilets and stinking lay-bys. 'We're treated like scum by the places we deliver to.' White men account for 94 per cent of drivers: the Commons report calls for more women and ethnic minorities but this is a culture that is hostile to both. Johnson, a member of the union Unite, tries to recruit other drivers to join the union, to improve pay and up the status and training, but eight out of 10 drivers are not members. 'We're all out there working on our own, and that's a hard trade to organise,' he says. In occupations where unions can get little foothold, a good government that regulates pay and conditions and organises training up a workforce is the only way to progress.

Once, wages councils set national pay rates and stopped companies undercutting each other. This system was abolished in the 1980s. Now Unite fears companies will use Brexit to drop EU regulations, such as the 48-hour working time rule. Many drivers voted for Brexit hoping to avoid the EU certificate of professional competence, a seven-hour annual course that is a vital safety backstop, for drivers themselves and also to protect anyone else on the road at risk from rogue lorries. Already the Driver and Vehicle Standards Agency – the regulator – is too under-resourced to catch all the cowboys.

The story of road haulage is mirrored time and again in British industry, with employers failing to work collaboratively and unions too weak to force good pay and conditions and sort out training. The state is the solution, but only if ministers make constructive use of its powers.

When Markets Fail

Left to itself the invisible hand is usually limp. Whatever economics textbooks say about perfect competition, the rest of us live in an imperfect world: rogue traders sell stuff that fell off the back of a lorry; cyber thieves steal passwords; counterfeiters knock off branded ware.

Private enterprise booms then busts, leaving Hartlepool, Bathgate, Corby and other communities bereft, throwing the costs of unemployment and social decline onto the state. Demand shifts or profitability drops and entire regions that had built up and adapted to servicing an industry or a market are abruptly declared redundant. Capital investment moves on, abandoning rusting plant or old-fashioned skills. In aggregate, over time, that creative destruction may be a recipe for economic progress as capital moves towards higher returns, benefiting the national bottom line. But people lose their jobs, families their income, communities their spine and places their geographical reason for being. What's good for the economy may be terrible for some individuals. Even the harshest proponents of free enterprise capitalism have never quite brought themselves to explain what should happen next: communities should fade away and die or 'get on their bikes', which in modern international terms means mass migration, camps, desperation and political turmoil.

Enter the state, to intervene against the weight of markets and the autarkic movement of capital. Who else but government –

councils, regional development agencies, central departments – is going to sweep up, bind the wounds or seek alternative sources of employment for the dispossessed? At least that is what government could do, if ministers believed in an active state.

Governments have no magic formula by which to regenerate run-down areas but state support can give hope to towns and cities, by endowing engines of recovery and renewal. Intelligent, creative planning of cityscapes recycles urban land. Critics say the state is bad at backing winners; what they don't add is that markets created the losers in the first place and are pretty inconsistent in backing winners, too. Theresa May's government renamed the Department for Business, Innovation and Skills the Department for Business, Energy and Industrial Strategy. Regular name changes such as this show how uneasy ministers, especially Tories, are about how to encourage and harness enterprise. May's new title at least gives rhetorical recognition to the state's role in identifying opportunity and assisting investment – as it has helped Jaguar Land Rover to build electric cars in the West Midlands, and an entrepreneur to make cabling on Teesside for a projected link to import hydroelectric power from Iceland. Of course private investors want state support; and of course the fate of any project will depend on commercial leadership and general trading conditions.

Nowadays the high bastion of finance, Canary Wharf was once abandoned after the decline of the London docks. Developers were simply not willing to invest in silted up creeks and rusting dock cranes that had, in their terms, negative value. To move on, it took the imagination and resources of the state, in the shape of the London Docklands Development Corporation, and inspired political leadership by Michael Heseltine. Thanks to public sector trains, roads and landscaping, subsequent private investors in the docklands eventually made a good profit. (The tale is also about unplanned over-expansion of London offices in the 1990s leading to the bankruptcy and replacement of Canary Wharf's original private developers, Olympia & York.)

Markets in property and places don't 'clear', as the textbooks suggest. It often takes the imagination of the state in the form of councils and development corporations to rethink uses for land and buildings. If, now, visitors are returning to Margate – which had largely been abandoned because of shifts in attitudes and holiday habits – it is because of public investment in galleries including the Turner Contemporary and the efforts of public bodies such as Visit Kent.

Councils can be place shapers. They worry about the charity shops moving into vacant sites on the high street when the estate agents can't or won't do anything. In many different ways, councils seek to arrest decline and inspire renewal. They string Christmas lights, organise improvement districts, cut deals, arrange rent and rates, lay new paving and manage traffic.

Only obdurate anti-statists deny that government intervention is a major part of the explanation for the historical success of economies as different as the US and South Korea. 'Industrial strategy' – rediscovered by Theresa May having been banished by David Cameron – points to the state's role in expanding knowledge and promoting innovations in products, services and business practice and (through patents, copyright and intellectual property regimes) giving originators a fair period in which to benefit from their innovation. Citing the internet and nanotechnology, economist Mariana Mazzucato argues that government investment has created spearhead technologies, from which the private sector comes along later to profit. Public investment in research has been critical in pharmaceuticals, defence spin-offs and IT. Innovation inside firms is patented, protected and utilised for profit; it can be circumscribed by the short-term perspective of shareholders. By contrast, investment by the state makes knowledge open to all and long-term: a common pool into which entrepreneurs can dip.

Maintaining Standards

After the Brexit vote many people woke up to the fact that EU membership had lowered rather than increased the cost of the common codes for labelling and weights and measures that international trade necessitated. Opponents of the European Single Market have never quite made clear how they would go about trading products and services without the level playing field in regulations that they find so objectionable. Voluntary arrangements are fragile, after all, and trust between distant trading partners breaks down easily.

The state has enforced standardisation for centuries: in the marketplace in Prato, near Florence, an iron bar is fixed to a wall, marked – as it has been since the 12th century – to show the accepted length of a standard unit of cloth. Traders may disagree but the commune arbitrates to smooth the path of commerce.

Business cannot be done without trading standards officers. We spend £1,160bn on goods and services a year. In 2014, consumers lost nearly £15bn through not getting what they ordered, and through substandard and otherwise dodgy service. Each year a third of us experience some consumer problem. Citizens Advice, to which many turn, gets a pitiful £18m a year in support and the Competition and Markets Authority spends only £6m on consumer protection. Total England-wide spending on trading standards was £165m in 2015–16: the council share, £124m, had fallen from £213m in 2010, since when staff numbers had been cut by half.

The upshot is that councils are now less able to protect consumers. But it's not just customers, as businesses themselves are damaged if norms are subverted or ignored. When Warwickshire County Council finds takeaway pizzas fail to contain the ham and cheese listed as ingredients, discovering processed meat product and non-dairy oil instead, reputations suffer all round, as well as taste buds. Trading standards officers, like the environmental health officers we visited in Chapter 2, have played a large part in monitoring faulty and potentially dangerous kitchen equipment and prosecuting nightclubs and other venues over fire safety.

A type of standardisation is knowing who owns what. Proposals have been made to sell off to the private sector the registration of companies and land ownership – destroying the credibility of the knowledge that these registers embody. During the coalition, Tory ministers were foiled in their attempt to sell the Land Registry. After the 2015 election they returned with proposals that would, in effect, have given the owner of the Land Registry every incentive not just to gouge clients but to pervert and degrade the information contained within it. But we'll establish a regulator, said Tory ministers, which rather concedes the point that this function should be as inalienable as the Domesday Book. A market-incentivised registry would have no a priori investment in truth or honesty or trust. Markets have to rely on a pre-existing culture and society for norms of good conduct and, for the enforcement of contracts and good behaviour, on the state. Estate agents

– hardly models of probity or popular trust – have protested most strongly against the prospect of this sale.

Keeping an Eye on Competition

Antagonists of an extensive economic role for the state can never quite make up their minds. Entrepreneurs such as Bill Gates or Mark Zuckerberg quickly lose their zeal for challenge and move to sew up markets by buying out rivals and preventing others entering their domains. Size and the fact of being first convey huge, sometimes unbeatable advantages. Mergers and acquisitions increase market share and once a company becomes the principal or only supplier of goods and services, it gets leverage over prices. But, short of monopoly, a cartel may bring useful stability and guarantee supply.

Only the state will run a Competition and Markets Authority, which must – if it is to be effective – have access to corporate detail and employ strong powers of investigation and enforcement, though a £66m budget for 2016–17 and 600 staff can only go so far. Especially when ministers are perennially tempted to succumb to the blandishments of business lobbyists. Sometimes they have a good case: size and concentration are important and investments may merit protection. The Showmen's Guild, representing fairground operators, rejected the charge that it stifled competition and failed to develop new rides and attractions: it said it regulated members for safety's sake, in conjunction with local authorities.[4] Right or wrong, government is inextricably involved with markets and trading: let's stop parroting tired slogans about the impossibility of bucking the market.

Who Else Will Keep the Lights on?

Energy offers compelling examples of the inevitability of the state, in production, distribution, in what consumers pay and – of course – on environmental sustainability and preventing further climate change. Unfortunately, global wellbeing, technological progress and consumer interest simply don't align. The state can't just hold the ring; it has to be a player. Certain risks – nuclear power for example – are just too great for companies to bear, even if they are well run. In some sectors, for example water and sewerage, the nature of the assets and the critical part they play in sustaining urban life mean that private ownership becomes a permanent and debilitating struggle between necessary regulation and profit maximisers. Where the state is a monopolist, it answers its citizens through the mechanisms of democratic accountability: ministers have to answer for the powers they wield. The irony and failure of the wave of privatisation by the Thatcher government is that state monopolies in energy, telecommunications, water and transport were immediately replaced by private sector monopolies, against which an increasingly elaborate and fallible regulatory regime had to be constructed. Ask commuters on Southern's railway lines into Victoria Station.

The Thatcherite privatisers of the 1980s held that markets would automatically sort things out; incompatibles would magically be married once the state was out of the way. The lights would be kept on, the planet saved from warming, fuel sources seamlessly adjusted as coal declined and gas rose. Consumers would behave as they do in the textbooks, each one collecting detailed information about tariffs and the fuel's relative greenness, switching easily between suppliers.

That fantasy has now run its course. The Thatcherites got it wrong on several counts. One of the reasons given for the necessity of privatisation – this was stated repeatedly by the 1980s environment secretary Nicholas Ridley – was that government could not afford to borrow. Once energy, water and other utilities were in the private sector, companies would tap the world's capital markets and investment blossom. But energy and water work on long timetables when capital markets demand instant returns, and so private owners had an incentive to minimise investment spending. For companies to profit, homeowners and businesses had to pay a surplus. When wholesale electricity prices plummet, household charges drop barely a jot.

Privatisation brought breakup and a futile attempt to abolish planning of supply. The state was left responsible for keeping the lights on and ensuring that energy was generated in ways that protect the planet – but it no longer commanded the means to do so. Even the energy transmission networks and grids had been sold. Why should a private firm bother to run cables far afield to encourage, for example, the construction of wind turbines in remote areas? In the Duddon Valley on the fringes of the Lake District, profit says build pylons; public opinion says bury the cables. In 2016, National Grid's 82,000 miles of gas pipes supplying 11 million households and businesses was sold on, with the China state investment company taking a large slice; the aim of this sale was not to secure future gas supplies but 'to increase shareholder returns'.

The professors of economics and ex-Treasury officials recruited to regulate the privatised utilities insisted everyone would behave rationally; all they needed to do was set a mechanical formula for pricing. But they did not realise how easily companies could refinance their borrowing, adjust the balance between equity and bonds, and end up making super-profits. As for sustainability, zero-carbon investment was not going to take place without state intervention.

Meanwhile the planet has continued to warm. Rain falls excessively or inadequately, making it even more necessary to plan water supply in different parts of the country over the long term. Markets turned out to have no intrinsic interest in assuring enough electricity at times of peak demand or even next year: the UK margin between supply and demand thinned to the point of panic. Electricity producers 'dashed for gas', because supplies of the fuel were cheaper, but not all hydro-carbon comes from benign Norwegians. The rise of Vladimir Putin has been gas propelled. Decarbonising electricity supply pointed to solar, wind ... and nuclear. But sustainable energy start-up costs are high and with the use of nuclear energy come big questions about who pays for security, decommissioning and technology.

The Tories botched the privatisation of nuclear, and Labour reluctantly renationalised the near bankrupt British Energy in 2002. Now another set of fantasies began. Labour made major commitments on climate change without reconceptualising the balance between public and private. The state had to be brought back, to some extent, in order to reform planning and remove obstacles. New nuclear would be built without subsidy. 'The private sector was confident in 2007 that it could build new nuclear without subsidy. That same private sector a few years later had to ask for a carbon price guarantee, and then for a long-term power price contract as well as a debt guar-antee. Even that wasn't enough.'[5] The ultimate indicator of the failure and the absurdity of privatising was the arrival of the French state to take over our energy supplies, in the shape of its company EDF. The same was true of the Chinese state – and it's worth asking to what extent the authorities of Beijing hold the British public interest uppermost.

From 2010, trying desperately to avoid the taint of planning, the coalition struggled with ensuring no blackouts. Ominously, in 2016 Theresa May downgraded the energy department and merged it into business, but altering badges won't reduce environmental jeopardy.

Ahead, one thing is certain, as the National Audit Office points out: household energy bills will rise. Going ahead with the new Hinkley Point nuclear plant will push up bills for decades to come. The UK government is guaranteeing £92.5 per megawatt hour of Hinkley electricity, more than twice the current market cost, for 35 years after the plant is finally constructed. And the state will carry the can for decommissioning the plant and burying it in concrete decades hence, and then the costs of guarding it for centuries. Despite those inflated household bills, despite direct subsidies and massive environmental distortions such as financial incentives to run diesel generators, by 2017 the 30-year attempt to remove the state from the job of supplying energy has failed.

Government must have a major role, promoting research (for example battery storage), insulating homes, cutting demand and adding flexibility to the grid. The perversity of today's policy is illustrated by the way sustainable energy from the sun has been treated.

In April 2010, Labour introduced a generous feed-in tariff to encourage the installation of solar panels. Cameron also backed renewables in the run-up to the election, trying but failing to fix a wind turbine on the roof of his Notting Hill home. Solar energy took off. Because of the feed-in tariff, householders could gradually recoup the cost of installation from selling the energy from their roofs to the grid. At the same time the cost of solar cells was falling fast. In five years the UK became the fifth largest user of solar, after China, Germany, Japan, the US and Italy, overtaking sunnier France and Spain.

The cost of the renewable energy subsidy was added to customer's bill, though it only formed a small fraction of the total. As it became clear that the subsidy was set too high, the government could have gently reduced it as solar became more cost-effective and needed less support. Energy prices were rising sharply and becoming politically contentious. Cameron was quoted as issuing an abrupt order, 'Cut the green crap!'

Suddenly, without notice, the feed-in tariff was cut – from May 2015 four successive reductions removed 87 per cent of the subsidy – upsetting the calculations made by all the homes, schools and small businesses that had borrowed to invest. Because it's hard to explain gigawatts and feed-in tariffs, the catastrophic loss of 12,000 solar jobs never hit the headlines. It deserved to.

———

Howard Johns, a long-time green energy campaigner, built up his company, Southern Solar, over 13 years. It employed 100 people in nine regional centres, turning over £10m a year, and each year doubling its business. 'The price of the equipment was falling fast and loads of new companies started up. We were installing solar in schools, colleges, swimming pools, businesses, expecting a stable market. Then overnight, bang.'

His company went into administration in October 2015, among an avalanche of others. Big orders were cancelled and he laid off all but 10 staff. That month 1,000 people lost their jobs as the Mark Group went bust, as Climate Energy and other firms tumbled out of the sky. Of 5,500 solar companies only 200 survived; 12,000 jobs were lost.

Among heavy losers were schools. Overnight their energy bills soared six to eight-fold as the tariff was cut, leaving them with debts for installation. One irony was that private schools, such as Winchester, which had also invested heavily in solar panels, were exempt from the subsidy cut because of their charitable status.

Johns says, 'Eventually new companies will spring up as the installation price keeps falling. There is no doubt solar has a huge future — if only the government had waited.'

Instead, in the panic at possible blackouts, in the winter of 2016 coal was given a big new subsidy to keep going a while longer, and 'dirtiest of all, most polluting, this winter they have given a big subsidy to diesel-generating stations'.

———————

The sabotage of on-shore wind is another curious act of vandalism. Just as wind energy was becoming self-sustaining and viable, Tory ministers empowered Nimbys, giving them effective veto rights, killing the industry. On the flip side is fracking, with new legislation that says however many people object locally, they can be over-ridden by central government.

The point is that all governments are forced to intervene and to subsidise. Whatever view you take as to what kind of energy should be generated and at what price, we all depend on active government to keep the lights on. But in the case of solar and on-shore wind, where Osborne once promised a 'march of the makers', he soon created a march of destruction, ideologically anti-green.

Disconnected Communications

Like energy, communications illustrate the beauties of the free ride. Why would shareholders bother laying pipes or stringing wires to rural, remote or poor areas? Without incentives BT would just set up its cabinets and cables in densely populated areas. In a market economy, after all, people who choose to live in villages or peripheral estates should pay a premium or move. Note how the invisible hand has a penchant for treating people as if they were completely mobile and had no roots or families, imagining that the perfect economic human will always put financial incentives above everything else in their lives.

People move around but they are in touch, by phone. Spectrum is the range of electromagnetic frequencies usable for over-the-air communications. It has to be regulated. In the 1920s, the American airwaves were a free-for-all; broadcasters started up all over the place and the result was cacophony. Stations clashed as they used the same frequencies and listeners couldn't hear a thing. Since then, it has been firmly established that the electro-magnetic spectrum is a public resource that has to be apportioned in some rational way by the state.

Even anti-statists seem to grasp the point. Canvassing for the Tory candidate at the Newark-on-Trent by-election in 2014, David Cameron complained about mobile phone coverage: he had similar problems getting a signal in his own constituency of Witney. Having managed to get the culture secretary on the phone, the Tories announced that phone companies would be persuaded to share masts. But the companies refused, pointing out they had invested in their own masts. As for national roaming, didn't the government realise that network differentiation – better signals from some companies in some zones

– was basic to their business model? The lesson, which the government ignored, is that intervention is required to ensure that coverage is wide and that no far-flung areas are ignored.

Technology is on the march, shifting the balance between fixed and mobile, voice and data services. Additional capacity is becoming available – the 700MHz spectrum band is being turned over to providers of mobile broadband. But the National Infrastructure Commission, lame and resourceless, says Britain is in the 'digital slow lane', far down the rankings for 4G coverage. The state, it says, must play an active role to ensure 5G readiness – before recommending that the instrument for change should be the weak local enterprise partnerships, which we encountered in Chapter 3 – boards of local businesspeople, uncoordinated and puny compared with the communications companies they would need to deal with.

Andrew Adonis, chair of the commission, says, '5G offers us a chance to start again and get ahead. If government acts now we can ensure our major transport networks and urban centres are 5G-ready in time to give British industry every chance to lead the world in exploiting its applications.'[6] But the action required is large. For 5G, a new network involving millions of 'small cells' is needed to bounce signals back and forth in order to ensure there are no delays. For an idea of how important this zero-delay policy would be, take driverless cars – if one of them were to lose coverage for even fractions of a second, the vehicle in front gets it. But how far can and should 5G networks overlap and compete? It's another classic case showing the necessity of state involvement.

Opportunities to exploit advantage and restrict competition abound: the honesty and effectiveness of the regulator, OFCOM, becomes ever more vital. As for broadband supplied through a cable, government is necessary not only to forestall monopoly and exploitation of customers but to ensure this utility is made widely available. Securing broadband connections to remote spots expands economic opportunity there, and not just for tourism. Only the state will do it. Unfortunately, the instrument the state chose – BT – turned out to be both monopolistic and unreliable.[7] The government allocated some £530m to rural broadband, in what became a vast welfare programme for BT, which took the money but hasn't yet supplied the goods.

State Ownership – What's Left of It

Even avid denationalisers come awry when big things need doing but companies see no profit or, as with the private owners of the high-speed line to the Channel Tunnel, go bust. The Tory model has become one where the state does the digging and building, with the aim of privatising later, at a discount. This describes HS2, which is being run by a government-owned company. (Though maybe in the case of this rickety, unjustified railway the reluctant marketeers have a point.) The failure of Railtrack in 2001 says clearly that major infrastructure and markets don't easily fit together but that has not stopped Tory transport secretaries such as Chris Grayling aspiring to the privatisation of Network Rail, the public sector owner of tracks and stations.

The government now owns banks, in the shape of RBS and Lloyds, but the Green Bank has been disposed of. The Royal Mint hangs on, showing that a business can be innovative while wholly owned by the state – because coinage remains an inalienable state function. There used to be Remploy, a decent state-owned company marrying social purpose and industry.

Set up in 1944 to provide work for disabled people, it finally fell foul of the anti-statist ideologists. Its last 33 factories were closed in 2012, lost havens for those who would find it hard to get other work. The jobs of 1,752 disabled people were lost. The rest of Remploy, by then a string of high street employment agencies, was in part sold off to the American giant Maximus.

The Forestry Commission is a successful state-owned enterprise that owns, conserves, develops and markets woodland and countryside. The coalition government tried to sell it off, but the shires would not countenance such an act of vandalism, affecting vital rural interests.

The history of the nationalised industries gets rewritten by their vanquisher, their performance removed from its technological and cultural contexts. Pre- and post-privatisation BT are simply not comparable. Once climate and pollution became important global concerns, the future of coal was going to be doubtful, regardless of who owned the pits. After a nationalised industry has failed, the accounting conventions that often stifled the nationalised industries' investment programmes are finagled into principled reasons why state enterprise never works.

Public ownership is not just about those functions where the state needs to be present to secure investment and fair access – to the roads, for example – but it is also about challenging and enriching those functions. In CalMac, the transport operation renationalised by the Scottish government, it not only assures connections to Mull, Islay and the Western Isles, but also has a means of promoting wider economic and social development.

What is peculiar about the Tories' animus towards direct ownership by the state is their resulting dependence on other, foreign states. There is a large oriental animal in the room: China. China's state-owned companies are starting to own great slices of the British patrimony. Dutch and German governments run British trains, at one remove; in London the 148 bus will whisk you to White City thanks to its owners, the Paris regional transport network. And we've already looked at the French energy giant, EDF, which provides much of the UK's energy.

Transport for London (TfL) proves the point. Over recent years it has built a reputation as a strong public institution with clear social purpose, good relationships with passengers and open democratic governance. It is part of the Greater London Authority group, answerable to the Mayor of London. TfL runs the tube, the buses, the Docklands and Overground railways, and other services are run by contractors. The public body specifies the service, coordinates ticketing and works to meld transport modes together – even the Emirates cable car folly ordained by Boris Johnson. It performs the dual tasks of both devising strategy carried out in part by contractors, and directly providing a service. Chris Grayling's bull-headed refusal to contemplate transferring London commuter rail services to TfL was a refusal on purely ideological grounds; unifying the south-east commuter services under public management made sense. Perhaps the Tory minister didn't want a well-run public service to show up the performance of the private rail franchisees.

His predecessor had previously refused to consider the evidence that a publicly owned rail franchisee can reach high standards of performance and profitability. In 2013, the Department of Transport wilfully ended the public operation of the East Coast franchise, which was popular and made money. Instead it was handed over to Virgin Trains, which also runs the West Coast franchise, giving it a near monopoly on rail journeys to Scotland from the south. So much for free market competition.

Moving About

Since Thatcher-era privatisation, the car and passenger ferry service from Portsmouth and Lymington to the Isle of Wight – Wightlink – has had four owners. The latest is Balfour Beatty Infrastructure Partners, which took over from Macquarie European Infrastructure Fund, owner in whole or part of National Car Parks, Thames Water and Arqiva, which compulsorily installs meters in households on behalf of ... Thames Water. During Wightlink's sojourn in the private sector, prices have risen and services are not obviously better. Islanders complain, as is their wont.

Suffice to say that investment decisions are not made with a view to coordinating timetables, joining up places or for the greater good of the Isle of Wight. The cost and availability of transport underpins travel-to-work areas and links to productivity, so the public interest is necessarily huge. The state has to regulate and should also be empowered to provide in this area.

This has not been the prevailing view. Take buses. Despite Margaret Thatcher's famous contempt for people who use them, they account for 62 per cent of all passenger journeys by public transport, giving access to education, jobs and public services. There's good evidence that improving bus services reduces social deprivation. Since the private sector took over bus services in England outside London in the 1980s they have declined sharply. Passenger numbers have risen in places such as Nottingham and in London, where buses were not deregulated but franchised, meaning private operators remained under strict public control. Elsewhere private companies run services as they choose, with councils paying for buses on specific routes, if they can afford to. Perversely, legislation introduced in 2016 expressly forbids councils from establishing their own transport companies, preventing others following the example of Reading …

————

Reading borough buses win national awards year after year – UK Bus Operator of the Year, Top Shire Operator, Best for the Environment – with individual awards in 2016 going to Reading Buses' Manager of the Year and Engineer of the Year. This is one of 12 councils that still run their own bus companies and they all outstrip commercial rivals: Nottingham has another top publicly run bus service, vying for the same prizes.

Reading council has been majority Labour since the May 2015 elections. Deputy leader Tony Page bristles with pride and a certain defiance as he talks of attempts over the years by Tory ministers to force them to privatise, ever since the 1985 Thatcher-era deregulation. 'John Major tried to get rid of us in the 1990s. Stagecoach would love to see us gone.'

Page was chair of Reading Buses for 20 years and now leads on transport in the council cabinet. 'We make about £1m a year, spending it on a better service joining people together, stopping social isolation, allowing people everywhere to get to work, to meet each other and keep in touch with family.'

Private bus operators would expect a 15 or sometimes a 20 per cent profit. 'If a route makes less than 12.5 per cent, they will close it down. Our strategic focus is on a comprehensive service, reaching everyone, so we go out into rural West Berkshire, South Oxfordshire and Hertfordshire.' Beyond the social importance of keeping an affordable link in people's lives, there is the environmental bonus of a good service. The Reading transport system is set up to prioritise travel by bus;

for example buses get priority at the traffic lights. As a result, congested roads are eased of cars, and 93 per cent of journeys within Reading are made by bus.

By Tory decree, private companies are free to set up shop and compete. Recently a firm moved in on one route in Reading with a fleet of old London Routemasters. 'We behaved like Stagecoach would have done facing competition. We put more buses on the same route, just ahead of them and drove them off the road. We bought the company up for £1, and extinguished their debts by selling off their old buses to Rio airport.'

Compare Reading with the miserable condition of bus services elsewhere. The Campaign for Better Transport says the devastation is as severe as the notorious Beeching cuts to railway lines in the 1960s. Councils are obliged to provide free bus passes to the old and the disabled, but often can't provide buses on which to use them.

We visited Shropshire, where many village households without a car are now all but cut off from the outside world. Shropshire Link used to run four buses a day to Ludlow and Bridgnorth, meandering around in the beautiful rolling countryside. Frank Taylor has no car, but he moved to a cottage in Chetton, beside the 14th-century St Giles church, knowing he could rely on the bus to keep him in contact with the world beyond the 36 dwellings in this small hamlet.

Then suddenly the service stopped. In an area with 5,000 people, all that was left was a bus driven by a volunteer on a Thursday taking people to Bridgnorth for an hour and a half before bringing them back. 'The Link had been our social lifeline. We all knew each other from different villages by using the bus. It took some to work, it took everyone to the shops and to hospital or medical appointments.'

Taylor had been an independent councillor for 20 years, and with others mounted a campaign. They took Shropshire council to court, assembling evidence of social harm. Once the Link bus stopped, pupils could never stay on for out-of-school activities or see friends after hours. A number of people lost their jobs without the bus to take them to and from work.

The campaigners lost their case. They had well-laid plans for combining school and other services and they did the costings for a minibus. But Shropshire county council – where the Tories hold sway – is not an activist place. Public services can be full of vim and vigour, but that requires political leadership and initiative. Reading and Nottingham have it, Shropshire doesn't.

―――――――

Transport isn't just a social policy concern – important though that is in ageing Britain. Jobs, getting people off welfare into work, schooling and training all depend on mobility. On mobility hinge productivity and profitability across the economy. And mobility depends on the state.

Whether it's road, rail, waterways or air, physical mobility needs the state as regulator, investor and provider. Companies won't build things that their shareholders or executive directors can't profit from – which rules out most infrastructure, unless they are guaranteed a monopoly for a long number of years, opening the door to exploitation and oppression.

Conclusion: What Needs to Be Done Next

It's time for a reappraisal and a general reworking of how the state interacts with markets. It's not that market capitalism doesn't work, but it can't be relied upon without supervision, planning and direct state involvement – above all in transport and energy. Public–private need not be a battlefield; there is no Manichean struggle between markets and collective action. We need to end the dialogue of the deaf between those who think the public unambiguously good and those with a no less binary view of the private sector. Interestingly this nuanced view is one that most private sector chief executives share. Business often acknowledges it looks to governments for connectivity, to ensure stable capital markets, protect intellectual property, build a skilled workforce, deal with climate change, address inequality and reduce poverty – but it wants the impossible: to do all this with as little taxation and regulation as possible.

Judging where public provision should end and private begin has been a matter of history and context and faith, not science. In Britain in recent years, the anti-statists have been on the march, powered by a stream of propositions from across the Atlantic masquerading as science or 'common sense'. They are in fact theories and dogma and they have damaged Britain. What is now needed is a great confidence-building exercise, boosting public assent and invigorating those who work in and for the public realm.

Chapter 6

Staffing the State

Humpty Dumpty has to be put back together again. The state's staff and managers have to be yanked out of the silos into which they have retreated. Civil servants ought to share an ethos and identity with council staff, people who work for the NHS and for agencies but instead carry different labels, rarely intermingle and spend far too much time in internecine battles. Our message is: unite – and fight. They have all experienced years of hard grind, pay freezes and pension cuts. Yet on them depends the reconstruction of our state.

Actually, let us rephrase that: it's not just staff and therein lies a problem. The staff of the state could (and often still do) provide a Rolls Royce service but we can't leave it up to them. That would amount to technocracy or rule by managers. In a democracy, public servants work for politicians, some of whom are ill-intentioned towards them and actively disparage the very work they do. Making a case for the state involves a paradox: people involved with government spend much of their time doing it down.

Public service is an ambiguous vocation, made all the more problematic by the occupational silence officials traditionally observe for fear of appearing politically partisan. Like the wise monkeys they do not hear or see their ministers or councillors, and never speak. They reel under the blows landed on them and hunker down in their teams, units and agencies, putting up barricades for protection, but thus running the risk of furthering the ongoing fragmentation and diminishing the public's sense of a unified state.

Yet public employees have kept the ship afloat. Despite pay cuts and denigration, the UK has not experienced 'unethical behaviour, inappropriate use of resources and corruption', the OECD reports.[1] Public employees have continued to serve, despite being constantly put down and diminished. As in most of the illustrations we give in this book, public servants are simply getting on with it. Yet by doing the best they can under trying circumstances they allow the austerians and their accomplices in the media and commentariat to say: look, public services are in fine fettle, you are crying wolf. By striving – in that hackneyed Whitehall phrase – to keep the show on the road, they end up as human shields for the austerity warriors.

We were led through a labyrinth of passages and doors marked 'strictly private' underneath the House of Lords to a vaulted room where we could sit and talk to Bob Kerslake. As a former head of the civil service, Lord Kerslake ranks as one of grandees of the British state. But grand he isn't. Unlike other former permanent secretaries he has turned out to be a remarkably effective legislator, deferred to on all sides for his expert knowledge of housing and urban conditions.

Truth to tell, despite rising to the top of the machine, he was never entirely embedded in a civil service system that, though its glory days are long gone, retains an insider, clubby feel in its uppermost ranks. Kerslake was set apart for two reasons: first, he has professional expertise as a qualified accountant when few permanent secretaries have studied post degree level, and second, he came to Whitehall late, after outstanding work as chief executive of Hounslow then Sheffield City Council and as head of the Homes and Communities Agency at a time when money was still being spent.

Indeed Kerslake's own career is an emblem of what should be a universal route to the top, if there were a joined-up, unified public service, with common training between national, local and state agencies, including the NHS. Kerslake is now chair of King's College Hospital NHS Foundation Trust, giving him the widest overview.

He is cautious, not wanting to increase pressure on former colleagues who have to handle ever deeper cuts and the shambles (our word) post Brexit. From our conversation emerges a picture of a public service that is stretched thin, with civil service numbers back to pre-war levels.

In 2010, the Tories were out to shake the civil service up when they arrived after 13 years out of power. 'Politicians have been unduly influenced by *Yes Minister*,' says Kerslake. 'That programme was out of date when it was written, and it's certainly out of date now. But Labour and Tory ministers all arrive suspecting we want to thwart them at every turn. That's just not true.' Relationships at the top were generally good but some ministers had strong views about the role of senior civil servants, he says. Francis Maude, in charge of Whitehall reform, wanted to give departmental heads – permanent secretaries – a new name, reflecting the less-than-secure tenure he thought they should have. They would be on their toes if employed on short-term contracts.

Kerslake reminds us how much life in Whitehall nowadays can involve senior civil servants having to manage challenging and sometimes even abusive behaviour from special advisers. So much depends on the qualities and capacity of the occupants of Number 10: some have been indifferent to what goes on inside departments, others control freaks.

Civil servants can be over-eager to please, he says. Where were they when they were needed to advise and warn Gordon Brown against his needlessly bureaucratic delivery of tax credits via HMRC? At communities level, Eric Pickles kept local government in order as councils protested at the level of cuts: 'He played whack-a-mole with them, using attack as a defence. This was an effective strategy but not a popular one.' Should civil servants have warned against services being pushed sometimes to the point of collapse? He acknowledges that the civil service system 'finds it hard to give sharp, challenging advice on consequences. It was clear from the start that a second round of local government cuts in this Parliament risked some critical public services – such as social care – reaching the point where they fell over. But there are no prizes inside government for being this honest.'

The truth is that senior civil servants struggle to defend the integrity and functioning of the state. They do tend to assent, even when sage advice might save ministers from themselves over policies that will have unintended ill-effects or are simply administratively impossible. But, says Kerslake, sticking your neck out 'is not the way Whitehall careers are made'. In local government executives can display their advice in open committees; their obligations are formally to the whole council not just the ruling party.

The critical question here is custodianship. Who speaks for the good of the state, who acts as steward of a past and future service? 'I'm not sure anybody truly does,' says Kerslake. 'There has been massive fragmentation, when we need a public service we all feel part of. The NHS used to have a unified management development programme, but it's gone.' The government, he said, fell for the idea that a large state crowds out private enterprise. 'They really believed that in the north and poor areas where the state was an important part of the local economy, something would fill the vacuum when they took all those state jobs away. They found that little did. The state was often keeping those post-industrial towns going.'

Despite all that, the civil service remains as popular as ever among bright undergraduates, with high numbers applying and few chosen after passing stiff exams. 'These applicants have a strong public ethos. They want to do good, and they want to get close to power and be influential. But Whitehall can eat up good people. I'd advise good public-spirited people not just to think about the civil service but to also look at local government, where councillors will be more likely to listen to them.'

———————

Is Kerslake's relative optimism a foundation for recovery? Some public managers are moving beyond their perennial dismay at the quality of decisions handed to them by ministers and councillors into a darker place. Some doubt whether the political system can ever deliver coherent policy lines, let alone the financial resources to allow managers to put them into effect. What if, in turn, politicians cannot interpret or put into practice the contradictory and sometimes impossible messages being sent them by the voting public? This results in populism, when they dare not resist.

Permanent Tensions

Government will always be a site of permanent tension between executive staff and elected politicians. Friction has grown with the ascendancy of ministers who believe in shrinking the state, meaning staff pay, pensions and prospects. The same politicians who cut so gladly are usually the quickest off the mark to condemn officials for letting the public down if they dare take action in pursuit of grievances.

Bob Kerslake was permanent secretary at the communities department, where in effect his message to staff went something like this: 'Please continue to put all your dedication into serving a minister who thinks you are overpaid, underworked, an active impediment to the good of the nation ... and by the way they think there are still too many of you even after staff cuts have been implemented. Please give Eric Pickles [the secretary of state] every jot and tittle of your administrative energy even when he stands on party platforms to mock you.'

The identities, skills and timetables of the two will always be different, bifurcating the state: public managers want to plan for the long term, whereas the time horizon of elected politicians is next week. Management is about numbers, organisational effectiveness, coping with multiple stakeholders; whereas political leadership is about language and persuasion, dealing with the immediate and boasting of quick results.

In our system, public officials answer to politicians, but may also have fiduciary responsibility – permanent secretaries, NHS chief executives and others are 'accounting officers'. Many are subject to codes of conduct and (this is tricky territory) a conception of the public interest that goes wider than serving the ministers in power today.

In the 1980s, the head of the civil service Sir Robert Armstrong pronounced that civil servants served the crown, which for all practical purposes meant Mrs Thatcher and her cabinet – allowing not a chink of any wider sense of the state and its purposes, nor an accountability that included MPs and the public rather than just ministers.

It's a threadbare doctrine. Ministers cannot be responsible for all that government does. Besides, ministers and councillors must observe a 'norm of responsibility', acting proportionately and with regard to the consequences of their action for the wider public interest. Most ministers are inept managers and haven't a clue what departments and arm's-length bodies actually do. Yet we persist with the assumption that civil servants only ever act in the politicians' names.

Teachers, clinicians, military officers, planners, trading standards officers, border staff – all legitimately exercise the powers of the state on the basis of their own professional identity. It runs alongside and complements political accountability. This isn't an argument for technocracy or rule by managers. Along with 'Yes, minister' should come: 'No, that is not what the evidence says or what my professional expertise supports.' And something else, which civil servants have rarely dared say: 'No, because that denigrates and denies a vital sense of statehood.' Civil servants should lay out options, challenge ministerial presuppositions and (much more than they do) think outside the box of their departments. Doing the best they can for incumbent ministers and councillors ought to include telling them that their plans are unrealisable within constraints on spending and may fatally damage the wider public interest.

Resilient Morale

As well as jobs, pay within the public sector has been frozen and increments curtailed. The rightwing media are negative, and politicians carp, where they are not actively hostile. And yet cuts and contumely have not hit job satisfaction and morale nearly as hard as might have been expected.

The OECD finds that public officials across other countries have decreased trust in their leadership. But in the UK successive surveys by the Cabinet Office garner both a reasonable response rate and surprisingly high returns on what staff think about their managers, pay and opportunities for learning and development. Since 2009, around 59 per cent of Whitehall civil servants are said to be 'engaged'. Morale remains relatively high among council and NHS staff, too. The reason could be pride in public service of the kind we keep hearing from the individuals we spoke with for this book. Some staff take an almost perverse delight in serving the state despite the negativity and noise from their political masters. They literally ignore the ministers they ostensibly answer to. And oddly enough dismemberment helps with this particular approach. Staff identify themselves more and more with specific teams and divisions – with groups of colleagues – rather than a wider conception of the public sphere or the state.

That's a loss. Take the staff at Jobcentre Plus, which handles benefit claimants. The Public Accounts Committee concluded that they needed a frame of reference extending beyond the Department of Work and Pensions into health, housing and family circumstances. They should see people in the round, understanding them as citizens and clients of the public realm, not just of a single department.

Public Managers: Finding Religion or Celebrating What We Have?

If the state were to be reconfigured, staff would have to undergo a kind of metamorphosis. They would have to throw off their current prevalent fatalism. Some would have to cleanse themselves of New Public Management precepts. A number are believers: they have taken to wearing the clothes of their political bosses and presenting themselves as heroic 'transformers' of public services. They became enthusiasts for cuts and contracting – without allowing history, experience or empirical evidence to dissuade them.

Under Thatcher, certain prominent civil servants and utility regulators became shills for radical downsizing of government, later finding jobs with banks and consultancies. Individuals found religion. Permanent secretaries, at the Treasury particularly, may try to be holier than the Pope. A senior official in the transport department says his purpose is to 'smash' the rail unions.[2] The permanent secretary at DWP tweets his 'regret' at the departure of Tory minister Lord Freud, the man who dismissed food banks as a stunt used by scroungers.

Reconstruction rests on a renewed sense of public service professionalism. The public may appreciate 'their' school, surgery, or even an HMRC contact across a counter or a quickly answered telephone. But they often go on to criticise managers in general. High levels of satisfaction are registered for specific services such as waste collection and street cleaning while people mistrust town halls and senior management. 'We love our bobby' – but the police service is overweening or bureaucratic. 'We appreciate our GP' sits squarely with suspicion of some unseen NHS superstructure. Junior employees may like their team but complain about the corporate centre, directors and excessive paperwork.

When pollsters were asked what words describe service providers, the terms 'faceless' and 'bureaucratic' came back. But it's impossible to make the case for the state without validating, even celebrating, management. When he was permanent secretary at the Cabinet Office, Ian Watmore – who himself had come into Whitehall from the consultant company Accenture – said something rarely articulated by his colleagues: public managers deserve credit for their operational management skills.[3] 'Nothing comes close to the scale and complexity of the tax and benefit systems.' Human resources, contract letting, public relations: the public sector had skill 'in spades'.

Here comes a busy public manager. Caroline Clarke is dashing in from a difficult finance meeting up on the second floor of the Royal Free Hospital in north London. She cuts an elfin figure, with cropped blond hair, tight trousers, boots and a snazzy jacket. She's finance director in charge of a £1bn budget and 10,000 staff; she is neither grey nor dull.

She buzzes with energy as she talks about why she loves her job, why she admires the people she works with, and why she would find working in the private sector so much less interesting and challenging – and less socially worthwhile.

We go downstairs to sit in the small pop-up coffee shop beside where the hospital vehicles park. Things are not easy here, as in so many NHS trusts. Her target was to make a £15m surplus in 2016–17; instead, she says she'll be lucky to come in with no more than a £30m deficit. Most trusts had to sign up to utterly unrealistic savings, which most will miss. Barnet clinical commissioning group, which contributes to the Royal Free's budget, was put into special measures for overspending.

When the heavy mob moved in, they cut by a third the tariff paid for Royal Free treatments. That helped Barnet's balance sheet, but simply passed the debt on to the hospital. It's a mad game of pass the parcel. You might think a senior finance officer would be infuriated by such idiocy, but not at all. She surfs the improbabilities.

Caroline studied economics and accountancy at the LSE where she was treasurer of the students' union. 'Accountancy is my way to show how you can use budgeting to change people's habits, by giving a clear and focused target,' she says. 'But I'm in public service for its values, expressing them through financial decisions.' She qualified with the Chartered Institute of Public Finance and Accountancy and joined the fast-track NHS management scheme, worked in one hospital for five years, moved on to work for the Audit Commission and then spent two years with KPMG. 'That helped me to learn how to use management consultants – and I hardly ever do. Small hospitals do sometimes need them for tasks beyond their strength. Whitehall uses them all the time because they can't be arsed to do the thinking themselves. I would never, ever use McKinsey, which does most NHS work, because they have a one-size-fits-all theoretical strategy and no practical applications.'

Headhunters chase her all the time: 'I just had an offer to run the Barbados health service, with an office on the beach!' She has had offers from Whitehall; she shudders at the thought. Mainly she is tapped up to go back to working for consultancies that want more NHS business. 'They want my address book and my mates.' She earns £182,000. 'Which is huge, far more than any of my friends. But that's still a third of what I'm being offered in the private sector.'

She is not tempted. 'I love my job.' The complexities please her, though the NHS is in perpetual turmoil. She has to observe the professional code of public accountants and political imperatives coming down through regulators and NHS England. 'I know I am always at risk. Something could go wrong, my head on a spike outside the hospital very easily.'

Maximising efficiency conflicts with the best treatment of patients, and they conflict with political and financial imperatives. 'I've had at least nine letters just in the last month from NHS Improvement: fill this template, this plan, do this, do that. The NHS feels fin de siècle right now and I can't quite see how this ends.' There are moves afoot to create hospital 'chains' to rationalise services, pathology, diagnostics, human relations and back office. The Royal Free belongs to the North Central London sustainability and transformation plan, bringing another set of conflicts and opportunities into play. The Royal Free Medical School merged a while ago with University College London Hospital.

If we were considering a chain of stores, the next move would be easy: close down the loss-making branches. Applying this model to London hospitals, one obvious efficiency would be to close the maternity unit at the Royal Free. It delivers 3,000 babies a year; to be economically viable, it should be 5,500. Other London hospitals could take their births. But the Royal Free can't turn expectant mothers away. Local protest would be deafening. Here's where the public sector is so much harder to run than a private business: decisions have to reflect politics, public sentiment, money and professional judgment (notably the views of doctors and nurses).

The trust operates expensive outlying neurology services scattered around 50 sites, including Potters Bar and Cheshunt: closing them would help cut back the deficit Caroline is faced with. 'If I was in a market, I'd drop all my unprofitables, wouldn't I? Look at dermatology: everyone goes there to have moles checked – but only 9 per cent turn out to need treatment.'

In the end, she says, 'It's going to be a game of chicken with the government. Who blinks first? I've got no bloody money. Demand goes up and up, our population rising. Look at this – 20 per cent of beds – yes, five full wards costing £2m a year each to staff – are filled with delayed transfer of care patients, frail and waiting for care so they can go home.' Cash-strapped local councils can't afford it.

The Treasury summoned her and a few other NHS finance directors recently for a working lunch. 'They think we NHS managers are not very good, and they make you feel it. I just want them to know that I work with some of the cleverest and best people there are.'

She's in her mid forties. Is there another cadre of the same calibre coming up behind her? 'Absolutely. The NHS fast-track management scheme is top or in the top three choices every year in the university milk round.' Do they still have the public service ethos? 'Yes, absolutely. I listen out for it. I'm a vicar's daughter, I know it when I see it, and our young managers have it. Though goodness knows, the NHS is a very hard place to be just now.'

Where Are the Voices?

That's unusual: a senior manager prepared to be frank in public hearing. They have a three-fold choice: exit, voice or loyalty. For Whitehall permanent secretaries and local government chief executives it's usually loyalty: they never walk out, though some go quietly out of the door or into internal exile. What you don't hear is voice. Ministers can go around rubbishing public servants and encouraging their allies in the tabloids and social media to mock and ridicule local authorities and civil servants – but public servants are supposed to owe dedication and silence. Some try for revenge in their memoirs, but by then it's too late; it's necessary to remind ministers and the public in real time about such verities as evidence, fairness, financial stability and respect for the state.

Instead, officials too often seem happy to play along; you rarely hear Cabinet Secretary Sir Jeremy Heywood utter a critical word in response to the briefings given by ministers' special advisers denigrating his colleagues. Abdool Kara, chief executive of Swale district and social policy lead at the Society of Local Authority Chief Executives, was exceptional when he asked in public how his colleagues could live with politicians' 'doctrinaire liberty to expound their beliefs, cherry-picking statistics', exulting in their ideologies.[4]

It needs to be asserted that speaking out is not undemocratic. Those who make government and public services work have a deep professional interest in the wellbeing of state and society, and they have a right to be listened to, perhaps even a right of veto. They aren't voiceless dogsbodies. Peter Hennessy's post-war history *Having It So Good* is peopled with panjandrums. Sir Edward Bridges, Sir Norman Brook, Sir Percy Cradock glide in and out of the story of Suez and the H-bomb like superior butlers, equal to ministers in most respects, including respect.[5] These days the ministers and the job are different and Hennessy's giants are long gone.

In the health sector leaders do speak out, as we heard. The NHS England chief executive Simon Stevens has a voice and uses it. Other leaders, from NHS Providers, the royal colleges of general practitioners, midwives, physicians, psychiatrists and nurses, get together and sink their differences, arriving at a common line. But usually it's a health line, disconnected from the wider space.

If you define yourself as the chief executive of one particular organisation, then a rivalrous, dog-eat-dog mentality grows up. Public managers lose the width to think across boundaries and to imagine themselves having a wider, generic identity whether they work in health, education, the civil service or local government.

This wider sense of state service has been shrinking. Apart from their weekly meeting – which is usually strictly government business – and occasional away days, permanent secretaries don't meet as a collective body, let alone to generate a common view. The local chief executives' body, Solace, is a pale shadow of what it once was. The Local Government Association and regional bodies such as London Councils retreat into silence, as their members cultivate the home turf. A decade ago, during the fat Labour years, chief executives had time to attend seminars to discuss wider issues, sometimes even write articles for the *Guardian* with lively discussion about roles and relationships. Now they hunker down, fixated on day-to-day survival.

In Praise of Process

That's regrettable, because it leaves the field clear for the state's enemies to bang on about 'bureaucracy'. Let's say out loud that spending public money wisely and well necessarily involves some bureaux. Offices, that is, management, procedure and orderly administration. Government office workers give planning permission, license vehicles and drivers, conduct diplomacy, regulate water companies and guarantee the probity of exams and professional qualifications. Bureaucracy means orderliness, predictability, doing things on the basis of rules. Public services depend on paperwork.

Process secures accountability. What's done by the front line has to be noted; public money spent has to be registered. Public services, whatever trendy thinktanks say, cannot be 'chaotic'. We can too easily take for granted the trust built up over many years in a managerial culture largely free from bribery and backhanders. Running these systems is far more complex than private sector management, which has just one simple bottom line to worry about. The public manager has myriad duties and targets to meet, some of them contradictory, as they keep the complex cogs and wheels turning under wide open transparent scrutiny. So if public managers themselves won't say it, we will: expert knowledge, planning, filing cabinets (and their digital successors) are fine things.

In Praise of Expertise

Michael Gove's throwaway remark about having had enough of experts has come to define the era, just as was the case with Margaret Thatcher's 'no such thing as society'. He appeared to speak it as a reflex during the Brexit campaign, but in fact that sentiment has a long Tory pedigree. With policing, education, in health and the law, Tory ministers have pursued de-professionalisation, seeking to diminish and deskill autonomy and dispense with passed-on trained expertise. Gove himself had already claimed you don't need training to be a teacher: the number of untrained teachers shot up under his regime, reaching 13 per cent of the workforce in his new free schools and academies.

The right had traditionally excluded one class of public official from its anti-bureaucratic narrative, one profession who were always heroic and virtuous in their eyes: central bankers. Now they too are suspiciously professional, with Mark Carney falling under the general contempt for experts, for acting and speaking with authoritative independence.

In our demotic age, when it's considered impolite to point to gaps in knowledge, public managers risk appearing arrogant or (the dread word) elitist. But knowing more is what state employees ought to do, thanks to the application of skills and foresight. The essence of the role is to plan using accumulated data, analysing it and then – a scandal in the eyes of the anti-statists – projecting forward in time.

Politicians and the public, however, have limited appetite for unpalatable truth, spiky evidence and discomfiting forward projections. They prefer gut instinct or 'common sense'. If you are the Chief Medical Officer, Dame Sally Davies, you know that homeopathy is intellectual junk: your professional standing demands a dismissive response to a health secretary asking for such treatments on the NHS. She spoke out, calling homeopathy 'rubbish', since when Jeremy Hunt has been mercifully silent.[6]

Knowing more implies some duty to plan. Government guarantees the future (think pensions and bank deposits) and shapes what is to come (training teachers, failing to train nuclear engineers). The state makes schooling compulsory because it has a concern for tomorrow's economy and society. The state seeks to reduce carbon emissions, makes pension commitments and builds transport infrastructure because it accepts responsibility for the future, and recognises that it is accountable for getting it right after the present politicians have left the stage.

In Praise of Planners

Planning encompasses projections from the Office of Budget Responsibility and the Government Office for Science along with enforcing controls on land use, calculating what roads, schools and sewers are needed as populations grow.

The function of planning is hotly contested and forms a clear line of demarcation between left and right in politics. On one side are those who believe government can and must make provision for tomorrow, deploying knowledge that markets and individuals don't have. On the other side are those who say markets will deliver and firms and individuals must be freed to make their own choices: the ideologues among them add that the state can never know enough to plan sensibly, pointing to the famously failed Stalinist five-year plans of old.

In this spirit, the government pushed through the Deregulation Act 2015, which forbade local planning authorities from considering construction and layout of new dwellings in emerging plans. This was Thatcherism in action. She had abolished the Parker-Morris minimum standards for the size of rooms and height of ceilings in 1980. Homes are now so small that Ikea has just brought out a new range of diminutive furniture. Under Theresa May there are proposals on the table allowing developers to avoid seeking planning permission from councils and instead allowing them to appoint an 'alternative provider' – potentially excluding the wider public interest from the decision as to whether a scheme should go ahead.

Local authority planning departments have been weakened by cuts, leading to retirements and redundancies; they have been battered by legislative onslaught and the drip, drip of biased and tendentious reports from business lobbyists and thinktanks.

However, Tory ministers have been far from consistent. They are ever mindful of constituencies where (whatever the Hayekians and the neo-liberals say) party support depends on protecting householders and property from market-driven change, which may include new dwellings on the field where they are used to taking the dog to defecate. As a result, planning has simultaneously been made highly complex and been deregulated. In the view of the Town and Country Planning Association (TCPA) the system is now 'frustratingly ineffective'.

———————

'We are optimists by nature,' says Steve Birkinshaw, head of planning and regeneration for Erewash borough council, the Derbyshire district centred on Ilkeston.

'We want to have a positive influence on creating places people like to live, and so a positive influence on the world. We really are a hopeful profession who want to make things better, and sometimes we can have a big impact.' But even as he says it, he falls back into periodic gloom. 'The truth is, the places people like best were all built before there were any planners, like cathedral towns.' The last 30 years have seen the Nimbys win the day, the haves holding on to what they've got.

'Concentrate on good design, I tell my team. We care about the richness of the street scene, the pattern and rhythm of the street where new buildings must fit in. But with so many restrictions on us now, often we don't have much influence.'

Every district has a target number of new homes it must find room for each year: for Erewash it's 350. Birkinshaw is all for more building in order to accommodate an expanding population, 'But we can't force the private developers to build. We don't own the land, so if they just land-bank the sites we nominate and refuse to build, there's nothing we can do. The next year we have to identify places for another 350 homes, most of which won't get built either.'

Why won't they build, when there is such high demand? 'Their bottom line is profit, not the number of homes built: they make more by building just a few, and not putting a glut of homes on the market in one place, holding onto the land.' Birkinshaw, along with the TCPA, says there is no chance of the government hitting its 1 million homes target, without taking action. 'Have you noticed how we planners are always getting the blame for the lack of building? If only the planning laws were relaxed, there would be plenty of houses built, ministers say. That's just not true. It's the fault of developers refusing to build.'

Each area draws up a local plan that is supposed to look ahead at future needs and allocate space for roads and services, but without money for councils it mostly remains a paper exercise. 'Our ageing population needs sheltered housing. But we can't make that happen. We can't insist that's the type of housing that goes into a new development. We may get a few but if we don't own the land we can't control it.' If the council refuse planning permission, because the quality is low or the plan unsuitable, their decisions are now routinely overturned on appeal to the Planning Inspectorate.

Birkinshaw is a senior and experienced planner who has worked in big cities, and for a while in the Department of Communities and Local Government in Whitehall. What keeps him going in Erewash is 'optimism!', he says. He has projects he is determined to carry through. There is a 100-hectare plot where he wants to see a new development for 5,000 people on the edge of Kirk Hallam, south of Ilkeston. He has a vision: 'I want a vibrant community there, a place people want to be, for young and old, incomes of all types, with jobs on the doorstep, by bringing in factories from around here.' Derby has train, plane and car factories, and their parts manufacturers. He laughs as he says, 'I am wrestling this to the ground. I am nearly there, with the council, the leader and everyone going in the right direction.' The landowner, he says, wants to make the most money he can: he wants a big out-of-town shopping centre. But Birkinshaw is holding out for the mini new town, and he thinks he's winning. 'That's what makes my job worthwhile.'

Celebrating Knowledge

Public services are for the most part the province of people with expert knowledge, backed by training and not inexpensive in-service refresher courses and development. That's one good reason why median public sector pay is higher than in the private sector: the proportion of the highly trained is greater than in the private sector – and the public sector spends more on training.

Studies show how excellence in a school reflects its teachers' professional confidence – and, as in top-performing Finland, a sense of national respect and admiration for them. For example, policing cannot be carried out with a rulebook in hand as officers need room for discretion: how well they use it is the measure of their professionalism. The police service is special – its members are called upon to put their lives on the line. But doctors, security personnel, restaurant and vehicle inspectors as well as social workers inhabit a similar dangerous terrain, where the penalties for a mistaken judgment taken in the pressure of the moment can mean lives lost or damaged, and disgrace, retribution and loss of livelihood for the professionals concerned. While politicians and top managers are highly unlikely to have an engineering degree, an inspector examining the containment vessel of that elderly Magnox reactor has to be trusted, without anyone looking over their shoulder to check their measurements.

If we can't allow them room to apply their expertise and make their own judgments about treatment or land use or the many other areas of public service, then their effectiveness is reduced. But trust can never be unconditional. Professionals have to account for resources and the quality of their decisions. History shows that professions can, if unchecked, become cartels that operate for their own benefit, not the public interest. Professional cultures can be exclusive and self-serving. How to remain humble enough to welcome patients, parents and the public into decision-making as collaborators and fellow stakeholders, while retaining the necessary superior knowledge, is a tricky democratic dilemma for public managers and politicians.

Reinventing Professionalism

Somewhere a balance has to be struck between respect for professionals and not letting them rule the roost. The police service may have been too financially squeezed – but senior doctors haven't done so badly. They make up 4 per cent of all NHS staff but their pay and pensions amount to 13 per cent of all staff costs. Like GPs they benefited from a pay hike during Labour's term of office and median earnings are substantial, even allowing for their years of training.

Most senior doctors dislike being managed, and are often tussling with NHS structures. They see themselves as answerable to the jurisdiction only of their own profession, its royal colleges and its disciplinary General Medical Council, though they will fall under NHS managers who are clinical directors, and are themselves doctors. But delivering public services efficiently and economically depends on strong lay management, for a simple reason. The public managers measuring performance by the police officers, doctors, nurses, health and safety inspectors and teachers are themselves professionals at public management, a serious skill in its own right.

Fair Pay

These immensely complex public systems need bright people, people who deserve decent pay and reasonable job security. With a time horizon far beyond that of the majority of private companies, the state has traditionally made attractive pension arrangements for its staff. Critics are often unclear why they dislike 'gold-plated' public pensions. If what companies offer is so much worse, why not turn their fire on the private sector rather than denigrate government, pushing to level up not down? All too often the state ends up paying for the lack of good private-sector pensions as those employees retire penniless.

When opinion turned against the outrageous growth of the earnings of the top 1 per cent during the years of extravagance before the 2008 crash, oddly it was often public managers who were most pilloried by the rightwing press. Before the pay freeze that began in 2010, parts of the public sector emulated the private sector free-for-all in top pay. The boards of some public bodies (notably arm's-length bodies and some NHS trusts) aped the worst mannerisms of City remuneration committees. Still, only £1 of every hundred earned by the top 1 per cent of earners is earned by public sector employees. Though their pay shot up, their pay packets paled alongside the stratospheric sums being earned in the private sector.

Public sector excess has a lot to do with fragmentation and marketisation. Often a naïve private sector chair will be brought in to a public board, bringing with them the contaminating excesses of his own industry, declaring that a trust executive merits the kind of money he himself is used to. It has only been after universities starting rejecting their identity as public bodies that vice chancellors have been paid sums out of kilter with the responsibilities of that position, as if bloated corporate earnings were a legitimate indicator of status.

Commissioned by Labour, Will Hutton tried to set out principles for managers' pay in the public sector. He found anomalies and concluded: 'The public has the right to know that pay is deserved, fair, under control and designed to drive improving performance – and that there are no rewards for failure.'[7] But a cap or test of fairness such as a 20 to one relationship between top pay and what organisations paid their least well-paid staff was rejected as inoperable across large and complex organisations, with different numbers of low-paid workers.

The chief executive of an NHS trust with nearly 7,000 staff looking after the health of thousands of people and with a turnover of £450m gets paid (in 2016) £185,000 plus pension. That is about the same as the permanent secretary in a Whitehall department, a very different job. What chief executives are paid depends on history and happenstance, luck and longevity. It's intriguing that some of the most highly paid chieftains of housing associations – an overpaid sector – have been in their jobs for ages, suggesting there isn't much of an active market in their skills. It would be going too far to say that the pay awarded to housing chiefs is irrational, but explicating any single amount is often hard, verging on impossible.

There are no hard and fast guidelines on proper pay, as public bodies must strive to be fair both to their employees and to taxpayers, who are easily indignant at professional salaries. The state should take the longer and wider view, so it makes sense to pay above the rock-bottom going rate to boost the wages of its lower-paid staff, setting a benchmark for the private sector to compete against. In times of high unemployment it's win-win for the state to pay above the odds, as it would only be subsiding low pay with extra tax credits otherwise.

Public pay has to be good enough to recruit and keep good people, whose high motivation often makes them willing to accept less remuneration than they might get elsewhere. But the taxpaying public will be watching jealously if they are paid too much above the norm.

It's not as if top public jobs are always secure: outside Whitehall public managers can face sudden dismissal. In the NHS and local government, chief executives are held personally accountable for service failures, and are summarily sacked if a public hue and cry follows some serious blunder by someone within their hyper-complex organisations. And however hard they focus on those amber and red flashing signals on their risks registers, 'untoward events' will happen. Andrew Travers, the chief executive of Barnet council, left summarily in May 2016 when ballot boxes were late arriving at polling stations. Did he bear sole responsibility? The Cabinet Office, which allocates money to pay for elections, admitted that it had struggled with the Treasury to provide enough funds. What responsibility did the elected councillors of the borough bear? Apportioning accountability between officials and elected members is never straightforward, and public servants usually carry the can.

When executives are, like Travers, on £187,000 a year, the tabloids will fire up with an indignant response that public managers are paid well enough to put up with some job insecurity. When those hostile to public servants make the sweeping generalisation that their average pay is higher, they conveniently ignore the effect of outsourcing. The state employs few manual workers these days, as a high proportion of this work is outsourced to private contractors, pushing up the median pay of the remaining more senior public employees.

When Hutton reported he called for more openness and scrutiny of pay setting. Well in advance of Theresa May's brief conversion to the idea, he called for employees to sit on board remuneration committees to help assess performance. Fearful that such reforms in the public sector would lead to parallel demands for companies, Tory ministers backed off. Instead, Cameron instituted a crowd-pleasing cap of top public pay, saying no new public sector executive should be appointed on more than the prime minister's salary, except in special circumstances. Of course, assessing the prime ministerial salary, no allowances were made for Chequers or for all the other perks of premiership, including the very large sums former office-holders can earn when they leave Number 10.

Instead of informed, mature debate of the kind Hutton hoped to stimulate, the Tories used pay as another weapon to further undermine, delegitimise and devalue the state and those who work for it.

Chapter 7

The Efficient and Effective State

Confidence in government has slipped a lot less than might suit the state's enemies. Ipsos Mori asks regularly about 'satisfaction' with public services, and the answers have gone up and down; there is no long-run trend either way, with today's satisfaction levels (55 per cent, the same as 1980s) and dissatisfaction (30 per cent) about the same. Other long-run studies such as British Social Attitudes point to somewhat worse or unchanged. One can add to that proxy evidence in the shape of complaints. Between 1990 and 2012, complaints to the Parliamentary Ombudsman doubled to 2,000 per year. Viewed in the light of relentless criticism and denigration from the rightwing media and their online accomplices, such figures are remarkably low.

Despite Labour's loss in 2010 and the Tory victory in 2015, grudging public assent to austerity, at least at first, has not signified any noteworthy shift rightwards in public opinion, except possibly on welfare benefits, which might be a mask for discontent over migration.

All the above suggests that the recovery in esteem for the state we are advocating here might not be so hard, at least in principle. People have to be willing to pay the price for decent, equitable public services delivered by a strong state. One precondition is confidence in government efficacy. To restore it, and prepare the way to better alignment of taxes paid and services rendered, government has to be seen to enjoy intimate relations with that old threesome: economy, efficiency and effectiveness.

Economy

Parsimony with public money is not an end in itself, but a means of cementing public trust and support for the state. Staff don't have to wear hair shirts or, like clerks in the Gladstonian Treasury, pare candle ends to save farthings. Working conditions within public bodies ought, generally speaking, to mirror those in society at large, for example providing staff with tea and coffee. Yet public managers ought always to betray a tic, asking themselves the reflex question: does what we are doing secure value for the public money we are spending? If staff have to make a long journey by rail but could be productive en route, they might sometimes travel first class. The appropriate response is not to tut tut but to ask whether the organisation has a plan for maximising discounts for advance booking and to check it has secured the best possible rail ticket deal.

To economise you need data. Compared with other countries the UK is reasonably well informed about spending. But figures may still be dodgy, despite the best efforts of the Office of National Statistics and the independent UK Statistics Authority. Managers, under pressure, may try to game the system. Statistics Authority chair Sir Andrew Dilnot says, 'It is no good to achieve a target that you are able to manipulate; there is only credit in achieving a target if it is independently measured.'[1]

Economy is often given the standard interpretation of pushing current spending into the corset of tight annual budgets. True economy is more strategic and thinks ahead: for example investing in measures and programmes for children early in life may reduce the need to spend on them as adolescents or adults. Much spending on schools and public health is investment not consumption and should be accounted for accordingly: cutting maintenance budgets shortens the life of these assets.

One of the curiosities of the British state is the juxtaposition of longevity with short termism. Through world wars, social upheaval and demographic flux, the state goes on; the Treasury is still paying out on loans raised in the mid 19th century. Companies get taken over, deserted by fickle shareholders, but the state goes on.

Yet it can be hard to see what happens across time when the numbers are discontinuous or missing. Too much of the data, especially spending figures, is in fact difficult to compare across time, or fails to clarify such elementary distinctions as capital and revenue, real terms and inflation adjusted, aggregate and per capita. Although the data is available, it is not necessarily workable.

In their prizewinning book *A Government that Worked Better and Cost Less?*, Christopher Hood and Ruth Dixon said we simply can't tell how far improvement resulted from IT or the rush to contract out services. They tried to compare the running cost of government over the past 35 years – the heyday of New Public Management – with satisfaction with public services. You can't do the sums – at least not reliably – because ministers kept chopping and changing and sometimes not even bothering to collect the relevant figures; permanent secretaries and Treasury officials did little or nothing to stop them.

Painstakingly, the academics stick the disparate data series together with Sellotape. They find that over 30 years, the running costs of central government rose. Civil service pay increased in real terms from about £15bn in the early 1980s to £16bn in 2012, despite a 200,000 reduction in numbers. Yet the running costs of central government rose in real terms from £15bn to £30bn. The disparity is explained, the study suggests, by the huge expansion in consultancy and contracting out. New Public Management has cost more yet hasn't made things measurably more efficient and effective.

All big organisations have spent but not reaped commensurate benefit. The New York Stock Exchange and Sainsbury's are only two of the many private-sector bodies that have wasted huge sums and had to abort big IT projects. But the state has also notched up big failures, responsibility for which is shared between officials, ministers and private contractors. Before the Inland Revenue and HM Customs & Excise merged, the former gave a £1.8bn contract to Electronic Data Systems (now owned by Hewlett-Packard) amid promises of great gains and efficiencies; there is no evidence of either.

The National Programme for IT launched by the Blair government became a watchword for overreach; Universal Credit, the flagship welfare reform project launched by Iain Duncan Smith in 2010, ditto. In a study for the Institute for Government, Nicholas Timmins describes an ill-managed programme that may only be delivered a decade after it was promised at considerably smaller scale and will cost billions.[2] Worse, it probably won't give benefit claimants any additional incentive to find work and won't deal with the huge problem of how poor households afford increasing rents in the areas where there are jobs. The project was bedevilled by the Tory determination to make the poor suffer the brunt of 'fiscal adjustment' after the crash and a dogmatic but out-of-his-depth secretary of state, Iain Duncan Smith.

Audit, Data, Reporting

The faltering progress of Universal Credit was scrutinised by parliamentary committees and the National Audit Office. It was not their fault that the government simply did not want to know. The UK possesses a formidable apparatus for gauging how public money is spent. Margaret Hodge, chair of the Public Accounts Committee said, 'We need to be able to follow where the pound goes and assure Parliament and the public that the pound has created real value.'[3] The devolved audit bodies and NAO perform the dual task of ensuring that money is spent lawfully and corruption is hunted down. For local authorities and the NHS in England there used to be the Audit Commission – but this was abolished by the coalition government.

Councils in England lose over £2bn a year to fraud. That's not disproportionate to what private firms and households suffer, but public money should be subject to special attention. And once upon a time this was the case. So we learned from visiting Brent town hall in Wembley, north-west London.

––––––––––

Asked what keeps her awake at night, Carolyn Downs answers, as council chief executives tend to: she worries most about children. At any time infants and young people are at risk of coming to harm; is the system safe, is the London Borough of Brent equipped to protect them?

But second on Downs' list as head of a major local authority is audit. The thinning out of her staff in management, administration and supervision means 'it could all go wrong. No one has time now to do basic checking. There is bound to be more corruption going undetected. I feel it in my bones. People are overwhelmed with work.'

The state gives things – money, goods, services – to the public and some are tempted to take more than their fair share. Within councils there is vast scope for theft and corruption – from the handing out of parking permits and disability blue badges to immensely valuable 'cash for keys' housing fraud, giving out high priced-housing in exchange for bribes. Procurement contracts offer multiple opportunities for such misconduct.

'The temptation is huge,' she says, 'and human nature doesn't change. With less checking, there is bound to be more corruption.' Take parking permits. 'The other day I asked why one single contractor has been given 19 permits. Why 19, I asked? No one knew. There was no real process, and permits are worth a lot: it's easy to Tipp-Ex over the registration.' One councillor asked why his high-priority constituent had suddenly been taken off the housing list. 'I didn't know but when I went to find out, I didn't quite get an answer. That sets alarm bells ringing.' She is sending auditors 'all over' the housing department. 'But I know I will be mainly relying on whistle-blowers who see something and report it.'

As the back room shrivels and those 'faceless bureaucrats' are diminished, the risk of dishonesty grows. It has taken centuries to grow a remarkably honest and well-trusted public service in this country – and we see how hard it is for developing countries to stamp out corruption once it's endemic. How easily and quickly all that trust can be lost once there is no longer a solid framework for reliable auditing and automatic everyday supervision.

Rob Whiteman is chief executive of the Chartered Institute of Public Finance and Accountancy, one of the principal professional bodies for finance staff in local government. He says, 'Without doubt, we are now entering the uncharted territory of unintended consequences. Local authority cuts of 40 per cent mean we have fewer finance officers and auditors, making staff more prone to corruption, especially as they have had no pay rises. People keep calling for yet more management and back office savings but it is reaching the point where it endangers all the processes that protect the public.'

Brent's accounts are still audited, says Carolyn Downs, but now by contractors. 'Our audit has been outsourced to external auditors KPMG, as the government prescribed, and they are rather nice about us. Too much so, I think.'

The disappearance of the Audit Commission may have put a relatively clean public sector in jeopardy, just when organised crime has become more sophisticated and online fraud is growing. Procurement contracts under £50,000 are barely scrutinised. A contractor holding several such contracts from various local authorities could be making a lot of money, which is hard to detect.

There used to be many more staff to check on housing fraud: is there really just a single person living in that home, paying reduced council tax? With fewer staff, local knowledge is lost.

Housing scams are high value frauds: right to buy fraud is increasing, and expected to rise sharply as housing associations are forced to sell their properties to tenants. Cases abound. There was a woman in Birmingham who fraudulently claimed a 70 per cent right to buy discount to buy her council house, while living in a second home that she had owned for over 10 years. Not untypical either is the head teacher who abstracted more than £7,000 worth of funds at a West Midlands primary: this is becoming more common as schools fall under less scrutiny, and head teachers have more autonomy.

Whiteman finds it ominous that less fraud is being detected. 'Ten years ago we had our own people who had that "auditor's nose" for sniffing things out that were not quite right. We used to be very good at catching the bread-and-butter fraud, like ghost employees on the payroll. Now we have external auditors, they are likely to be less good and they now have to rely on weaker information from internal systems that don't work as well.'

The audit professionals' list of what to look out for is long, warning of risk in all kinds of procurement contracts – money laundering, false slips-and-trips insurance claims, businesses making fraudulent applications for exemptions and reliefs, new public health contracts recently passed to councils, cyber crime with false diversion of money to bogus accounts, double invoicing, grants for voluntary work that was never done, staff pensions still paid to deceased ex-employees, staff diverting council money to personal accounts – and a great deal more.

Nonetheless, whatever malign media and axegrinders may say, the flow of money into government and out to services is still traceable and transparent. Controversy around the Private Finance Initiative was in large measure about the covert way in which deals were refinanced and profits hidden from public view.

Secrecy is the private sector way. The annual reports of public companies are usually uninformative. The action takes place in private briefings to analysts and share dealers. Millions in the private sector are squandered on excess pay, on botched decisions and failed mergers that enrich only their fixers, yet company accounts provide little basis for scrutiny and company shareholders are rarely interested in these details, especially if they only hold shares for nano-seconds. Firms increasingly invest in intangible assets that do not appear on their balance sheets.

By contrast the state is rife with self-reporting. Gov.uk churns out masses of accountability data, as do the devolved governments, arm's-length bodies, NHS trusts and local authorities. It is not always as intelligible as it could be and presentation varies, but it is augmented by the oversight of multiple watchdogs.

Public bodies not only report, but their board meetings are often open. That said, beyond a few people – who are either dedicated or come for the tea and biscuits – the public are never going to have the time or energy to invest in scrutiny or assiduous reading of minutes and reports. Instead they need confidence in government's peculiar reflexivity, meaning how it monitors and corrects itself.

As well as auditors, the state invigilates itself through inquiries and runs umpteen corps of inspectors, who patrol health, social care, police, probation, prisons, schools and colleges, childcare, the railways and environmental health, as we saw in Chapter 2. But, as with open documentation, this exposure can and often is used as a weapon against the state. The growth of watchdoggery is often a tool to undermine public confidence in public provision. This has been the stock in trade of Health Secretary Jeremy Hunt.

The Mid Staffordshire NHS Trust is a case in point. It was badly run and the public inquiry set up in 2010, led by Robert Francis QC, produced a narrative from which all healthcare providers could learn positively. Instead Hunt used the Francis report to declare all NHS care to be in crisis, encouraging wild generalisation from the experience of one trust. He wound the

Care Quality Commission (CQC) up to become a bludgeon and bully. Coaches hired by the CQC pulled up outside hospitals and clinics to disgorge scores of inspectors determined to find fault. OFSTED, the inspection regime for England's schools, has by and large managed to resist such conscription.

But inspectors, like auditors, usually say their job isn't to criticise policy decisions, including spending. In recent years that has meant their judgments have lost value: what's the point of critiquing the lack of nurses or the rising deficit in one hospital trust, when the cause of the problem lies not in that hospital but in policy made elsewhere?

Assessing Efficiency

In 2013, the year of the Francis report, other essential reading offered a comparison with the sins of the private sector: the report of the parliamentary banking standards commission, chaired by Tory MP Andrew Tyrie, depicted boardroom failure and inadequacy. These two reports defy any generalisation about the superiority of public or private sector when it comes to 'corporate governance'. The same goes for 'efficiency' and the notion that on any like-for-like basis, profit-seeking companies are better at securing their outputs at the lowest possible price sector.

The first base for assessing efficiency is to understand what public bodies do. This work goes far beyond crude comparisons of cost – such as that seen on travel websites. In 2010, the coalition made great play about securing efficiency by requiring public bodies to publish all their spending figures so that the public could assess value for money. Communities Secretary Eric Pickles envisioned armchair auditors clicking online to examine every penny of expenditure, and then arraigning their local councillors and officials. Look at this extravagance, his spin doctors told their media pals – this huge annual bill for flowers being delivered to that town hall. It took a while for the penny to drop: town halls celebrate weddings and weddings tend to attract floral decorations, for which the town hall receives the initial bill, and couples and their families later reimburse the council.

Of course public spending bears close scrutiny; not all public bodies can say with confidence what their purposes are and how well their spending achieves their aims. OFSTED, for example, finds only an uncertain relationship between the quality of services for children in need and the amount spent by councils in England.

Benchmarking may show variation in performance between similar departments, NHS trusts or local authorities. This can be used to suggest scope for improvement. But public bodies are attuned to the political and social circumstances within which they operate. Carting the refuse from a block of flats is a different operation from collecting the bins in suburban streets. Reasons for disparity in spending on, say, child protection have less to do with bad social workers than entrenched deprivation and family breakdown.

Efficiency isn't an end state. How often in recent decades both left and right have called dramatically for 'reform', as if a one-off magic shot in the arm such as privatisation or extra spending is all it takes. Efficiency is a permanent work in progress: organisation and delivery of services can always be improved. On stepping down as chair of the Public Accounts Committee, Margaret Hodge compiled a long list of inefficiencies, along with persistent delinquents in Whitehall departments and elsewhere. In her book *Called to Account* she asks why repeated inquiries find the same mistakes made in the same areas, defence procurement being a particularly expensive example.[4] Successive reports from the NAO, added to studies by the Institute for Government, say UK central government could be more fit for purpose, more effective and probably cheaper, too. The Institute for Government's Julian McCrae sums up the problem. 'For over half a century, Whitehall has conspicuously failed to develop the commercial, financial and project management skills necessary to run a modern state.'[5] How far that is due to political failure – an unwillingness to think hard and long about the permanent machinery of government – or inertia and conservatism on the part of the mandarins is moot.

Anti-state ideology says public organisations are condemned to inefficiency because they lack the spur of competition. Let's ignore the obvious fact that competition only applies to markets in fits and starts. If it drives down price, it usually degrades quality in public services and in health, say, where quality is paramount. It also demotivates staff and, as we saw in the previous chapter, it undermines their professionalism.

Public organisations can, it is true, tend towards inertia and inefficiency, so stimulus towards innovation and economy has to be built in. Striving to minimise outlays while securing the best possible service is a perpetual challenge. Public bodies need constant prodding, preferably from a critical friend, who is able to compare performance and provide benchmarks while respecting the qualities of public service. That critical friend should be able to distinguish between genuine efficiency savings and cuts to service; ceasing to maintain grass verges, for example, is doing less, not doing the same better.

That critical friend should be listened to, in the way that too often audit reports aren't. A gap too often separates analysis and remedy. We probably need a new Office of Performance with a remit to carry into effect all those recommendations from the PAC and other audit bodies that cause a one-day-wonder news report and then disappear into the ether.

How to Be Efficient: A Smarter State?

'Modernity' involves an entire slate of problems that have no clean-cut solutions. In defence, for example, the never-ending dilemmas involve keeping up with technological change and expensive new weapons that the other side has developed. Or new regional threats that keep changing: tanks were declared redundant in the defence of Europe after the Berlin Wall fell in 1989, but now thanks to Vladimir Putin's bellicosity they are back in the front line. How can a decade-long government procurement timetable keep up?

The state can't, however, duck the challenge. As Cameron said, it has to keep getting 'smarter'.[6] But as on so many other occasions, his talk was hollow. A smart state needs well-paid, well-respected staff and should be led by ministers who believe in public purposes realised by well-financed government. If you reckon the state is bloated and the people who work for it are timeservers and second-raters, which is the view held by several cabinet ministers, you aren't likely to appeal to smart people.

A smart state might speed up its IT and cut costs as more people connect online with councils, the NHS, income tax, benefits and government agencies. But it's not smart to ignore the large numbers of poorer and older citizens who may never cope online.

Government digital has made progress: towards biometric passports, a single sign-on so people don't have to re-identify themselves to different public services and more online bookings and transactions. We're still in the foothills, says Kevin Cunnington, head of Government Digital Services, which runs the common platform Gov.uk. The DWP and tax offices still only share minimal amounts of data, forcing members of the public to repeat data entries and slowing down payments to and from government. But it's an exciting frontier.

However, beware those – Tory ministers especially – who say they have a magic bullet. You hear this all the time about the NHS. A whopping £22bn is to be saved by 2020, yet no health economist believes it. Tory civil service minister Francis Maude saw 'transformation' as a way of cutting the body count among civil servants, failing to see that numbers matter. Maude singled out the Department for Education: 'It is halving in size, but its radical programme is changing the face of secondary education.'[7] As we saw in Chapter 2, the formula is turning out to be a recipe for educational anarchy, forcing the department to appoint regional commissioners and staff to step in and sort out the multiplying examples of waste and duplication among academy schools.

What Has the State Ever Done for Us?

Efficiency means getting services at minimum cost, while effectiveness is about seeing a result. The public care about outcomes – minimizing salmonella poisoning, say. But government often seems to spend too much time worrying about inputs, such as the number of inspections of restaurant kitchens. One depends on the other, but the public just see the tip of the iceberg. Private companies don't have this problem: their owners only have to worry about profit. The state's problem is that tax and costs are highly visible while the public service or process they pay for may be out of sight or unsung.

The state's trumpet goes unblown and the *Life of Brian* question does not always get the full answer it deserves. I've paid my £1.5m in tax, said Godfrey Bloom, the former UKIP MEP, and all I've got to show for it is a measly £500 a month state pension.[8] This reductionist and naïve view is all too common. The response he got on Twitter was apt: here is someone who apparently has lived for 50 years 'without using a road, hospital, GP surgery' to which can be added that he clearly has never breathed clean air, used a regulated market, eaten trustworthy food in a restaurant, spent state-guaranteed money or, as one online wit observed, used a public toilet.

Yet such a list is a reminder of how diverse the public realm is and how it suffers from lack of 'brand identification'. The problem is one of concentration and focus and it starts in the middle. In a governmental system often characterised as overly centralised, the centre is surprisingly weak. The centre of UK government has been called a Bermuda Triangle. Bounded by the Treasury, Number 10 and the Cabinet Office is a dark terrain where no one assumes responsibility for curating the state.

A strong centre could secure the pan-Whitehall cross-government collaboration on which the effectiveness of most policies depends. Take wellbeing, which hinges on exercise, income, education, housing, access to leisure centres and so on. Labelling one pot of money as 'health and wellbeing' and allocating it to a single department results in a narrowing of focus. Making the state more strategic means uprooting entrenched civil service attitudes, subordinating sectional for the general interest and improving branding efforts such as a single digital presence and HM Government identity. It would also mean giving the 'centre of the centre' in the Treasury, Cabinet Office, Number 10 and their devolved equivalents more authority in securing a common line.

Towards a Common Public Service

Too often public servants splinter and fragment, putting up obstacles to cooperation and failing to see the bigger picture. Take something as obvious as securing economies of scale through procurement. Despite the efforts of the Cabinet Office – under successive prime ministers – interdepartmental collaboration is weak; the government fails to act as a single purchaser, utilising its combined bargaining power. Government recognises that it needs to act as one customer to exploit its buying power in the market – and yet it cannot pull itself together in order to do so.

Recently, the Cabinet Office has made more effort to strengthen purchasing power by building up and sharing commercial expertise between departments – in part by centralising buying and management of common goods and services through what is now called the Crown Commercial Service. This agency reckons Whitehall departments buy 'common' goods and services worth between £8bn and £15bn a year that it could be procuring on their behalf. Would it be an undue restriction on the Department of Culture or the Environment Agency if toilet paper for staff loos were bought in bulk? Too often what is missing is collaborative and flexible behaviour by departments, and within departments.

Help for those with mental health problems is split when it should be shared between NHS clinicians, the police, council housing and social work staff, as well as family and neighbours. Around half of people with lifetime mental health problems experience symptoms by the age of 14, but counselling is available in only a limited number of schools – and the fragmentation of education in England has not helped. Services helping people with mental health problems get back into work are not joined up between the NHS and the Department for Work and Pensions, and these problems are compounded if they fall into the clutches of private sector benefit assessors who have a financial incentive to ignore or underplay their condition.

Turf Wars

A selfish spirit also runs through departments' arm's-length bodies. Made worse by the recent governments, the landscape in health is pitted with fortifications built to protect pieces of turf: Monitor – now NHS Improvement – duplicates the work of NHS England and both have a jagged relationship with Public Health England, the Health Research Authority, Health Education England, the National Institute for Health and Care Excellence and so on down a dizzyingly long list. Functional differences cannot be wished away, but they need to express an underlying commitment to the same objects – notably, the health of England.

Public service professionals will always need breathing space to exercise their own judgment, based on their training and experience, as we saw in the previous chapter. Teachers see a child differently from social workers and police officers. All those perspectives are valid and may demand separate organisations to accommodate them. But a pathology of public service has been the construction of barriers between departments and functions. The public are bemused when – especially in child protection – services can't or won't communicate with one another, or share their findings and reports.

Increased sharing between public services could also help the public sector make itself more attractive to new recruits, thus deepening its talent pool. Career paths within the public sector should be aligned with a single online portal for advertising management roles and common induction and entry training, opening the doors for middle and senior managers to work across the public sector and private sector – deepening their opportunities and experience.

Don't Call It 'Engagement'

Effectiveness means more than just listing government objectives and recording whether targets have been met. The public has to be convinced. The public sector word here is 'engaged'. But people don't use this word – or rather, when they do they mean getting betrothed. It's partly a matter of vocabulary, partly to do with the way the public sector has been trying to ape business jargon. Oddly, the recent cuts do not seem to have deflated the bubbles of the new vocabulary, which includes localism, community, choice, contestability, 'reform', innovation, partnership, vision, governance and – king of the heap – transformation. Instead of continuous improvement, it's revolution. Inflated rhetoric is pumped into documents where theorists of the new cry: heed us or you die, radical change is inevitable.

Jargon, acronyms and sometimes, you suspect, deliberate obscurantism in too many statements and papers are objectionable because they exclude the public and take the state even further away from daily comprehension and appreciation. All public bodies ought constantly to make their paperwork and websites intelligible to a public that may only have basic levels of literacy and numeracy and who don't recognise acronyms or the complex architecture of public service.

A guide to written content on the Gov.uk website sensibly divides communications within the system (where acronyms and shortcuts may make sense to insiders) from mainstream messages to citizens, taxpayers, companies and the public. Yet the state is too often mealy-mouthed, if not downright obtuse.

———————

Here is the British Council advertising for someone to supervise the teaching of English, no less:

'Regional English Language Policy Project Manager is responsible for the successful implementation of a 30-week project in two regions of Peru. The project aims to establish a replicable model for English policy implementation at regional level. This directly impacts regional leaders and influencers who need to strengthen their English language skills in order to empower themselves to build commitment and action plans that allow them to implement the policy successfully. The project also aims to collate key baseline information that allows the UK education sector to engage effectively with regional leaders, influencers and stakeholders to offer continuous partnership and support for bilingualism targets.'

Here is Stockport NHS Trust explaining why they will not, after all, appoint a second nurse – and possibly not wanting to be entirely honest:

'We are proud of the Parkinson's service we provide here at Stockport Foundation Trust. In an effort to continue to provide the highest quality service we have identified the Parkinson's service as key to the Stockport Together Proactive programme delivered as a Vanguard model of care. This will mean a slight change of service alignment within the Foundation Trust by moving it from the traditional Medicine Business Group to a more Community-based setting. This change will have no negative impact on the quality of the service being delivered and will only help us to fully understand the demands on the service when delivered in this way and work with Commissioners to determine if our current resources are sufficient.'

For anyone who thinks they may have been marked unfairly in an exam, here's the Office of Qualifications and Examinations Regulation (Ofqual) and its clear-as-mud explanation of what a marking error is:

'The awarding of a mark or the arrival at an outcome of Moderation which could not reasonably have been given or arrived at given the evidence generated by the Learner(s) (and for Moderation, the centre's marking of that evidence), the criteria against which Learners' performance is differentiated and any procedures of the awarding organisation in relation to Moderation or marking, including in particular where the awarding of a mark or outcome of moderation is based on: an Administrative Error, a failure to apply such criteria and procedures to the evidence generated by the Learner(s) where that failure did not involve the exercise of academic judgment, or an unreasonable exercise of academic judgment'.

———

Government needs to watch its language, its visual signals, its websites and its public messages and speak in human terms. The state should be brisk, concrete and demotic (meaning ordinary!). 'Deliver' is what you do with pizzas, not priorities.

'Results' are better than the ubiquitous and woolly 'impact'. 'Facilitate' is either unnecessary or can be replaced by 'do'. And so on. We need to be wary of falling into the trap set by the anti-statists, who imply that complexification is a sin unique to the public sector. Government bodies are many-sided organisms and in their internal dealings inevitably use shortcuts, common understandings and acronyms. As do banks, retailers and Barnardo's. Some professional language rests on esoteric knowledge: what doctors and software designers do may be impossible to express in everyday terms.

A distinction should be made between rococo language and procedure. A 55-page form – for tax credits or rural payments – may be justified by the conditions set for getting the money applied for. Make them simpler and financial accountability might suffer, and opportunities for fraud grow. Advocates of a basic income that would sweep away all the form filling are dishonest if they don't admit that the basic income would have to be set very high, at a prohibitive cost, if benefits were to be really simplified.

Charles Dickens is often enlisted in the anti-statist cause because of *Little Dorrit*. But his indictment of the Circumlocution Office was that it stopped government doing things: the novel was powered by his anger at obstacles to action over social injustice.

The Value of Complaints

One way of measuring the effectiveness of an institution is to examine how it is perceived by the public, and how happy they are with its service. In 2015–16, the Local Government Ombudsman received 11,833 complaints, against 18,020 in

2009–10. Quite what that measures is not obvious. If police numbers are down and the speed at which you get help and attention from an officer has been cut ... if waiting times at A&E are up ... if your library has shut ... you might well be in complaining mood. But what's the point of belabouring the council manager or the NHS chief executive (especially the latter) when what she or he can provide is entirely conditional on spending decisions made by ministers?

Yet access to a reliable system for complaints has to be part of sustaining public confidence in government. A good manager will even value complaints as a way of gauging how well a service is delivered.

The trouble is that complaints are used by enemies of government as a weapon rather than a learning and improvement mechanism. This is one reason why complaints handlers have proliferated. As well as the Parliamentary Ombudsman, there is apparatus around councils, the police and courts and schools. However, few complaints mechanisms allow for the effect of central government spending cuts. Nor is it made clear enough how complaints can be dealt with when a service has been contracted out. Where do parents go if they are not happy about the latest free school? Or if they're unhappy that the free school has leached money that would otherwise have been spent on their children's education? Some contractors have elaborate schemes for complaints, but do I go to them or the council if litter is deposited outside my house on bin day?

Front-of-House Friendliness

How do most people come face to face with the workings of the state? Often accidentally, erratically, maybe only via some lowly employee, or not even an employee but someone working for a contractor, or a temp agency for a contractor. That first encounter will be freighted with importance – the hospital porter, the door keeper at the job centre where you go to enquire about your pension, the school or doctor's receptionist, a bin man, a post office counter, or a hundred others, each one carrying the public sector's reputation in their demeanour. Citizens may forge their view of the whole organisation and maybe even the state itself at the point of contact between themselves and 'front of house' public employees – and they pass on that pleasant/hostile impression to their friends and family. Yet often those first faces of the state are the least monitored, the last people considered by boards, senior executives, councillors or ministers. They are wrongly regarded as too lowly to bother about: treated badly and disrespectfully by their institutions, they may pass that disrespect on to the public.

'Do you really want to know why folk don't bother to report crime?' a blogger responded to a story in the *Echo*, the paper covering Southend, Basildon and other parts of south Essex.[9] 'First you have to call a number, which often rings for ages. Finally you get through to an officer who sounds so harassed, you feel you are a nuisance. If you can get over feeling embarrassed about bothering them, then you get fobbed off that someone will call you back, then someone will take a statement (often several days and even a week or so down the line, when your memory is fading with important details). You get asked to attend Canvey Police Station, where the officers demand who sent you down there, when the phone officers simply give you a date and time to attend – you feel so degraded, so punished enough, you simply walk away, too upset to want to take it any further.'

Our Canvey Island blogger went on to offer his/her remedy to the Essex police, and other organisations will take heed. The message may be unoriginal, but the fact it needs repeating says much. 'Please make the initial calls easier to get through to a person, not leave a recorded message, please come out for statements within 24 hours max and please be more welcoming to those who have been brave enough to come to you for help.'

————————

The complaint has an all-too-authentic ring about it. A snotty GP's receptionist, a grumpy school caretaker, a rough nurse or, as here, an impatient desk officer in a police station: these may help explain the great paradox of the first decade of the 21st century. Why, despite such growth in spending on services, and extra staff numbers in many of them, did the public fail to applaud, or register improvement?

Perhaps one answer is that, in our increasingly individualist age, people's sense of their dignity and self-worth have grown, making them more sensitive to slights and signs of 'disrespect', which itself has become a key word in the way other people and organisations are perceived.

People form their views from a variety of sources – from hearsay, random chat on- and off-line as well as personal experience. One bad personal anecdote may be passed on to dozens of people, leading to a widespread negative perception of the system or service: bad stories travel further and faster than the tales of good treatment. People big up crime in their area if they themselves have been victims or if they believe the area is run down or neglected – whatever the objective evidence says. Statistics rarely trump stories.

The media matters too. Police forces now publish crime maps, with details about offences in the vicinity, but people still rely on media reports, usually exaggerated and prone to emphasise individual stories. Crime is the easy staple for the local press and TV; it's cheap to report stories in court, without bothering with any general context that would say how far and fast crime has fallen since the mid-1990s.

The state, in other words, often faces a credibility gap that hostile forces – not exclusively but notably the *Daily Mail*, the *Sun* and their online equivalents – seek to deepen. A problem is that perceptions of quality, reported in surveys of customer/patient/citizen experience, may be formed ad hoc, and randomly, because people may judge quality not by improved medical outcomes or more crimes solved, but by the way they are personally treated.

Chapter 8

We Need to Talk About Tax

Our ways of thinking have been dominated by economics. Of course numbers matter: income, spending and the proportion of what we earn that is shared with the organism that makes the earning possible in the first place are all essential to our wellbeing. But the terms of the cost-benefit calculus are often too narrow; they cannot be confined to what is immediately quantifiable. Taxation is never just about money: it is the seat of wider attitudes towards society and government.

Tax should be fairer. Those who have more should pay more. The tax net embraces us all, including big companies that trade overseas. They should no longer be allowed to evade and avoid taxation. The tax net should also embrace our assets as well as our income. Authoritative reports say time and again that the UK system of taxing property – through council tax, inheritance tax and stamp duty land tax on purchases – is inefficient and inequitable. The state could be much more effective in collecting money owed, through back tax and fines; HM Revenue and Customs should be one of the principal governmental departments, not a backwater.

Paying More

Tackling tax avoidance and evasion is not, of course, a substitute for citizens actually paying income tax, VAT or other charges, or explicitly making the link between what the state can do and its revenues. At the end of the day, we can't duck a basic proposition: paying for decent public services means raising tax and for the most part that must mean decisions about how much to levy on income and property. Is that so painful? The alternative to tax is barbarism: in how we treat the disadvantaged, the sick and children. Tax is the price we pay for a civilised society.

Yet the debate about tax, such as it is, has been framed as if we were a nation of rugged individualists fending off an assault on our hard-won money. Previous governments, especially those on the left, could have done so much more to enrich this social conversation and emphasise reciprocity. It's not just that our economic being and our ability to earn depends on the (tax-financed) state, it's also that tax is a way of sharing – paying our neighbour's pension, schooling for the child in the flat opposite. It's a simple truth: if we want a strong NHS, good education, beautiful public buildings and parks, let alone decent care when we are old, and secure borders, we must share our income to provide them collectively – through the state.

The UK is middle of the road in international comparisons, with other European countries on one side of the street and the US and white Commonwealth on the other. Tax revenue in the UK was just under 33 per cent of GDP in 2015, compared with just over 50 per cent in Denmark and 36 per cent in Germany. The US figure was 26 per cent, which is lower than in Canada and Japan (both just over 30 per cent) but similar to Australia. So how much of what conventional wisdom calls the tax 'burden' do inhabitants of the UK bear?

Undertaxing not Overspending

One charge levelled at the Blair–Brown governments was always false: Labour did not overspend, it undertaxed. Raising taxes would not have had to mean higher income tax. With courage, Labour might have grappled with a longstanding failure to tax property and wealth effectively and fairly. Taxes on above-average-value properties might have prevented the housing market bubbling into excess. Labour turned away from proper taxation of inheritance, even as a device to pay for meeting the growing cost of social care for older people. Cameron, Osborne and opportunist Liberal Democrats attacked Labour for spending the nation into deficit; a fairer charge is that fiscal cowardice produced no sustainable basis for very necessary spending.

In ageing Britain more will need to be spent on healthcare, pensions and long-term care – the Office for Budget Responsibility estimates the costs at an extra 1.8 per cent of GDP during the decade after 2020, just to stand still on quality and keep up with the demographics. That approximates to twice today's revenues from inheritance tax, stamp duties and capital gains tax. Older people tend to have accumulated assets and, increasingly, enjoy generous post-work incomes. The question of tax is unavoidable.

Yet it's taboo. 'Policymakers rarely step back to consider the design of their national tax systems as a whole,' said the Mirrlees Review, convened by the Institute of Fiscal Studies. 'Public understanding of taxation is limited. And the political and public discussion of tax design is woefully inadequate.'[1] People don't understand National Insurance – they think it pays for the NHS when it's an additional income tax that goes into the general pot. They certainly don't understand council tax – they think it pays for councils when the bulk of local government is financed from grants and business rates.

In government, spending is the route to glamour, excitement and career advancement, except possibly in the Treasury – though even there, the grubby business of raising revenue is delegated to a separate organisation, HMRC, its headquarters now physically adjacent to the Treasury in Whitehall but lower in status. Spending is prime, despite the logic that insists raising the money has to come first. Ministers, councillors, executives – and auditors – devote most of their time and energy to programmes and policies. No one wants to be the back legs of the pantomime horse and raise the revenue. For every hour public managers, councillors, MPs and ministers spend thinking about spending, they devote bare minutes, sometimes just seconds, to thinking about how that spending is funded. If they did, public services would be in a much healthier condition. One of Margaret Hodge's achievements was to shift the attention of auditors towards the effectiveness of HMRC, the state's ability to levy tax and reasons why individuals and companies seemed able to dodge it quite easily.

Call it the great asymmetry. Judged by conference themes, pamphlets and seminars, the proportion of total time and effort given over to taxation is minuscule. Staff are not – when surveying flood plains or organising adult social care – going to say to citizens: you do realise, don't you, that these services depend critically on our collective willingness to muster tax payments? We, service providers, need to make you aware as service users that taxation is the key to our relationship, and the quality and volume of the services we can offer.

The reason for tax silence isn't just that the Treasury is historically jealous of anyone else getting involved with money matters. In British central government we observe the peculiar convention that budgeting (the core financial activity of the state) is a personal act by the Chancellor of the Exchequer. 'The Treasury', said the Mirrlees Review, 'is a remarkably powerful institution and, as far as tax policymaking is concerned, has become more powerful in recent years, as it has taken on much of the policymaking capability of HMRC. There are no checks and balances within the executive. Parliament has a rather weak oversight role, particularly when it comes to more complex areas of tax policy.'

Tax silence also stems from the strength of individualist ideology, as if payment were a private transaction, which should be closely guarded. However, since the financial crash and recession, attitudes have shifted and economists are no longer so willing to give a malfunctioning market system a cover story. Attention has switched to obligations, especially on the part of banks and companies, which so clearly depend on government for their survival and prosperity. The old reflex against tax has given way to fiscal common sense, and more widespread understanding that decent services have to be paid for.

Borrow Today, Tax Tomorrow

To pay for the revival and reassembly of the public sector, governments have either to borrow or tax. Trading one against another has been one of history's large gears for many centuries, turning the fate of monarchy in 17th-century Britain and now, in democracy, working the main lines of politics. Tension recedes only when states such as Saudi Arabia or Norway have access to revenues from extracting a lucrative natural product – at least as long as the dollar price of oil remains high.

Limits on borrowing were never as precise and forbidding as rightwing economists and Tory ministers once claimed: note how they are less vocal now that circumstances have trumped 'laws'. With the loudhailer press behind them, the Tories sold the public a false comparison between state and household borrowing. There are limits to what governments can borrow, though no one quite knows in advance where they fall and calculations are very different since 2008.

Some have moral objections to making tomorrow pay for today's consumption (revenue spending) but with capital investment, tomorrow actually benefits from today's spending. It seems to have taken the Tories seven years to learn the difference, and even Osborne's successor, Philip Hammond, has chosen to raise investment levels despite urgent infrastructure needs – for example, one reason for the UK's low productivity is its poor transport system. The state's capacity to borrow is much greater than the advocates of austerity admitted: because of historically low rates of interest the state could maintain high levels of indebtedness. But it's taxation that must cover interest payments and, as and when, pay down outstanding debt.

Across the OECD countries, tax on income, social security (National Insurance) and consumption (VAT) have been the state's principal revenue. As a proportion of total take, tax on business has fallen – which ought, according to theories espoused by marketeers, to have unleashed more enterprise and growth than has been evident. Instead this has been reflected in a race-to-the-bottom contest between countries, in which all lose out by raising less than they could and should from company profits. States 'had to' compete by cutting corporation tax, said the prophets; the injunction fell apart on the rocks of the financial crash, as the selfish tax models adopted by the Republic of Ireland, for example, were exposed. A special dogma applies to corporation tax; cutting it is deemed to be good for the economy when its effects on employment may be non-existent and its fiscal consequences are to put extra unfair pressure on those paying tax as they earn.

Raising tax need not mean bumping up tax rates. Revenues should grow as the economy expands, when rates are stable. If tax-funded state efforts to promote GDP growth succeed, the Treasury benefits and the public realm becomes self-sustaining. Taxation now can reduce the need for tax tomorrow. This is the argument that Labour should have made before 2010 and all opponents of austerity should have mounted afterwards: wildly cutting spending meant the state did less to sustain economic momentum and pushed down revenues.

Tomorrow's Tax

Jobs are changing and with them the basis for taxing incomes from employment. The gig economy is tax-light. The OBR notes that an employee on £30,000 could cut tax payments by as much as £3,300 by operating as a company rather than as an employee. Unsurprisingly, incorporation – the creation of companies – is rising by 5 per cent a year, much faster than the annual rise in employment (0.4 per cent), opening up a tax loss to the state of billions.

A muted, hesitant HMRC has often failed to anticipate schemes designed to avoid if not evade tax and, sadly, other parts of the state have made its job even harder. The BBC, local government, the NHS and Whitehall scored a dreadful own goal by allowing well-paid employees, consultants and contractors to avoid tax by putting them on special arrangements and channelling payments through artificial company vehicles designed to minimise their tax payments. For public bodies, avoiding tax is like hara-kiri, ritual disembowelment.

Equally as dismaying as the loss of revenue was lack of self-awareness. How could a local authority that rigorously prosecuted humbler residents for non-payment of council tax at the same time collude in non-payment of tax by their own senior staff? Fortunately many public bodies recognised this hypocrisy and such arrangements are now uncommon.

But they are all too common across the private sector, where companies themselves devote huge resources to what is euphemistically called tax planning. The Public Accounts Committee uncovered 'a vast and sophisticated industry which supports aggressive tax avoidance by wealthy people and large companies'.[2] Thanks to its efforts, which were not welcomed by Whitehall or by the companies concerned, they shone the spotlight on Google, Amazon, Starbucks, Shire and other international firms that had created labyrinths of shell companies and intra-firm transactions, consuming precious brainpower not on producing goods and services but on subverting tax laws. It's an industry at which the UK excels and, post Brexit, many are anxious to turn it to the UK's comparative advantage. The City of London advertises itself as the epicentre of evasion, spinning ruses and avoidance schemes.

Tax is getting harder to collect but that's in part because online companies have been allowed to collude. Take value added tax. By making basic changes, Amazon and eBay could require sellers to display valid VAT numbers, so reducing evasion. But they don't. Not our responsibility, they say with the insouciance typical of these multinationals. The state still has a long way to go to assert its rights – on behalf of every tax-paying citizen who is cheated by this corporate high-handedness.

Collecting What's Owed

Alongside an honest approach to raising revenue, more work needs to be done to collect what is already owing. As of March 2015, an estimated £24bn was outstanding, two-thirds in taxes levied but not yet collected, the rest in fines and tax credit over-payments. This figure is less than what the state should receive if companies and individuals met all their tax obligations, declared all their income honestly and so on – the Treasury itself puts this 'tax gap' at £36bn for 2014–15. HMRC says the sum is shrinking, because since 2013 employers must report information in real time, instead of waiting until the end of the year. HMRC prefers to be assessed on the additional revenue it generates through its activities, plus the losses it has prevented; in 2015–16, this compliance yield was estimated at £27bn, though £7bn of this will probably never be collected.

From 2010, the PAC began to shift lackadaisical attitudes towards tax collection, which had persisted during the Labour years. It raised questions about the myriad reliefs and measures allowing firms to avoid general rules and not to pay tax. The government chooses not to levy huge amounts of tax owing, by giving these exemptions. Newsworthy gimmicks are invented at budget time, then stick to the tax code like barnacles. With most of them we neither know what they are worth or whether they work. Do companies given a tax holiday on the condition that they spend it on research and development really go ahead and invest?

To the gap between what is owing and what is receivable, the NAO adds the value of transactions that are criminal, fraudulent and off the books, which might be worth a further £50bn a year. If the state collected the £100bn notional total of lost income, it would cover two-thirds of the annual running cost of the NHS.

Discussion of the gap is often skewed. The huge sums owed to HMRC dwarf losses incurred by the social security system and yet attention still focuses on the latter. Whatever the tabloids tell their readers, benefit fraud and error was estimated by the DWP at £3.1bn in 2015–16, or 1.8 per cent of benefit payout. That figure also includes errors by staff and is worth comparing with the value of underpayments at £1.8bn and the lack of effort made to ensure the vulnerable get what they are owed.

Clearing the Backlog

Enforcement also means retrieving money from poorer households who have overclaimed or been overpaid tax credits, for example from people from outside the UK. Some people get squeamish at this point. Councils in England were owed £2.7bn in unpaid council tax in 2015–16. Michael Finch, a partner at lawyers Moore Stephens, noted that councils 'are acutely aware they have a fine line to walk between being assertive enough in dealing with serial debtors who are deliberately avoiding paying, and not being too heavy-handed with honest taxpayers who are in genuine financial difficulties'.[3]

Various non-tax debts are also owed to the state, in uncollected fines and payments from magistrates and criminal courts. Courts have ordered confiscations, but as of 2016 £1.6bn was outstanding, much of it more than five years old. HM Courts and Tribunals Service says that realistically only £203m of this is collectable. But that is because the number of financial investigators has been cut and the use of restraint orders to freeze offenders' assets has dropped, either because lawyers are now scarce or ministers are softpedalling. The Foreign Office could be much more active in finding and repatriating assets transferred overseas – and Brexit will only make this more difficult. The PAC has complained of a lack of any central strategy to manage outstanding debt.

The NHS is estimated to be owed £500m by people with no right to treatment, which is not a large sum in terms of the total health budget but still significant. In hearings, the permanent secretary of the Department of Health indicated that passports would have to be shown when patients turn up at GPs or clinics, provoking controversy in the context of Brexit and the respective healthcare of non-UK EU citizens in the UK and UK citizens in other EU countries. Some NHS staff protest that it's not their job to ask for proof of nationality; but others are privately bitter about the abuse of the system that they witness. Logic points to a scheme for national identity, a provocative subject that we will return to in Chapter 10.

Joined-up enforcement, reinvigorated administrators, better IT – recommended in successive reports on HMRC – could bring in a chunk of what is owed the state. But better IT should not mean confining the link between taxpayer and state to an impersonal online transaction. Paying tax online is a boon, at least for the minority who make a declaration and do not have their income tax deducted by their employer through PAYE. But practicalities also matter. The Driver and Vehicle Licensing Agency (DVLA), part of the Department of Transport, abolished the paper tax disc motorists used to have to display on their windscreen that showed to every passer-by that vehicle excise duty – popularly known as the road fund tax – had been paid. The immediate response was a rise in evasion, from 0.6 per cent in 2013 to 1.4 per cent by 2015, with a loss of some £80m a year. Evaders made the entirely rational calculation that without a significant measure of enforcement – online checks by inspectors that a given vehicle was taxed – no one would be any the wiser. The DVLA has frequently been praised for its efficient use of IT and online applications – without anyone noting the lack of enforcement caused by fewer staff patrolling on the ground, another case of the austerians' self-defeating cuts.

HMRC – Why the Poor Relation?

The state's problem with tax begins and ends with HMRC. The giant department has been curiously inert as well as subordinate.

A genuine austerian would have cherished HMRC and pumped money into enforcement, in order to maximise the tax take. Instead the older Tory instinct of 'don't let's be too hard on our business backers' has prevailed. HMRC was ordered to cut staff by 5,000 a year, which was daft when for years it could show that each extra tax official brought in substantial sums. The Association of Revenue and Customs (ARC), the senior tax managers' union, said every £312m spent on tax officers brought in another £8bn to the exchequer.[4] Scrutiny of high net worth individuals with assets worth more than £20m brought in £1bn 'extra' between 2009 and 2014, the financial secretary to the Treasury claimed.

When HMRC made 5,600 staff redundant in 2014–15, the effect on taxpayers was immediate and damaging, with calls left unanswered and cases left to fester. The next year it had to re-employ 2,400 staff to stabilise the service. Complaints are still running at record levels – 80,400 in 2015–16. No wonder HMRC's score for employee engagement is 45 per cent, well below the Whitehall average of 59 per cent. Everything was made worse by contracting. A contract with Concentrix to tackle fraud and error in tax credits went spectacularly wrong, creating a backlog of 181,000 incomplete cases. HMRC was so embarrassed by the catalogue of failure that it cancelled the contract.

HMRC spending is to fall by a fifth by 2020. Offices are being shut, with 137 out of 170 offices closing by 2020–21, affecting 60,000 staff, who are to be redeployed into 13 regional centres and hubs or made redundant. In their place are to be 'regional hubs'. Jenny Manson, a revenue officer for 35 years, says staff used to identify with districts, with their networks of relationships and expertise.[5]

Alongside technological change has come a needless and regrettable loss of local tax presence on the ground, replaced by long-distance, understaffed call centres. For our book *Cameron's Coup* we talked to the senior partner of Howsons Chartered Accountants in Sheffield, who bemoaned a loss of local knowledge and expertise, which affected both quality of service and revenue as his local tax offices closed. 'Before, you could call a local inspector who knew us and knew the client. You could talk to someone who knew what you were talking about. Now you get a call centre somewhere and someone who just takes notes but has no idea what you mean. They say someone will call you back but they don't. They tell you to write, they don't reply.' Clients struggle with self-assessments, unable to get any advice, and investigations are left hanging for years. That's a story we heard from the inside too.

———————

The Walsall tax office closed its counter to the public in 2014, and now it is running down the rest of its office, as its functions and some staff move to a large Birmingham regional office. It is one of the 281 face-to-face offices closed by HMRC and as a result, the people of Walsall have lost yet another direct connection with the state, a human face beyond the cold and often confusing algorithms of online form filling.

For Walsall the loss of any jobs is a blow, as the West Midlands is an unemployment black spot. Some 60 jobs are going in this tax office closure: some employees are moving to the Birmingham office and commuting, others are having to move there. As 90 per cent of the staff here are women and most of them are family carers too, the extra commute is more than many can manage. Sahin can't make the journey as she cares for her elderly parents in the early morning and needs to get back to them straight after work. When we met her she was looking for a Walsall job for when the office finally shuts, but so far with no success.

In the name of efficiency the functions of the state are being downsized everywhere, and nowhere more than in back offices, home of the maligned 'bureaucrats' that all politicians pledge to cut back, as if they weren't an integral part of efficient, smooth-running services. But at what point does the relentless efficiency drive turn self-defeating?

Sahin talks of how the public used to come in all the time to seek help with tax forms, to ask difficult questions, to have the system explained to them. The tax official wasn't a faceless monster but a person, like Sahin, who could explain how and why, and what tax reliefs or tax credits could be claimed. Large numbers of people can't cope with complex self-assessment online forms, those such as the growing number of local self-employed builders need help. The rapid rise of semi-bogus self-employment forced upon low-skilled workers in the gig economy requires them to fill out tax forms for the first time.

But at a higher level, local accountants found the personal contact useful too, for advice on subtle tax questions, in a regular to-and-fro of local information about their clients' business. 'People still come to our office looking for advice, because they don't know we are now closed to the public,' says Sahin. She and her colleagues suspect less tax will be collected in the long run due to the closures: 'Local knowledge matters. The staff who live here, we know what goes on. We know people and we hear things.' She means the person driving a flashy Merc or BMW but claiming virtually no earnings, or the thriving burger bar claiming they make no profit.

As more and more people are doing fragmented jobs or doubtful self-employed work, it gets harder to keep track of the earnings of part-time bar workers or zero-hours delivery drivers. 'One DJ claimed he only did a little occasional work, a few gigs now and then, but a young girl in our office knew at once it wasn't true. She said she knew he was DJing every night.'

The public are losing a helpful service while the state may lose revenue over the years as all over the country its officers are pulled away from their roots, out of touch with local taxpayers. HMRC loses valuable experience in all such reorganisations: in

Walsall many seasoned staff took early retirement or voluntary redundancy rather than shift to the new office. These losses are ineffable, and while short-termist bean counters win the argument with their numbers, they are often proved wrong in the long term.

HMRC needs to be relocalised, and reprofessionalised. The chippiness and peculiarity of Gordon Brown's adviser Damian McBride came in part from his origins in the unhappy HMRC, before being elevated 'up' into the Treasury. Within Whitehall, HMRC has to be given more status. If getting the money in precedes spending it, the permanent secretary of HMRC should cut a bigger dash. HMRC is classed a 'non ministerial department' on the unconvincing grounds that a minister might interest her or himself too much in tax affairs. Behind that lies a cultural cringe. Tax is deemed 'private' when in fact it is the acme of public participation. HMRC insists the tax affairs of businesses are confidential matters, deserving the utmost secrecy: it took much effort by MPs to lever out of HMRC the extent of deals made with businesses and obligations unenforced.

In Praise of Professionalism

The success of HMRC, as of all public service functions with a policing element, depends on our trusting its professionals and giving them space to make judgments about how to maximise the public revenue. Crimp their discretion and their effectiveness drops; extend it too far and they may become sloppy or even dangerous.

Dave Hartnett, the former permanent secretary for taxation, epitomised the tensions. Hartnett was in the eye of the controversy over HMRC deals with big corporate taxpayers, among them Goldman Sachs and Vodafone and, after leaving government service, has become an adviser to some of those selfsame corporate giants. But even Hartnett's most trenchant critics recognised his expertise. In his heyday Hartnett exemplified inspectorial enthusiasm for the cause of raising the revenue: someone who got out of bed in the morning to follow the money and win the battle against corporate lawyers and accountants and their fancy avoidance schemes. Vocational spirit is vital; it needs to be praised, cosseted and paid for. If it isn't, then, as with Hartnett, it may be tempted to cross to the dark side.

Investing in the Future

Tory chancellors are deeply ambiguous about tax raising. (Labour chancellors are also markedly inconsistent.) In the shape of George Osborne they say many of the right things and do some of them, but half-heartedly, as if embarrassed about empowering the state even to collect what is legitimately owed.

Osborne simultaneously presided over cuts to HMRC effectiveness while extending its powers and enacting tougher penalties for evasion. HMRC has been recruiting extra numbers of lawyers to hear appeals resulting from its crackdown – despite going ahead with staff cuts at the same time. More cases are going to tribunals but the PAC complained of an enormous backlog, with 43,000 cases pending.

The coalition government invested nearly £1.8bn extra in measures to tackle avoidance and evasion between 2010 and 2015 – which included money spent on IT upgrades. Efficiency has improved, especially PAYE and online VAT and that is welcome. HMRC has moved to rectify losses through illegal sales of goods and services over the internet. A post-Brexit anomaly is that while trade outside Europe is being talked up, especially with China, HMRC is being urged to clamp down on Far Eastern companies trying to sell in the UK without paying VAT. HMRC seizures of assets to recover debt this year have been rising. In 2015–16, more assets were recovered than ever before: some £255m, which includes the recovery and repatriation to Macau of £30m of proceeds of corruption.

HMRC's move to digital and online services is supposed to cut costs, but 'making tax digital' – putting in place fully automated tax reporting for individuals and businesses – has been slow to get off the ground. And collecting taxes has in fact become dearer, though costs have decreased relative to how much VAT and income tax has come in. Yet in HMRC, as throughout government, there is virtually no evidence that big spending on IT has had any effect on efficiency: it's simply the case that no one knows. Jon Thompson, chief executive, talks of transforming HMRC 'into one of the biggest digital organisations in Europe'.[6] The danger with such hyperbole is that it puts the cart before the horse. What he should be seeking is a transformation in public attitudes towards paying tax, making it as easy and attractive as possible, using whatever methods people find suitable. It's all well and good that phone centres and webchat may, as he says, 'sweep aside' time-consuming processes rooted in paper, but mouseclicks or taps on a smartphone screen run risks. Paying tax isn't like paying a credit card bill: it's an act of civic participation, and it's elemental.

International Mobilisation

Taking sterner action is vital if the obligation to pay is to be equalised between citizens and companies at home and abroad. Meeting in Paris in November 2016, representatives of 99 countries gathered to sign an OECD convention to combat 'base erosion and profit shifting', following similar agreements on closing loopholes and data-sharing. Such collaboration has a long way to go. In its crown dependencies and territories the UK supports many tax havens; the president of the EU Jean-Claude Juncker has yet to recognise – let alone apologise – for his role as prime minister of tax haven Luxembourg, beckoning tax avoiders to move artificial headquarters to his country.

But since the crash, a new spirit has entered the tax departments of many countries. MPs of all parties have been pressing the government to tighten the status of the UK's 14 overseas territories, forcing them to disclose the ownership of companies registered there. These territories – including the British Virgin Island, Turks and Caicos, Bermuda and Gibraltar – are one of the UK state's guiltiest secrets. Their ambiguous status has allowed successive governments to tolerate their collusion in tax evasion and, possibly, money laundering and the financing of drugs and terrorism.

In April 2015, George Osborne introduced the Diverted Profits Tax, with the aim of stopping multinationals from moving profits out of UK reach and into countries colluding with them by levying exceptionally low rates. Companies have come to invest large amounts of time and energy in using legal tax dodges, such as putting their brand name in a tax haven. Johnnie Walker whisky was just one of many to employ this strategy. The subsidiary company owning the brand name charges the main company a colossal sum for use of the name, sucking all the profits away from the main company and into the tax haven. The tax on diverted profits is being set at 25 per cent, higher than corporation tax, to encourage onshoring of activities. HMRC says it is beginning to see evidence of behavioural change in the right direction but no receipts came in from the new tax in 2015–16, so time will tell.

Making Everyone Pay Fairly

Tax evasion has lost some of the cultural cachet once attached. The performance of the likes of Sir Philip Green in selling the staff of BHS down the river has been widely linked to his domicile in a tax haven, where he transferred at least £400m to his wife, who is a Monaco resident: what price a knighthood for someone whose fiscal commitment to the UK is so thin? More than 2,000 Britons who live in Monaco are costing the UK economy £1bn a year in revenue, according to an investigation by Transparency International. It may be time for the international community to get as tough as General de Gaulle: infuriated by some particularly unjust tax dodge, he surrounded the principality with troops and turned off its water supply until they relented.

But Tory chancellors have only been prepared to take modest action. Banks, accountants and lawyers who market avoidance schemes are to be fined more heavily and – an important break-through – named and shamed. But, again, paper proposals depend on enforcement, which means the HMRC has to have more bodies. 'The means are not there to deliver,' says Prem Sikka, professor of accounting at the University of Essex and a leading voice in the tax reform debate. 'We simply do not have the judicial capacity.'

Chapter 9

The State Ahead

A tide is flowing towards more not less government, towards rethinking and remaking the capability of state to provide more not less. Look at what is on our doorsteps, let alone what lies ahead, and increased collective action is unavoidable. And for this, we need plans.

This conclusion results from a dispassionate look at the UK, its problems and people. But politically, it's a different story. The May government appears to be less overtly dogmatic than Cameron's but the same ingrained Thatcherite beliefs remain – witness her ministers' reflexes on transport policy, criminal justice and across social policy. Brexit exposes a multitude of decisions where their anti-statism will be on trial.

Dealing with Brexit

The Leave campaign was powered and financed mainly by state-shrinking private marketeers, who want to cut taxes and – whatever the pledge on the bus said – abolish the NHS. Brexiteers fantasised that their little England might be magically unified and united, dispensing with most regulation, welfare and public services, once the beast of Brussels was slain.

But during the campaign and afterwards it became clear that, whatever else it may entail, Brexit means expanding the reach and size of government. Deloitte earned the wrath of Number 10 for calculating that an extra 30,000 civil servants are needed, in addition to the extra 500 people already being recruited by the government to staff the Brexit departments.[1] The Institute for Government points out that the Home Office, which will be 20 per cent smaller by 2019 than it was in 2010, has to deliver Brexit, reduce net migration to below 100,000 as promised and seal the borders without spending extra. The former head of the civil service, Lord Bob Kerslake, is blunt: 'It's not possible.'[2]

And that's before the consequences for public services of emigration (forced or voluntary) of their EU staff. The NHS employs an estimated 55,000 EU staff. Agencies started to have difficulties filling vacancies during 2016. Recruiters fear a perfect storm: cuts to funding for nurse training reducing the number of UK entrants to the profession piled on the deterrent effect of the EU referendum result.

The Brexit mantra was 'taking back control'. The libertarians among them seem utterly confused. If control does mean control, that means more not less government. Markets are supposed to be about freedom of movement, whether for capital, goods, services or people. But now the latter is deemed to be in special need of control, which must imply many more staff and new huge state databases: visa schemes, regulation of labour markets and business, including scrutiny of small firms.

When Theresa May was Home Secretary, queues at Heathrow forced her to abandon cuts to the Border Force budget and to recruit replacement staff. Half the passengers arriving in the UK come from other EU countries, and in future the purpose of their visit, length of stay, right to remain and their jobs may need checking. Now May is prime minister, every option points to further strengthening of the force's numbers and functions. Customs has 5,000 staff and the Border Force 8,000, which is a very lean operation by international standards. KPMG says that leaving the EU customs union will require at least 5,000 more customs staff to check tariffs on all incoming goods. New IT systems are proposed but however fancy they won't stop companies failing to declare goods subject to duty if 'self-regulation' comes in.

We interviewed Border Force staff, under strict anonymity, meeting them miles away from Heathrow for fear of disciplinary action if they are caught. Here's what they say about their work, where passenger numbers have risen by 20 per cent since 2010, and are set to rise by a further 43 per cent by 2030, while Border Force's funding is cut: spending per passenger is down 25 per cent. Technology was supposed to reduce the need for staff; but the e-borders project has been abandoned, at a cost of £1bn.

Heathrow staff screen 225 million arrivals passengers each year. After the row over gigantic queues before the 2012 Olympics, strict targets were set: non-EU passengers must only queue for 45 minutes, EU for 25 minutes and fast-track first class 15 minutes. These targets were to be met 95 per cent of the time.

In reality these targets are only met 70 per cent of the time. Untrained staff from elsewhere in the Home Office were being deployed every shift in each of the five terminals. 'After just three days mentoring, all they can do is a basic passport scan.' But our interviewees say training matters: 'We can feel when something is wrong, in who the arrival is, where they've been, for how long and how often. We notice their demeanour, their nerves.' It takes experience to notice children being trafficked, they say.

If the public complain that too few passport desks are open, staff must reply from a printed drill sheet: 'All available officers are currently deployed and working to protect the public; border security remains our number one priority.' In truth they want to say: 'We haven't got enough staff, we've had enormous cuts, we're on our knees working all hours and still missing targets for queues, with too little time to scrutinise passengers. Sorry. Did you vote for public service cuts?'

To staff desks in order to keep the queues down, people are taken off customs duty, with the result that many fewer checks are made on suspect goods and luggage. 'Guns and drugs don't seem to matter as much as queuing times for the public,' one officer says. A perverse effect is that government fails to get the £2,000 fines due from airlines that bring in people without the correct documents, because claims must be filed within five days and that deadline is often missed, losing large sums the state should be collecting. 'As it's all hands to the front desks, the paperwork on doubtful immigration and asylum cases piles up behind the scenes.'

New staff are now on less favourable contracts that allow managers to oblige officers to work overtime, extra days or cancel holidays at short notice: 'A nightmare for parents with childcare.' As a result, there is high turnover. 'We're at least 300 short in Heathrow,' they reckon. Official safe quotas for the right number of staff per port have been abolished, because they would never be met.

Amber Rudd, appointed Home Secretary by Theresa May, paid an early visit to Heathrow, the nation's busiest entry point. All the desks she saw were fully staffed; there were minimal queues at passport control and everyone smiled. What she didn't see was passengers being held back from entering the arrivals hall. Was she told that desks were open only thanks to HMRC tax apprentices from Newcastle upon Tyne, who were being put up in Heathrow hotels? And it's not as if HMRC can easily spare them, when there are tax forms to be checked.

Problems start overseas, where visa offices have been closed. One officer who used to work in a UK visa office in Africa says the checks are now much weaker, with face-to-face applications in country of origin now abandoned. 'You can't rely on written references and qualification certificates. We used to have local staff to detect people who were not as educated as they claimed or not speaking the right local language.' There are now fewer forgery specialists on duty at all ports to inspect suspect documents.

The NAO warned that the Advance Passenger Information System – giving advance notice to border agencies of incoming passengers to check anyone suspicious – was only collecting 86 per cent of inbound arrivals. The system can't check them all 'in sufficient time to prevent high-risk travellers from starting their journey to or from the UK'. That means 16.5 million people a year are not checked before arrival.

Control Is Difficult

Control isn't just administered at the border. Managing work permits is going to be complicated and staffing-intensive. Brexit will require more officials to round up overstayers and illegals and do closer checks on who leaves the UK; that means more inspections and more inspectors. Migration control is likely to bring more work for the police, an impossible additional burden on today's staffing levels: police numbers have been cut by 14 per cent since 2010.

Brexit won't do anything to stop refugees trying to get to the UK, nor people who just want to come, regardless of their legal status. The pressures powering migratory flows are not likely to diminish. The share of the world's population living outside their country of birth rose from 2.7 per cent in the mid 1990s to 3.3 per cent in 2015, adding 85 million to today's total of 245 million (of which refugees are about 10 per cent). Many migrate successfully and integrate well; many don't. And the consequences – for the labour market, housing and social adjustments – fall on governments. Even Tory MPs are reaching for the state and expecting it to take strong action. We spoke to Charlie Elphicke, Tory MP for Dover, whose every instinct is to diminish the role of government but who at every turn starts arguing for more checks on vans and lorries, looking for contraband goods as well as people. He endorses the view of our Border Force officers that too many hard-pressed staff are being taken off basic customs work to concentrate on migration, causing revenue loss and greater risk of guns, drugs and bombs getting through unchecked.

The Consequences of Limiting Capacity

Brexit has crystallised a problem that has been growing in severity over recent years – the consequences of shrinking government. Tory ministers never seemed concerned about the consequences of austerity and fragmentation on our ability to respond with resilience to threats old and new. Mega projects are started – HS2, Hinkley Point, Universal Credit, possibly now revamped border control – without a strategy or any overall look at resources and staffing. The UK construction industry will not be able to handle the simultaneous demands made by these projects for engineers, quantity surveyors and steeplejacks, let alone software designers and IT people. It seems that if you don't believe in government, you don't bother ensuring government works.

Here's one example of how fragmentation reduces basic ability to get things done. It came up when MPs were worrying about asbestos in school buildings, where fibres from the now banned material are especially dangerous for young lungs. Academies and free schools are setting up, often in older buildings, which are liable to have been built using asbestos. The government established a £1bn slush fund to buy properties, which would then be given to those groups wanting to establish schools. They have been randomly established, damaging existing institutions, and no one worried that this 'more autonomous schools system' could not even monitor the estate it occupies. Who checks for asbestos? Not councils, though they have years of experience in surveying and dealing with the problem in already-maintained schools: they were told to have nothing to do with academies. One place to turn would be the Health and Safety Executive, which has expertise in asbestos and other hazards, but it has been starved of funds. It just about survived the demolition of quangos after 2010, but has been severely cut back as the long-time punch bag of anti-state jibes from Tories, the tabloids and trolls about intrusive ''elf and safety'. If academy pupils are endangered by asbestos, we won't know for many years, too late to regret not just austerity but the damage caused by deliberate disorganisation.

National Risks

An underspent past is all too present in today's inadequate buildings and infrastructure. Chips and tarnish ought to be a daily reminder that a responsible state should plan. There exists an apparatus for looking ahead but it is rusty and unused. Part of it is the National Security Council created by Cameron, except its orientation is abroad. A full definition of 'security' would see that so many of today's and tomorrow's issues are at home and abroad at the same time – including terrorism, subversion, energy supply and infectious disease.

Fragmented as it is, the state makes only intermittent efforts to scan the horizon and assess risk. Every company, institution or public body these days has a risk register for the board to study, but not the state. There is something called the National Risk Register but it focuses on natural disasters and terrorist attacks. The Office for Budget Responsibility tries to take the long view, projecting spending on, for example, health or student loans into the 2030s and beyond. But its work is not tied in to the ad hoc forecasting done by the health or communities departments or by the Ministry of Defence, which has its own internal thinktank on the future. The Government Office for Science does its forecasting in glorious isolation from the rest of government.

So we get the grand-sounding 'National Policy Statement on National Networks' but it turns out to ignore regional railways and east–west connectivity, for example how to get a container off a ship at the Seaforth terminal on the Mersey and onto one waiting on the Humber. Only a few months after its publication, during his whimsical conversion to the idea of a 'Northern Powerhouse', Osborne discovered the urgent need to join Hull and Liverpool, albeit not until some time in the 2030s. Only in fits and starts, or often stops, is there any strategic planning.

Business complains about the absence of a forward view, without acknowledging that cut-throat competition and short-term investment decisions by company boards are also part of the problem. Yet, the chief executive of O2 warns that Britain is being left behind on the switch to digital. He may have a commercial axe to grind, but he is entitled to ask for some sort of national plan to ensure mobile phone masts offer genuine cross-country spectrum coverage. 5G needs 500,000 new masts in London alone. Where will they go, with what degree of public consent, especially when local planning departments have been so severely diminished? Some kind of projection would be useful.

The Commons Public Administration Select Committee doesn't buy the usual excuse that permanent secretaries and ministers are too busy with the immediate policy agenda, or that old Macmillan cliché – events, dear boy, events. It sees a generic resistance to the state trying to think strategically. The greatest obstacle is the Treasury, which resists all arguments about spending more now to forestall more expensive sudden crisis needs in 10 or 20 years' time, even when those crises can be quite clearly seen looming up ahead. But that may be no accident. What if the Treasury doesn't like what it thinks the future will bring?

Fred and Ginger used the future conditional in their famous song; in fact there is *inescapably* trouble ahead. You name it: the horizon is filled with problems that are going to demand more not less government activity, whether by councils, Whitehall or arm's-length bodies.

Bugs and Jeopardies

Finance and the banks still threaten possible future catastrophe, and there are lessons still unlearned from the last crash. But consider for a moment the other threats. Grim warnings abound over the effect of automation on white collar and middle-income jobs – including the state itself, where 25 per cent of jobs are said to be doable by machine. Threats such as blackouts, obesity, climate change and pandemic flu may be exaggerated, but they are also real, and the duty falls on the state to prepare and protect, whatever their scale may turn out to be.

Markets won't offer this protection. The interests of private companies and the public diverge. Take the battle against drug-resistance: either pharmaceutical companies see no profit in it, or there is a risk that they see the chance for a massive mark-up for the winning solution.

Halting the race between drug-resistant bacteria and new anti-microbial drugs is a prime example. GPs were too lax in handing out antibiotics and patients were too avid for a pill. Either way, antibiotics became overused, allowing common infections to build up resistance. A commercial response – further investment to produce new therapies – won't work; the cycle will simply speed up. Rather, it demands widespread changes in public behaviour. Dame Sally Davies, Chief Medical Officer for England, says, 'We need patients and the public to understand that most of the time they don't need antibiotics.'[3] But the credibility of voices such as hers along with the research needed to keep up with evolving pathogens depends on a strong commitment to state action in order to widen the message and halt the cycle.

Health and Lifestyle Future

Who else, except Davies and her devolved counterparts, is going to marshal evidence and resist business interests? Looking ahead, technology will improve monitoring; medical diagnosis will continue getting more precise; pharmaceutical companies will keep innovating, if the state keeps investing in basic science. Government has to allocate resources between people, between conditions, between areas for innovation, for the obvious reason that otherwise the markets will ignore millions with unprofitable conditions, as in the US. The US makes a huge commitment of national resources to health at upwards of 17 per cent of GDP but leaves millions unable to afford basic healthcare, causing third world rates of morbidity and mortality.

Government alone can align demand and supply in this area, by encouraging people to live more healthily. The voices of Davies and her colleagues sometimes grate but she has no option but to persist. Public health cannot be an oxymoron. Although smoking prevalence has fallen dramatically, nearly one in five adults is still a smoker. In the lowest socio-economic groups, the rate rises to over one in four. Physical inactivity is estimated to cost the UK £20bn a year. One in four adults in England is obese, and by standard definitions, 60 per cent are overweight. The consequences for onset of diabetes, heart disease and multiple morbidities including cancer and mental health are well proven.

Changing lifestyle to combat this is hard, and doctors and public service managers only have any chance of success if they can work together. In ageing, fattening Britain, parks, outdoor gyms, pools and leisure centres are more necessary than ever. Some GPs, for example in Liverpool, now prescribe walks and gardening. The East Riding of Yorkshire council IT system allows surgeries to book patients directly into exercise plans at the local leisure centre. And the reality behind this is that bad health and harmful behaviour are facets of inequality, so that even governments of the right can't duck the fact that income and wealth disparity ends up creating expensive extra health needs.

What Happens When the State Fails to Plan

The right derides manpower planning but the alternative is skills anarchy, which will be incompatible with post-Brexit demands for border control. The state must peer ahead and envision tomorrow's workforces – anticipating and encouraging new courses at universities and further education colleges and apprenticeships. Getting the alignment absolutely exact between occupations and trained personnel may always be impossible – but leaving a great lacuna when future skills needs are clearly foreseen is a dereliction of duty. For austerians the temptation is always for the state to cut back on expensive training now, and let others worry about the shortfall later. But in fields where the state is the principal employer, there is no excuse for failing to prepare enough staff.

———————

Few skills are more obviously necessary than those of doctors, nurses, radiotherapists and other clinicians, and it is the job of Health Education England (HEE) to allocate training places each year. With the number, age and frailty of NHS patients growing by the year and with population predictions reasonably accurate, it shouldn't be too difficult to allocate the appropriate number of places. The government talked sanctimoniously about not saddling future generations with our debts – but they can also be saddled with gaping holes in necessary skills that will need to be filled more expensively one way or another.

NHS training is expensive – £610,000 for a doctor, £70,000 for a nurse. As NHS budgets were squeezed, so was HEE. Training places were cut despite the growing demand for staff, forcing trusts to hire agency and interim staff at exorbitant rates and recruit from abroad.

The John Radcliffe University Hospital in Oxford has all the advantages of its prestigious reputation – but that hasn't saved it from a serious nursing shortage. The vacancy rate in the Thames Valley Region, where the John Radcliffe operates, is 10 per cent; this is only worse in London, where 18 per cent of nursing jobs go unfilled. By chance, the day we visited the John Radcliffe's Chief Nursing Officer, Catherine Stoddart, the Care Quality Commission had suddenly descended.

There was an irony in this, for it was the CQC that exacerbated the sense of crisis in nursing. Responding to the Francis report into Mid Staffordshire Hospital, where nursing cuts were one of the causes of extra deaths, the CQC demanded signs be put up on boards in every ward announcing exactly how many staff were on duty on every shift. That requirement alone instantly created, or revealed, a shortfall of 24,000 nurses.

The John Radcliffe has been frantically recruiting from all over the world, mainly from elsewhere in the EU but also from the Philippines. Stoddart herself was newly arrived, headhunted from Australia. You might expect there would be a central NHS bureau seeking out staff from abroad for the whole service, but instead each trust is on its own, hiring private recruitment agencies. Staff from different trusts compete with one another and, insanely, each trust tries to offer better inducements than the next. This has been one result of the fragmentation of the NHS into competing units. Recruiting costs are high: in 2015 the John Radcliffe spent £1.4m bringing in 448 nurses from the EU.

What happened with nurses was not so much a planning as a political failure. In 2010, the coalition government cut training places to save money. By 2015, Health Education England was training 3,100 fewer nurses than a decade ago, a 19 per cent cut. As a result, 2015 saw one of the lowest ever cohorts of newly qualified nurses. There is no shortage of potential recruits: 37,000 applicants for places are turned away each year. Now add to that the attrition rate: only 60 per cent of newly trained nurses enter the NHS, as the long-enforced 1 per cent pay cap means they can earn more in other occupations. At John Radcliffe, after pay, the reason nurses cite for leaving the profession is intensifying pressure of work due to lack of staff, in a self-perpetuating downward spiral.

Post Brexit could be the time to seize control of clinical training and properly plan for a knowable future. Instead, further cuts to HEE risk creating an even greater shortfall. As of September 2017, bursaries for trainee nurses are being abolished: the government says that cutting the state's cost of training may paradoxically help colleges create 10,000 more places. In theory, it frees colleges to scoop up £9,000 a year in fees from all those 37,000 applicants previously turned away. Will it work?

Catherine Stoddart fears it will have the opposite effect. Saddling these not highly paid nurses with thousands of pounds of lifetime debt will deter many from going into the profession. 'I worry particularly about the older ones, as a third of our trainees are healthcare assistants who train up for a full nursing qualification. Already they have to give up their pay while they train, so they will be reluctant to take on debts as well when they have families and high living costs in this area. Those with healthcare experience are the most valuable recruits and we can't afford to lose them.'

—————

As Stoddart hurried away to supervise the day's shifts, the arrival of the CQC to inspect only added to the sense of pressure and disunity within the NHS, with each hospital competing for everything in short supply – nurses above all.

Demography and the Life Cycle

The UK population is projected to increase to 81.2 million in 2065 and we are not preparing for that demographic fact. Its composition is shifting. Because the UK birth rate grew in the 1950s and 1960s, many more people will reach the state pension age from 2020, even if pension age is pushed ever later. If it does rise to our late sixties and beyond, much more public effort will have to go into keeping people healthy enough to extend their working lives, or else they will be living on disability benefits. In 2016, 2.4 per cent of the UK population was aged over 85. By 2065 that proportion will be 7 per cent. Average spending on health increases with age, as a fact of nature.

Pundits talk about generations as if they were self-identifying blocks within each decade – as if, for example, people born in 1960 had the same outlook and interests as those born in 1969. It's less rigid than that, but age does strongly colour perceptions and interests. Progress through the life cycle means people see the importance of different services at different times in their lives, soon forgetting what once seemed vital.

At any one time, a relatively small proportion of people have children in schools and parents only use maternity services for a very short time. Nurseries are of concern for perhaps five years in a family's life and university likewise only for a while, and then are too often forgotten. Young adults use fewer public services and may see less point in paying towards them, until they have children. Crisis conditions in social care take most families by surprise when an aged relative suddenly has new needs: old age, everyone discovers, is no place for rugged individualism. Standing on your own two feet is harder when you need a Zimmer frame.

Of all the public services, concern for the NHS is the most universal at all ages because everyone fears they might fall ill or under a bus at any time in their life. The problem for local councils is that maybe only one person in 50 is a heavy user of its most expensive care services at any given time; people are paying in taxes all the time, but needing a service only occasionally. In the middle of all this sits government, obliged to look at present and future in ways that markets can't or won't, obliged to at least try to care for all.

Surveys show that the public has yet to come to terms with the expansion of life expectancy. Some find the prospect alarming; they are gloomy about growth in the dependency ratio, the proportion of the 'retired' and the very young versus those of working age whose taxes pay for this dependent sector of society. Others see a slow process of maturation, during which time the capacity of older people to continue working will grow and, as the state pension age is raised, the affordability of ageing also increases. Whichever viewpoint you adopt, there is one certainty: the UK cannot deal with age except through state action. Only the state can secure the flows and transfers of income that will guarantee people security once they stop earning and only the state can ensure that when people's health starts to fail, care will be provided.

Will Society Step Up?

The right holds to a peculiar sociology, assuming things will sort themselves out automatically if the state would only step back. Without regulation and without the welfare state, everything will be all right: families, philanthropy and charity will take up the slack. Markets will cure the decline of industrial sectors through ceaseless creative destruction – so long as workers are prepared to get on their bikes, abandoning homes, family ties and community to accept whatever wages the market offers.

That is what makes benefit cuts acceptable to Tory MPs who probably wouldn't see themselves as cruel: people need to be set on their feet after too much state support has sapped their morale and drained their initiative. The bedroom tax may oust them from a family home, but it ensures best use of scarce square footage – though the greatest abundance of such spare resources is, of course, in the untouchable private sector. Cut back the Employment Support Allowance for sick and disabled people and they will go to work – never mind the failure of the chivvying private contractors to find them vacancies. A state that cares for people in times of need, or protects them from abrupt industrial change beyond their personal control, is a dangerous liberal delusion that weakens the moral fibre and the work ethic of a nation. So say the right.

This doctrine helps explain the right's blindness to social changes that result from economic 'progress'. Rightwing think-tanks and their intellectual allies in academia and consultancies look at the growth of public expenditure and blame lobby-ists, public sector unions and lily-livered liberals. What they ignore is the pressure of socio-economic change, the growth of inequality and other ill effects of markets that only the state can alleviate.

Government has become more difficult: not just because the power of global companies has grown or because of the internet, but also because people, households and communi-ties have become more demanding, and as their needs grow they do not 'self-heal' as the theorists think. Markets simply fail – housing is a contemporary example, creating a great backlog of need and demand because builders don't and won't build without making a stonking great profit. In reality, it's only the state that can hold things together in a fragmenting, fissiparous world.

The Next Generation

Future growth depends on a general improvement in the quality and education of the workforce, investing in the common pool of talent and skill and creating more parity of opportunity so that more can succeed. This will also have a positive effect on standards of equipment: when workers are very cheap, low pay means employers need not bother with investing in more productive machinery as it is cheaper to increase manpower.

A high standard of skills training, good education and above all high quality in early-years teaching sets a population on the path to higher output per head. Study after study shows that with every year that passes for a child, the harder it becomes to reverse a disadvantaged background. The Early Intervention Foundation (EIF) puts the figure of £17bn on failure to take early action that would probably prevent later problems such as unemployment, domestic violence, depression, drug and alcohol abuse and youth crime.

Tory ministers promised expansion of nursery education but then failed to make it affordable, or to ensure that premises and teaching were of sufficient quality to make it worthwhile. (The evidence shows that mediocre nurseries that simply warehouse young children have little effect.) One of the most short-sighted moves by the coalition was drastically to scale back the Sure Start children's centres that it inherited from Labour. By mid-2016, 800 centres had closed; many were no longer getting professional support from health visitors, speech therapists or even a visiting teacher, becoming instead holding pens rather than a springboard for young children. What was once designed as a universal service for all families has shrunk back into being 'focused' on those families with serious problems.

However, some good children's centres continue, managing to keep going against the odds, kept on by dedicated councils in the poorest places.

In Sandwell, West Midlands, Springfield Children's Centre survives. Depleted of some services it used to have but still rated 'good' by OFSTED, it's a lifeline for families teetering on the edge of calamity. We met Janice and her three-year-old son, Dillon, who found their way here in a state of despair; by sheer luck she had been told by a friend that this was the place to come for help. Her ex-partner had attacked them with a knife. He was arrested, but broke his bail and turned up again, this time pouring petrol all over himself and the house, threatening to set them all alight. A family support worker at Springfield arranged for panic buttons to be installed in her home in case he attacked them again.

'This place has been a home for us,' Janice says. 'I suffer bad depression, and I'm on a waiting list for treatment but the doctor says it might be months. I worry about Dillon, because he saw it all. He plays at pouring petrol and setting it alight and he's scared his dad might do it again. But they have helped him so much here, he's a different child.'

She found him hard to handle, but parenting classes made a difference. 'They give you techniques for getting him to bed on time every night, how to have reward charts for good behaviour. I feel I'm better in myself, not so many panic attacks, better with him and his behaviour has really changed.'

She has had advice for debt problems left by her partner, but still has little money. 'I can never take Dillon anywhere, except the library, but here we've had a trip to Dudley Zoo, and other outings. I feel he'll be ready for school next year, after the help he's had.'

Her support worker talks of how much better they both are. 'You'd hardly recognise her from the person she was when they first arrived.' Now Janice volunteers at the Springfield Centre and plans to take a course in childcare when Dillon starts school.

———————

Can Springfield and Sandwell council's remaining children's centres survive? The council is determined to try, but with each year comes a new round of cuts, falling on top of 40 per cent already sliced away, making it far from certain that the Sandwell centres won't have to go the way of so many around the country.

The original vision was that every child, every family, would be helped early in life, and that every child would be ready to start school on an equal footing with their peers. As health visitors are cut back again, school nurses are usually spread so thin that they each cover more than ten schools. Everywhere there is less prevention, leaving the state to cope with severe crises that could have been avoided. Child protection will always be a fundamental duty of government. The number of children taken into care is rising at huge extra cost. Most recent figures show that there are 70,440 children in state care in England, with numbers having risen significantly, by 15 per cent in 2016, from the previous year. Wide variations among councils show that some invest in social workers supporting families at risk, while others end up spending even more on taking increasing numbers of children into care. The EIF reckons that for lack of early help, these children grow up to 'cost' £5.3bn in terms of extra health needs, crime and joblessness.

Expanded early years and good nursery provision remains a prize waiting to be grasped. Of itself, state action would not guarantee a better future, but a new deal for the under-fives has to be a major component in any programme for inclusive growth. Needless to say, leaving it to the market is the same as doing nothing: motivated and well-resourced parents will seek out such provision as there is, though often at great sacrifice in cost and family wellbeing – but all the rest will struggle and fall behind.

Social Intervention

We were tempted, in Chapter 6, to include in the list of public officials who had 'got religion' the name of the formidable

Dame Louise Casey. She came into the civil service renowned for her work on homelessness and rough sleeping. She had impressed Blair and colleagues with her energy and straight-talking enthusiasm. Working at the Communities department, Casey took on the 'troubled families' programme – which focused resources on 400,000 households across England. Criticism of the programme's sociology and statistics was justified, but may have missed the point. The problem with 'troubled families' was the practicality and scale of invest-ment, given the context of local authority and other spending cuts in which the chosen families were supposed to be 'turned around'. The problem was not the principle: the state can and should intervene to improve the lives of people, and this requires involvement in the details, not just the broader picture. But because Tory ministers clearly did not believe in active government, their espousal of troubled families looked like a form of social cleansing. There was too little money invested in the programme, and the official evaluation, when eventually published, was excoriating. The National Institute of Economic and Social Research, commissioned to carry out an official study, found the scheme had no signifi-cant effect.

Casey's next project was to scrape away at the sore of inte-gration and ask to what extent minority religious and ethnic groups (meaning Muslims) are joining the mainstream – itself a problematic concept in a society where in 2011 13 per cent were foreign-born, 20 per cent identify themselves as belonging to an ethnic minority and 27 per cent of 2014 births were to mothers born outside the UK, predominantly Polish, Pakistani and Indian. She found some wards where 85 per cent are from Pakistani or Bangladeshi origins, highlighting Muslim women trapped at home not able to speak English and held back by 'regressive cultural practices'.[4]

The Kobi Nazrul primary school in Whitechapel in London's East End became briefly famous in 2014 for all the wrong reasons when accusations were made of infiltration of the governing body by Islamicists, with one governor a senior member of the radical Islamist group Hizb ut-Tahrir. OFSTED moved in and put the school into special measures, slating its teaching and the children's behaviour.

Governors and the head teacher were replaced and since then the school has improved to win a rating of 'good' from OFSTED. The new head has done all she can to involve parents, with workshops of all kinds, and has provided free English classes for mothers. They are encouraged to join classes, which are organised on the school's behalf by the Deesha project, a charity, not just to learn English but to make friends, learn how to help their children grow their self-confidence and help them to travel around London: some had never been on the tube.

On the day we visited, some 20 Kobi Nazrul mothers were studying a sheet with text messages, so they could understand their children's texts, with all the abbreviations and expressions. All but one wore a hijab, two wore face veils and were notably more subdued than the rest. But the conversation was lively, with much laughter and much puzzlement over text expressions such as CWOT (complete waste of time), FTF (face to face), and MON (middle of nowhere). Most can now speak reasonable English, encouraging and correcting each other: although there were more Bengali speakers than others, a multiplicity of languages stops anyone lapsing back into their own tongue.

They talked with pleasure about expeditions they had been on together. Recently they all went to the V&A Museum of Childhood in Bethnal Green. None had ever been to a museum before, didn't know how to get there, whether they had to pay, or if the donation box was compulsory. The rule is that once they have been taken somewhere, they have to repeat the visit, taking their children on their own. 'Once they get up the confidence, it's easy for us to show them so many places to visit,' said Samantha Campbell, their teacher. They now have a WhatsApp chat room where they swap news together all week.

'This class was just two hours, but we asked if we could go up to three,' said one mother, Ayesha. The head teacher, Belinda King, explained that she had to find the money to pay for it, £18,000 a year from a sharply shrinking school budget. 'But it's worth every penny!' she said. The charity bears the main cost, but can't pay for it all. 'We can only take in the number of mothers we have funds for.'

She says she sees the benefits very soon in the children of mothers who attend, as the class shows them how to read with their children, even if their reading is not perfect. 'The mothers from this class, once they learn enough, come and volunteer at the school, which is really useful.' Some go on to become teaching assistants – and, when we asked, all of them said their aim was to get a job. One had already found care work, another was working in a clothes shop. One forthright mother, Saaed, talked of how much help they had from the scheme, 'I can read, I can write, I can explain things, I don't need an interpreter – but yes, my children sometimes help me with my homework.'

The mothers' test results have been very good and participants almost all significantly improved literacy, numeracy and computing skills, reporting themselves confident in talking to their children's teachers or doctors. The women's lives are being renewed: windows are opening on the world, as they are drawn out of their homes into making friends and taking part in a society partly unknown to them until now. They are hugely enthusiastic, eager to talk about its value and convert other mothers. All the women here said they would like to do more classes if they were available.

Casey called on the government to fund a good English for Speakers of Other Languages (ESOL) course. But in 2011, after David Cameron delivered a diatribe declaring the death of multiculturalism – which had been responsible, he said, for separating out cultures into their own silos – the adult skills budget was cut by £400m, with severe effects on ESOL funding.

No one says social interventions are easy: many efforts are doomed to fail. Take the social fact of divorce. During the past four decades a rising proportion of marriages ended. It's not a trend governments 'caused', nor one they can much influence, despite many decades of Tory ministerial hand-wringing. More divorce can mean gaps in childcare, poorer children and inadequate child maintenance. The latter is something governments have tried to do something about, without huge success, mainly because in the final years of the Major government they ignored all advice and set about it disastrously. As a result the Child Support Agency, and now the Child Maintenance and Enforcement Commission, failed to get errant fathers to cough up: they simply refused, en masse, and the state never effectively obliged them to pay, leaving mothers with huge back payments owing. Had they refused to pay tax, the state would have jailed them, but owing money to their ex-partners was never quite as pressing.

The fact is that family composition has changed; women are often self-sufficient now, and therefore need to be out earning. As a result they are not available to be full-time carers for frail family members. Families are simply not able to save enough from their income during a working life in order to pay for their own care in older age. But nor could most families a century ago, when even fewer of the elderly were cared for by families than now, due to so many families living in tiny cramped quarters. In those days many elderly people ended up in workhouses. There was no mythical golden age when women did all the caring and the state was absolved of all obligation.

Social Care

Older people account for 62 per cent of all hospital bed days and 52 per cent of admissions that involve stays of more than seven days. Inadequacies in care result in increased use of A&E and longer delays in people leaving hospital. Four in five UK local authorities offer insufficient care, according to the Family and Childcare Trust – that's 6.4 million people aged 65-plus living in inadequately served areas.

At every turn, more provision is needed. In 2015, two in five of those receiving residential care are paying for it themselves or being helped by their families. But despite growing numbers of those needing such care, the number of residential beds is falling. That's because councils can't afford to fund the other three in five places and have been tightening eligibility, cutting the fees that they will pay by 5 per cent in the three years to 2016 as costs rose. The withdrawal of local authorities and the NHS from direct provision of social care has been the major strategic shift over the past three decades. Companies piled in, scenting opportunity; by the end of 2016, Care England, representing private providers, predicted four out of ten homes would close in the medium term.

The big 2011 report into social care for the elderly from Sir Andrew Dilnot, warden of Nuffield College, Oxford and chairman of the UK Statistics Authority, remains on the table. As he was writing the report, Dilnot spoke movingly to us about a visit to a dementia unit. 'What kind of models of economic rationality and statistical probability could ever capture the humanity of the care I witnessed? Call this the confessions of a repentant economist,' he said. His report suggested a way to smooth the path a little, to help people cover the cost of their care, but it still left in place a jungle of eligibilities, varying charges and uncertain allowances.

Before completing his work, scandal broke. Shocking pictures from a BBC *Panorama* programme about the mistreatment of adults with disabilities at Winterbourne View, a privately run unit, melded into the sudden bankruptcy of Southern Cross, a private company with 31,000 residents in 750 homes. Until the scandal broke, few realised the extent to which the care home industry had become a target of predatory capital funds, stripping away the property values and leaving the rest of the business financially vulnerable. Now equity capital is moving on and out, not being able to make the business pay. Care home chain Four Seasons publicly blames the enforcement of the living wage for its staff, and inadequate fees for its patients, for closing its homes, but it is also weighed down by interest payments after being bought up in a debt-fuelled deal by Terra Firma.

The Care Quality Commission's 2016 State of Care report said 'sustainability of the adult social care market is approaching a tipping point' with nearly three quarters of care homes in special measures and one in ten nursing posts vacant.[5]

Housing and the Old

The housing crisis shows no sign of solution without a radical change in direction. On some reckonings, in theory it could be solved if the existing housing stock could be better matched to households – but that would require intervention on a politically unimaginable scale, applying bedroom tax principles to the entire population. If there is scant planning for new families, there is even less for future demographics and the elderly. The tax system could encourage the elderly to move out of homes that are too large for them, and could do more to help release their capital to pay for their care. Wealth has accumulated among those who already do, or will in the future, need care, and releasing that wealth, as Labour had proposed in the 2010 election, makes sense: politically it was doomed as a 'death tax', but something of the kind will eventually be necessary. As more people need care at home, the layout and size of Britain's homes make them unsuitable and inaccessible for many as they age or become disabled. Too many of the homes now being built are too small to fit even basic furniture, let alone wheelchairs and orthopaedic beds that might allow longer independent living.

The Government Office for Science conducted a foresight exercise on housing. An additional 1.42 million households will be headed by someone over 85 by the mid-2030s, which translates into a 70 per cent increase in demand for specialised accommodation – yet construction of specialised housing has been declining. Poor quality housing is already adding to the costs of the NHS by £2.5bn a year, with homes suffering from damp, lack of insulation and unsafe stairs, to name but a few of the problems. For older people, moving to more appropriately sized accommodation is going to depend on sale and purchase prices matching: an active state would offer bridging finance, and through new building seek an altogether better fit.

Housing and the Young

The UK is an old country, relying on bricks laid by Victorians and tunnels dug in the 1930s. Buried pipes, tubes and wires get forgotten and patterns of land use get fixed. Green belts become inviolate; neighbours vehemently object to new homes next door and 'densification' of sprawling suburbs becomes impossible. Impossible, that is, if councils and the Homes and Communities Agency are not allowed to use powers to plan, compulsorily purchase and build.

There is no perfect ratio between housing tenures, between owners and renters or between private and social landlords. But the state can be strategic about land use and provision of enough homes near to jobs, where people can genuinely afford to live. In Chapter 6 we heard the frustration of a local authority planner: there is so much that could be done to ease housing for the future, but it has only ever been done, in the interwar years by Attlee, Macmillan and Wilson, through a massive state-organised programme, where half the new homes built in the UK were social housing.

The concept of 'affordability' is malleable; the government now chooses to define it as housing available to buy at 80 per cent of market price or market rent, still wildly beyond the means of many across the country. Failure to build by developers despite rampant demand damages the wider economy, which needs people to be able to move to take jobs. Market rents and prices distort society and harm wellbeing – by stopping people having children, preventing them looking after relatives, forcing them to live too long with parents or in bad conditions that harm their health and their children's prospects. Successive governments failed to intervene as warped economic incentives made investing in homes more desirable than investing in productive companies, sending house prices soaring as people used them as piggy banks, as pensions and as speculation. Without state intervention, buy-to-let was a better investment than shares, and the benefits of incumbency (sitting on a pile while it grew in value) increased, squeezing out younger people and families. Home ownership fell drastically, to just 51 per cent of tenures in December 2016 according to the Resolution Foundation.[6]

House building did pick up after the recession but the number of homes available to people on modest means has fallen. In 2015–16, only 32,000 so-called affordable homes were built in England, fewer than the previous year and significantly fewer than the 58,000 constructed in 2009–10. Borrowing to build new social housing, even in high-price London, local authorities could pay off the debt after a maximum of 26 years with all subsequent rent turning a profit for the years ahead, but that was not permitted by the Treasury.

Such figures have to be viewed in the light of a 30-year assault on the very idea of public ownership and construction. What's needed is reinvigoration of the idea that government (whether through councils, housing associations or other public developers) has the right and duty to address shortfall with a strong housing strategy. The reality is that at any given point at least a third of the population will never be able to own their own homes, on any likely distribution of earnings.

It's not that government has abandoned housebuilding, the problem lies with the inadequate scale and ad hoc nature of its involvement. Following abortive moves by Labour and Cameron to proceed with garden cities, the May government is allocating smallish sums for housebuilding in garden villages, extending Long Marston in Warwickshire for example and Deenethorpe in Northamptonshire. The principle is sound; the practice is piecemeal and parsimonious. Several of these schemes involve state land, usually former military bases and airfields. But this is alienation, rather than recycling public assets; the traffic is in one direction only – towards diminishing the patrimony. The state should also be buying land, in anticipation of future needs and uses. Meanwhile, the dwellings being built in these schemes are often poorly served by roads, hospitals or schools, let alone buses or care for the homeowners when they get old and frail. Relaxation of permitted development rights has led to tens of thousands of new homes being created without the requirement for planning permission, particularly through the conversion of commercial buildings and offices into homes. That means little or no thought is given to the most basic issues, such as whether there are enough doctors' surgeries in the area or where children will be able to play.

One lesson is about investing in order to save. The balance sheet for housing development has to be long term; while developers think of their current share price, only government can think and spend over the many decades it may take before investment in bricks and mortar bears fruit.

For the post-war new towns, the state bought land at agri-cultural-use value using compulsory purchase where necessary. They built housing and industrial estates, sold some land, rented units and over the years the enterprise broke even. In Harlow, public spending and revenue balanced decades ago. Yet the new towns were never just a way of alleviating housing shortage. At their best they were planned with employment and transport in mind, and some were created as poles of regional growth. In Crawley, Stevenage and Peterlee, employment was assured before foundations were dug.

Of course not all the towns succeeded. Corby was stricken when the steel production it was built around collapsed in the 1980s, over-reliant as it was on one employer; towns such as Skelmersdale and Cumbernauld could never be emancipated from the fate of their regional economies. The lesson taken from these failures must be to think long and hard about diverse employment, for young and old, women and men, before designating a new town. Another evident lesson is that the state, whether in the shape of development bodies or councils, can be effective and entrepreneurial.

———————

Thurrock Council wants to show it can outdo private property developers. 'We can build better than they can, better quality, creating the developments we want for our community – and make a profit,' says chief executive Lyn Carpenter. Remember, this council is dominated by Conservatives and UKIP, not Labour.

Even under restrictions imposed by the government, Thurrock has been able to pioneer its own development company, wholly owned by the council, which can borrow at low rates. It started on brownfield land, on a site needing lots of preparatory work. Their new development is called Gloriana – to commemorate Elizabeth I and her association with nearby Tilbury docks – and now has 128 homes at a reasonable price.

Private developers require a 15 per cent profit margin while the local authority can make its financial arithmetic work at 7 per cent: if property prices fell, then 3 per cent would be OK, they say. In Thurrock, private developers are sitting on land with planning permission for 8,000 dwellings, but they won't go ahead and build. Instead they just land-bank, because undeveloped land sits on their balance sheets as a comfortably growing asset. Lyn Carpenter says she wishes the council had the power to rescind planning permission in order to force them to build, 'but we can't'.

The council is eyeing up Grays shopping centre for redevelopment, with extra housing to complement a new mall. Other local authorities are flocking to visit Gloriana, to find out how they pulled it off, says Carpenter: 'Birmingham are copying us, because we can prove councils can do better than private developers.'

Planning for the Future

Once a hotbed of anti-statism and an enthusiastic proponent of less government/more market, the OECD in the 21st century has seen some light – although this may be less ideological conversion than a reality check about market failures. Its work on cities is indicative: cities 'are incredible generators of growth and wellbeing, yet poor planning can turn them into inequality traps' says secretary general Angel Gurría.[7] Government – state, city or regional – has to forecast, plan and move resources around spatially.

It's worth harping on about planning. In British towns and cities, the function of mapping the desired shape of an area then mobilising resources to achieve it – including constraints on markets – has fallen profoundly out of fashion. Across the country planning departments have atrophied, and graduate planners now look for careers with developers and consultants, not public authorities. Polls show most professional planners to be pessimistic about the future. The Royal Town Planning Institute says budget cuts and Tory attacks on planning powers stop the state ensuring that schemes make any wider sense. Central government has seized the right to overturn local decision-making, and usually sides with private developers.

Anticipating Climate Change

If the state can no longer plan, developers will seize the chance to build where they can turn a profit, flood plains included. Meteorological records show that six of the seven wettest years since records began occurred from 2000 onwards so the risk of inundation can only grow, and the water won't spare those who simply deny man-made climate change. On present evidence, no likely course of action by the UK government – let alone the Americans, Indians and others – is going to decelerate climate change. Bank of England governor Mark Carney and former New York mayor Michael Bloomberg convened a task force to urge companies to disclose to investors the impact of climate change on their businesses. If they don't – or more likely won't – government is left trying to save markets from their own short-sightedness.

The UK has an economy-wide target to reduce greenhouse gas emissions by 80 per cent by 2050, from a 1990 baseline. The coalition didn't abolish that target, though it made its realisation considerably less likely, and the May government removed the phrase 'climate change' from the ministry responsible for action. A large gap persists between the target and the UK's current trajectory on emissions.

At the same time, the state must deal with the effects of climate change. Over the coalition years, flood defence spending did increase overall compared to the previous five years thanks to the panic that took hold after the winter floods of 2013–14. But the scale of the problem is huge: around 5.4 million properties in England (one in six) are at risk of flooding from rivers, the sea and surface water; annual flood damage costs are rising, with the cost of the winter floods of 2015–16 up to £5.8bn.

The state alone can redistribute funds to help the people at risk. Only it can coordinate the engineers, planners and emergency services – and keep learning from 'last time'. Yet here again, the austerians have diminished the size and presence of the key anti-floods body. The Environment Agency is damned if it does and damned if it doesn't – though it turns out dams are not always a solution. In the West Country, where the Axe, Brue and Parrett boards drain – or rather don't drain – the Somerset Levels into the Bristol Channel, the cry goes up for dredging. But what is required is upstream work on the land with sumps and tree planting, and extensive involvement with farm practice and land ownership. And all that will have to be paid for – but the downstream property owners who are so vocal about sandbags and dredging are also mainly Tory voters who are generally unenthusiastic about any government proposing to raise taxes in order to pay for this work.

Denying man-made climate change won't secure coverage if your home falls in the expanding red zones on insurers' maps. The mass refusal of private insurers to face the growing risk of flooding forced the state – even when led by the Conservatives

– to step in. It's not that Axa and Aviva are malign: they see losses not profit so why should they write a policy? The government's response was the semi state-backed insurance package, Flood Re, which we cited earlier as an example of confused boundaries. It is accountable to parliament but depends on an insurance industry levy, which is capped. If claims exceed a threshold, those claimants won't be paid. Meanwhile, adapting to the likelihood of more floods, housebuilding materials need to be refashioned. Here is another example of where the state can and should be supporting the growth of useful knowledge, which is then made available to all firms. Instead, the Building Research Establishment is no longer state-backed but a charity, dependent on contributions from industry.

The Science of Productivity

Join the chorus. Productivity, which is the ratio of the value of output to the number of hours worked or people employed, unlocks growth; squeezing more out depends on knowledge, research and innovation. Mark Carney, governor of the Bank of England, describes productivity as 'the ultimate determinant of people's incomes, and with it the capacity of our economy to support health, wealth and happiness'. The UK has fallen 30 per cent and more behind comparable countries: a French worker produces in four days what it takes a British worker five days to do. German productivity is 35 per cent ahead.

In response you could, like the ultra-Tory authors of *Britannia Unchained* – cabinet ministers Elizabeth Truss and Priti Patel among them – proclaim that 'British workers are among the worst idlers in the world'. More analytically, you might look at sluggish directors, sitting on large sums they won't invest in research and development or technologies, preferring to pay dividends to shareholders or buy back a company's own shares to increase the share value on which directors are judged and rewarded. Business gets over £9bn a year in research and development tax credits, but it's hard to identify what is genuinely new research. Entrepreneur's tax relief costs the government another £4.6bn, for what may be normal business activity.

Alternatively you might, like the Confederation of British Industry, wring your hands. The business-lobbying body wants better education, more connectivity and improved business practices. After years of predicting a better national minimum wage would destroy jobs, the CBI now says that higher rates will push firms to innovate in how they use staff and machines. What the CBI won't or can't say is that the UK's productivity problem is a classic exhibition of its – especially business's – problem with the state. Employers could start running schools or tarmacking roads, all of which would improve productivity, but when they had their chance in the 19th century they demurred and it's unlikely their response would be any different today. It's government alone that can turn the key to higher output. The precondition is open acknowledgement of the state's role – and this is not something that most Tory ministers are willing to do.

They worry that research is not being taken up by firms and applied in devising new products and services but stop short of funding the transitions and translations needed – which could imply state banks and state risk funds. Policy won't go there, staying with the easy bit, which is UK research. Easy, that is, in the sense that the UK research record remains highly impressive despite austerity. Whether it will survive Brexit is another matter. What is missing, predictably, is a wider scheme for growing and enriching knowledge and making it available to developers of products. Useful organisations such as Innovate UK don't join up with each other. Lines of strategy here; plans there. A large-scale reorganisation of the research councils is taking place, for realisation in 2018 when UK Research and Innovation will be unveiled. The potential is huge.

———————

In a smartly renovated old railway building in Sheffield, Magnomatics Ltd is one of Innovate UK's beneficiaries. The company is developing a magnetic gearbox with no contact between moving parts, first invented by Sheffield University. In two quiet rows upstairs the engineers (eight of them PhDs) sit at their computers. Designing variants at high speed, each computer on its own generates a thousand possible solutions to technical problems, and then evaluates them itself. 'No,' says Peter, one of the engineers, 'it will never take over from us humans. It can only do so many tasks, but it needs a human brain. AI will never do my job!'

Downstairs in the workshops are arrays of gearboxes on the benches. Some are being designed to fit a hybrid electric car, some for a Formula 1 team, others for wind turbines, marine engines and something secret for the Ministry of Defence. David Latimer, the chief executive, shows us round, picking up one piece of machinery after another. He has long experience of the slow process of developing a new idea from a university laboratory and getting it to market. That takes patience and funding, both often in short supply in Britain, he says. But when it works, it lasts: his first business was working on air-conditioning compressors used in VC10s, devices that were still in use 30 years later. An engineer by training, and serial nurturer of start-ups springing from universities, he has both the enthusiasm and the patience. But the frustrations are many, he says.

'This gearbox,' he says, cradling the large circular steel casing, 'is the only magnetic one patented. It has half the moving parts and it saves 35 per cent in fuel, yet costs the same as a conventional one.' Then it must be an easy sell to investors? 'No, not at all. Motor manufacturers are ultra cautious. They ask where has it been used before, and when you say nowhere, they back away. We have to put it into a car and demonstrate, so their board members can drive it. It costs half a million to build a demo car.'

Why wouldn't venture capitalists seize this chance? 'They want a fast turn-round within five years,' says Latimer. He compares UK investment attitudes to the Japanese: 'Toyota has 3,000 people working on R&D and they think in terms of a 30-year horizon.'

This magnetic gearbox was invented in 2000, with six people working on it for five years. Getting it 'across the chasm' from university to business took time. In 2006 the six moved over with their patents to start the business, but that was only possible with government start-up funds. They also subsidised themselves by working as engineering consultants to other firms. By 2012 they realised they couldn't get any further without raising significant capital, and taking them up to 2016 they got £2m from mixed government money and EU funds, and that helped raise £2m from IP Group, venture capitalists specialising in university technology spin-offs. But that would never happen without the matched government funds and the confidence that brings. Latimer says IP hope to sell their 40 per cent share for £30m in due course.

'Due course' is the problem. 'It'll be 2018 before we have full-scale demos of all these technologies, with a large motor for a wind turbine, one for a ship and one for a hybrid car.' But, he adds, 'the earliest possible date you could see a car in the showroom with our gearbox would be in 2022.'

That's 22 years after it was first invented. 'The inventors wasted five years at the start, when if they'd had the investment they could have moved faster.' But otherwise, yes, that's the kind of timescale it needs – and neither manufacturers nor enough venture capital investors think that far ahead. Then add in the risk that it won't work: a previous innovative electric car Latimer worked on, spun out of Imperial College, was sold to GKN, but in the end didn't suit their mass-market needs.

Investment in Magnomatics could bring about 'a lot of manufacturing jobs, with large energy-efficient engines, a business that will continue to grow'. Latimer notes, 'that brings in tax revenue. We have sponsored an engineering design business with 20 highly skilled engineers, just what the country needs. We spot the brightest engineering students in Sheffield and give them internships to keep them going. Our latest, Rob, had job offers from Roll-Royce and McLaren, or could have gone abroad, but he came to us because our innovative work is more exciting.'

Dealing with Future Technological Threats

Innovation isn't just for legitimate business. The increasing number of internet and online transactions are fertile ground for fraudsters, thieves, mischief-makers and agents of foreign states making war by a new means.

Overall reductions in recorded and reported crime conceal increases elsewhere, especially in cyber crime. The National Crime Agency says we are simply being outpaced. The Office for National Statistics counted 5.6 million incidents of online fraud and computer misuse in England and Wales in the year ending June 2016; it is now the most prevalent recorded crime. But e-crime expertise has been lost with cuts to council trading standards. National Trading Standards, which is under the wing of the Department for Business, Enterprise and Industrial Strategy, costing barely £15m a year, prosecutes a derisory number of cases – there were a mere 83 convictions in 2015–16.

Hacking and disruption are daily dangers for institutions and individuals. RSM, the accountancy firm, says cyber fraud attacks are increasing in frequency, breadth and sophistication. The state gets portrayed as an oppressive gatherer and hoarder of data. But only the state is going to be able to research and defend when hackers and cyber criminals come calling, and for that it needs data. Only the government might step in when the commercial interests of internet giants start to make intrusive use of the mounds of personal data they collect in order to make money. The government's National Cyber Security Strategy accepts that the state is the last resort, the last defence: 'Although key sectors of our economy are in private hands, the government is ultimately responsible for assuring their national resilience.'[8] The state has to draw on all the intelligence it has at its disposal and knock heads together.

That includes patrolling banking and finance security. During 2016, a cyber attack on Tesco Bank threatened not just its account holders but wider confidence in the system. In principle, the finance sector could gird its loins and come together to devise stronger defences. In practice, it takes government to mobilise its expertise, via GCHQ and the finance regulators, both to protect public systems and to share knowledge with the private sector. When perpetrators may be sponsored by Russia or China or other foreign states, government must be involved in defending the country from foreign interference. In December 2016, Alex Younger, head of the Secret Intelligence Service, broke cover to warn of fundamental threats to European democracies.[9]

As technology advances and, for example, the cost of drones falls to the point where parents start considering them as Christmas presents, people will demand state action. With the spread of drones comes risk to aviation, and on a more local level the nuisance and disruption of neighbours' lives. Calls for regulation start to be heard, as well as calls to the police and council for the protection of the public interest. Yet police numbers have been significantly cut and the skills of traditionally trained officers may not be up to the new challenge: investment in retraining and new recruitment is needed.

Contours of Change

New offences upset social order, producing calls to action – female genital mutilation and forced marriage are examples arising from increased migration. The contours of threat change constantly – from returning jihadis, home-grown extremism and easier access to weapons. These are not just matters for the police force; all public services are potentially in the front line. Anti-extremism policy cannot safely be delegated to security specialists or headteachers in isolation: all public staff need to be alert.

We don't live in some Hobbesian state of war, but we do need protection and assurance that changing security risks are not just under observation but are prompting clever countermeasures. The different classes of risk grow, from Putin's Russia, from the collapse of failed states, from China – which is simultaneously a trade partner and a threat. Once, Tory ministers would have said: trust us, we are the people to buttress the military while cutting back the social and economic dimensions of the state. If that were ever convincing, it is not now, because threats and countermeasures involve people, communities and flows of goods and capital investments.

That is not to say warnings from military officers should not be heeded. Sir Richard Barrons, after his retirement in April 2016 as head of Joint Forces Command, says a Russian air campaign would quickly overwhelm Europe. He blames over-investment in a small number of hugely expensive ships, platforms that the UK cannot afford to use properly. After the Russian invasion of the Crimea, the spotlight shone on the atrophy of the UK's conventional strength, the rundown of armoured strength and the deterioration of advanced warning aircraft strength. MPs say the Royal Navy's destroyer and frigate fleet 'is at a dangerous and historic low'.[10]

Some of this is UK-specific, some to do with wider trends outlined earlier in the book towards outsourcing and fragmentation. Examples abound of the consequences of the doctrine, and not just in the UK. A senior officer at the Szczecin headquarters of NATO's command centre noted that the former West German government once had thousands of flatbed wagons at its disposal for the movement of tanks and other vehicles to NATO's likely front line. Now, keeping barely 20 on standby was difficult and expensive for NATO, because rail operators across Western Europe, including Deutsche Bundesbahn, have been privatised or subcontracted and rolling stock has been broken up or eliminated, as 'just in time' deliveries increased. Vladimir Putin has duly noted.

The Future of Defence

Defence is the prime duty of the state – and that means sustaining companies that produce the aircraft, ships, communications systems and technologies of war. This means disregarding market ideology. The military industrial complex is real enough, a symbiotic intertwining of state and private interests. If that's OK for defence industries, why shouldn't the state similarly intervene in other vital national interests?

From Cameron, the May government inherited a shipbuilding strategy for new frigates, and what are now called global combat ships. But ships don't build themselves nor do disabled destroyers refit their own engines; a navy needs yards and specialist skills that cannot be turned on and off like a tap. That in turn means partnership and collaboration within the private sector.

When the boss of Rolls-Royce warns against allowing his company and others in the defence industry to 'wither on the vine', he is negotiating contracts, yes – but he has a valid point to make. A report by an industrialist who has been on various corporate boards with an interest in the sector, says the government is too reliant on a single firm, BAE, for ships.[11] But you can't magic new shipbuilders out of the rarefied air of defence contracting. Besides, BAE was once state-owned, and remains highly state-dependent, providing at least a benchmark for costs and investment.

Debate has waxed and waned over the potency of the nation state as international trade and capital movements expanded. The 21st century has so far not been kind to the Cobdenites or exponents of the 'end of history' theory. Prophets of the inevitability of globalisation have found it hard to account for the obvious signs of basic nation state militarism in China and Russia and elsewhere. The bottom line is that only idealists and fools ignore defence and that only the state will shoulder the responsibility.

The illusion that history had ended and with it the need to maintain soldiers, tanks, ships and planes has lasted too long on all sides of politics. It has led to the rundown of barracks, bases and training grounds, which the NAO reports are still deteriorating, regardless of the increasingly fraught security situation. By the end of 2016 there was a £8.5bn gap in the finance needed to maintain the UK defence barracks, buildings and land to a decent and effective level.

In defence the government is usually the only buyer so it is inevitably drawn into pacts and arrangements with small numbers of companies: the only remedy against potential corruption is maximum disclosure in fields where degrees of secrecy are necessary. Why companies and the state can collab-orate in defence – and produce weapons systems and (often) promote technological innovation – and not elsewhere is not clear; yet the anti-statists often draw an imaginary line.

In defence contracting, governments may simultaneously be owners, procurers, regulators and promoters. Take the missile producer MBDA, which is owned jointly by Airbus, in which the French and German governments have large stakes, by BAE Systems of the UK and by Leonardo-Finmeccanica of Italy. Its entire production goes to supplying various govern-ments around Europe, and the UK government signs treaties about the use of its products with other states. How far it can be said to be a private company is debatable: it represents industrial strategy, planning and the deepest involvement of politicians and officials in strategy and finance. If this works in defence, why not in other fields of vital national importance such as energy or transport?

All the future tasks we list in this chapter are pressing, unavoidable, and can only be done by the state. A future in which the state does not step up will be bleak indeed – for the elderly, for the young, for climate change, for productivity, for the security of the nation itself.

Chapter 10

The State of Balance

If you have come with us so far, a nagging question remains: how can the state be made capable for the tasks ahead? It's a tightrope walk across a chasm. We've focused on one side of the gorge, where the anti-statists have mustered their firepower in recent decades, attacking the public realm, its staff and purposes, using their media strength and ideological channels to poison the public mind against tax and against the idea of state activism.

But there is danger on the other side too. There lies the authoritarian state: you can see it in Russia and emerging in Hungary and Poland. The state and the nation merge; dissenters are silenced and marginalised. Freedom is crushed – at least the freedom to express dissenting views and agitate. The policeman becomes the agent of an oppressive state. In China, the party and the state merged long ago and is now symbolised by hooded operatives milling outside the home of a daring would-be escapee from the approved order, an artist or dissident or member of an ethnic or religious group – or in Hong Kong a young person who refuses to kowtow. State power without checks and balance tips into tyranny.

Fighting for balance between state and individual, and mobilising on behalf of proportion, are not slogans to raise the pulse. But recent events in the US show both the wisdom of the founding fathers and the fragility of their settlement: how difficult it is to sustain counterweights that prevent excess yet allow enough power for effective government. In the UK, the pendulum analogy is the most apt: at present, the pendulum has swung too far in the anti-collective direction. We are trying to wrest it back, but that's not to say we advocate an extreme alternative.

A Third Way?

You may say that all this is painting the world in black and white, when it's speckled like a Seurat painting. Among the dots, triangulated between public and private, sits the third sector, which includes charities, mutuals and non-profits. The word 'charity' is full of biblical warmth, but as we have seen with the Garden Bridge Trust, not all non-profits are equal. Macmillan nurses, Age UK, Shelter and Barnardo's would top some lists of reputable charities; but what about private schools or BUPA, which to all intents and purposes are private businesses? Charity requires state-enforced regulation to give donors and the public assurance of their trustworthiness. The state is already involved through tax relief: every time someone puts a pound in the tin for a donkey sanctuary, the taxpayer adds another 30p willy-nilly.

On his path to power, David Cameron for PR purposes painted a vision of a Big Society to fill the gap when the state was withdrawn. Meek charity trustees imagined they were about to inherit the earth. Charities did indeed do their best to repair the great rips in the social safety net torn apart right from Osborne's first budget. One of the most visible has been the admirable Trussell Trust, previously a tiny Salisbury charity that sprang up to open some 500 food banks nationally by 2016, mainly in churches, giving basic three-day food parcels to over a million people, many of whom were working families with children.

But charity could never fill the gap. Voluntary sector interests are particular – hedgehogs or autism. Unlike the state, they have no obligation to offer universal services and some are necessarily very restrictive.

Since the 1980s the function and character of charities has changed. Some have become contractors competing fiercely with the private sector to do public work, in children's services, health, care for the elderly and more. Since 2010 that transformation has accelerated, at the same time as charities are increasingly threatened if they dare speak out on behalf of the people they aim to serve and challenge the cuts.

———————

Not all became quiescent. Over 60 children's charities, including the NSPCC and Action for Children, are grouped together in Children England. Its voice is Kathy Evans, chief executive, and it is powerfully outspoken.

We talked to her not so long after the shocking sudden bankruptcy of a large and famous children's charity, 4Children, which ran Sure Start Children's Centres, nurseries, out-of-school clubs and activity centres. Its children's centres were rated among the best.

But Kathy Evans says contracting went too far. 'In these public service markets, charities are routinely treated as just another commercial business and they are expected to subsidise low-price contracts with their own funds. But this isn't an ordinary commercial market where demand is always good and repeat custom is brilliant. More demand from children in need is a sign of society's failure, not success.'

Contracting is what did for 4Children, plunged into bankruptcy after seeming so solid. 'They grew rapidly, they borrowed, they relied on promises of contracts.' Then the cuts came. 'They didn't factor in the withdrawal of local government grants. It's happening in health and social care for the old and disabled too: cuts have overturned their business models, with the politicians always wanting more for less.'

In late 2016, Children England published a Declaration of Interdependence, calling for an end to competitive contracts, and their replacement with long-term partnerships between state and charities to run services together. It declares: 'We believe that the reliance on price-driven competition is eroding, rather than building, our sense of common cause in achieving this vision.'

She bubbles with indignation over social impact bonds. 'Snake oil!' she says of £80m of bonds sold to investors such as Goldman Sachs on payment-by-results for each problem person turned around – young offenders, the unemployed or families. 'They are promised an 8 per cent return, 8 per cent on each success! When exactly is a problem person officially "cured"? That's putting a price on the head of the vulnerable.'

―――――――――

After the dream of the Big Society faded away, as it quickly did, the Tories waged war on charities' autonomy, legislating to impede their campaigns and even proposing to cut tax relief on donations. The collapse of Kids Company was turned to political use, as the tabloids seized on its connections with the BBC and some figures on the political left – though Cameron and Osborne had also been strong supporters, channelling money towards the charity and even inviting its charismatic founder to speak at the Conservative party conference.

The government appointed a hawk to chair the Charity Commission (Sir William Shawcross) and started criticising charities for daring to speak out or lobby MPs; at the same time it told them to cut their costs, except when it came to the Charity Commission, which proposes to charge them fees for being regulated by it. Charities did indeed have vulnerabilities: a few were paying fat-cat salaries of over £300,000 to their chief executives, and stories of these mega-salaries were eagerly fed to the Tory tabloids.

Charities and voluntary bodies should be awkward, a thorn in the side of state and society. They should take the side of people in need and speak out. A good state should heed them, however provocative. But the quid pro quo is probably that charities should not grow too big and be careful about becoming social services contractors and recipients of government grants.

The Question of Constitution

The place to look for balance within the state ought to be the constitution, meaning the codes and conventions for how we govern ourselves. Lately, however, we have tended to veer from tradition-encrusted veneration to naïve shouts for plebiscites on everything amid public indifference to such major changes as devolution. The constitution never seemed to address public services, especially where the state was active in people's lives through local authorities, arm's-length bodies and contractors.

The notion that Great Britain has somehow lacked a constitution, or more specifically a written constitution, was always misplaced. Fundamental law has been in place since at least the Act of Settlement 1701. What it lacked was codification, though in recent years efforts have been made, for example the Cabinet Manual, which brings together myriad conventions, hard and soft understandings, fixed procedures and statute law.[1]

Some of this will need substantial revision when the UK leaves the EU. As for the other anomalies, for example the crown dependencies, questions remain: why does the UK subsidise Isle of Man residents, for example, who pay so little tax? What nonsense is our semi-theocracy, where 26 Church of England bishops in the House of Lords make our laws, and sometimes carry strong influence, as in denying the right to die legislation? In the 21st century we go on languishing under such higher mysteries as the 'royal prerogative', which is basically a way of the cabinet spending money without legal permission.

From the way the House of Commons operates to the oddity of the office of prime minister, whose occupant has to swear an oath as a Commissioner of the Treasury to get paid, the system drips with antiquity. It is full of black holes. What management sense can we make of the prescription that parliament 'will normally' understand that ministers cannot be held responsible for administrative decisions? Why shouldn't the cabinet secretary be appointed transparently, through open competition, rather than 'on the advice of the retiring cabinet secretary who will consult with a number of [unnamed] individuals'?

As for the electoral system, it is regularly gerrymandered by whoever is in power, with votes purchased by a handful of plutocratic party donors who are either rewarded publicly with absurd honours or in unseen ways by other business favours.

First-past-the-post voting bars new parties, discriminates against smaller parties and forces probably a majority to vote not for what they want, but for the least worst of the only two prime ministers on offer. State funding of parties and a proportional voting system are a bare minimum of requirements to correct the grotesque distortions that tend to disenfranchise large numbers of voters, generating a lack of trust in the authenticity of whoever is in charge of the state.

Ghosts from the distant past still haunt us. In any UK conversation 'we' is problematic, because of felt identities among residents of Scotland, Wales and Northern Ireland. English identity is a puzzle for fiction writers of the John Buchan persuasion, academics and flag-wavers in the Albert Hall during the last night of the Proms. But the 'we' question is unavoidable as we talk about the state. Its writ runs in a bounded space; obligations and benefits fall on a designated population. How actively should the NHS pursue payment by non-citizens? How are non-citizens to be identified? Under Labour, proposals for national identity cards were couched in terms of combating crime, terrorism or benefit and NHS fraud as well as for controlling migration. That was a popular idea – until it was proposed in such a cackhanded way, whereby everyone would have to pay £75 for a compulsory identity card. For a better, stronger state we propose there should be better evidence of belonging, of obligation, of a citizen's rights and responsibilities, which a national identity scheme could provide. A passport currently costs £72.50. Why not issue every citizen at birth or naturalisation with a free British passport, as a gift and an emblem of belonging, as a positive good, not as a state threat?

Can the State be the Enemy of Freedom?

Clothing themselves in the garb of constitutionalists, the left and liberals have often undermined government, despite their general support for an active state. What upsets them is what the state knows about us all – its data.

But if the state can be trusted to redistribute income through taxation and benefits, it should be empowered to collect and guard information for the sake of delivering public services accurately and deepening knowledge to further improve these services. By setting themselves against that idea, some on the liberal left aid and abet the Adam Smith Institute and the anti-collectivist right. Stirring up an anti-state paranoia, they adopt strongly individualistic stances on data collection, crudely casting the state as oppressor.

Of course there are genuine threats regarding data use that need eternal vigilance: Silicon Valley libertarians say that data will eventually do away with the state. What it turns out they mean is that their giant companies, averse to paying any tax, will control everything and amass huge financial and cultural power. Those naturally suspicious of all data collection struggle, trusting neither the Scylla of Google on one side of the straits nor the Charybdis of the state on the other: their incoherence is personified by Edward Snowden, preaching resistance to the oppressive surveillance state from his lodging at Putin's elbow. The hacking, manipulation and fake news interventions by Russia and others in the 2016 US election campaign put paid to residual optimism that data was somehow not subject to Gresham's Law and that good data (numbers, facts) would drive out the bad (fake news).

It is also true that the state can go too far: the Investigatory Powers Act was not unjustly called the 'snoopers' charter' when it became law in November 2016, with its sweeping powers for the state and communications companies to collect and store bulk data on telephone and email records and internet browsing, with access given to a long list of government agencies. While supporting legitimate use of this data, Harriet Harman, as chair of the Joint Committee of Human Rights, spoke for many when she protested at the refusal to exempt MPs' communications, or confidential communications between lawyers and clients.

Data and Transparency

All organisations, private sector and public, need a 'private life', but campaigners demand total transparency. People are encouraged to belittle expert and esoteric knowledge; they tend to paint the subtle, often tacit, dealings between professionals and their clients as a conspiracy. Meanwhile, the Taxpayers' Alliance and related rightwing groups bang the transparency drum as an instrument in their noisy campaign against taxation and against the state.

Elizabeth Denham, the Information Commissioner, talks about balancing the right of access and the importance of transparency with the 'need for government to have room to do its job'.[2] This is again a call for that much-needed balance: the public deserves to know what the state is doing in their name, yet also needs to give officials the benefit of some functional freedom.

Freedom of Information (FOI) has been abused. It has been exploited by commercial contractors trying to winkle out extra details to help them with their bids. Labour often found the freedoms it had introduced were used as a blunt weapon in the anti-statists' longstanding campaign against waste, as a way of suggesting that all active government tends to squander taxpayers' money. Blair, Jack Straw and other Labour ministers later berated themselves, asserting that FOI had made government less effective. Responding to information requests can be costly for public bodies; a number of such requests are frivolous and some are trawling expeditions by hostile media seeking any nuggets for campaigns against the public realm. How much did they spend on biscuits, how often did they use an official car? As always, there is a balance to be struck: ministers and officials should be accountable, but they also need a modicum of unmonitored reflection and the right to talk privately amongst themselves. FOI has encouraged better record keeping but perversely it may mean more private conversations in which nothing is recorded.

Data paranoia does impede good government. Currently, absurdly, fewer than 10 per cent of files relating to the same individuals are shared between the DWP and HMRC, a recipe for unnecessary administration and a much less joined-up state. People are infuriated by having to give the same information – say over the registration of a death – over and over again to multiple officials and offices, yet it is often the suspicious anti-collectivists and anti-statists who stall rationalisation of data collection. It is interesting to note how rarely they focus on companies' private collection and sale of data, the ones that chase purchasers around the internet with unwanted ads, related to what they already know about their buying habits and goodness knows what else. These companies are not subject to freedom of information.

Real damage has been done by paranoia over the use of health records. The NHS has been stymied in vital research projects by over-rigorous data protection that goes well beyond detaching patient names from data about conditions and treatment. In every visit to a GP, information is generated about various medical conditions and the effectiveness of the drugs and treatments, making the NHS a data goldmine. Data-sharing ought to be a 'no brainer', said the chief executive of the Medical Research Council, Sir John Savill. Potentially, the NHS – combined with the UK's unique longitudinal research studies into cohorts following the lifetimes of children born in 1946, 1958, 1970 and 2000 – has the richest social and medical data in the world. Yet those who Savill called 'consent fetishists' have severely impeded data use and a brilliant opportunity has been squandered.

Marketeers were partly to blame. The Tories' Care.data plan for the NHS aspired to 'turn the UK into the best clinical laboratory in the world'. The Health and Social Care Information Centre and NHS England drew up a sensible plan where anyone who didn't want their data to be used (even when anonymised) had the right to opt out. This is broadly how the system works in Scotland. But the scheme went awry because Tory ministers and their advisers were determined to sell NHS Care.data information to private companies, most of which are American and avaricious. Research to benefit medicine and the NHS was one thing, but commercial access spoiled the whole project, alarming GPs and their patients, despite all the careful protocols put in place. The question became, 'Would you trust Jeremy Hunt not to sell your precious personal data to an insurance company, which would then double your premiums because of what your GP's notes say about you?'

Evidence from focus groups suggests the public take a broadly pragmatic attitude and are happy to follow the lead of experts they trust – particularly NHS clinicians – in making the case for data-sharing where they saw it was likely to benefit society, themselves and the nation. The regime put in place by NHS Digital now discourages even data-sharing between councils and the NHS and damages the state's capacity to do good.

The Media's Influence on the State

The power wielded by the *Daily Mail* and its proprietors, Associated Newspapers, has been immense, ever since Alfred Harmsworth, Lord Northcliffe, hit a sweet spot in English political and cultural attitudes – mean, judgmental, selfish, suspicious – through brilliant headlines that simultaneously created and followed those attitudes. The newspaper is coercive, but no one coerces its readers into endorsing its reactionary views, which are generally both aghast at the need for a social state and clamorous for the state to censor and intervene.

The state is closely enmeshed in broadcasting and online media, regulating content and competition. Newspapers claim they should be exempt from any check on their accuracy, beyond what they choose to impose on themselves: any outside overview or redress against their abuses would be an affront to democracy. For the claim to hold, you have to believe that newspaper owners are upholders of democracy, rather than ideologists and maximisers of their own power and profit. The Murdoch dynasty controls nearly 40 per cent of mainstream daily newspaper circulation, and in his broadcasting empire Sky is now far larger and richer than the BBC. So, do you believe that Murdoch is upholding democracy? Or do you believe that he is maximising his own power and profit?

In a curious letter to the *Guardian* in December 2016, Rupert Murdoch claimed never to have asked a British prime minister for favour.[3] In fact, in 1998 he asked Tony Blair to intervene with the EU commission over an £800m deal allowing Sky to expand on the Continent. Since taking ownership of the *Sun* in 1969, Murdoch's game has been trading political support or opprobrium for regulatory openings and exemptions: the UK was something to be manipulated for commercial advantage. Was it to please Murdoch that the BBC was savaged with a gigantic cut of £700m in revenue and forced to pay the free licence fee for over-75s from 2020? In the US, his Fox channel can claim to have made an American president, and no doubt will expect its pounds of flesh.

The disclosure of grotesque routine telephone hacking within the Murdoch empire led to the Leveson inquiry. The judge's conclusion was that the power of the newspaper press needed checking; he proposed an elaborate mechanism to give readers and the public rights of redress against media abuse. This involved government approving a panel of independents who would approve a regulator; the media could face higher court costs if they failed to join and faced libel actions. But Cameron and Theresa May after him backed away from implementing the recommended regime.

An independent press regulator would not stop the *Daily Mail* and the Murdoch titles from debauching good governance at Westminster, intimidating ministers or warping the public interest with their bully-power. But it might stop press persecution of individuals and give some rights to those defamed by its editors and sensation-seeking columnists. The state rightly treads gingerly where free speech is concerned, but nothing Leveson proposed would have interfered with it.

The reputation, culture and function of the British state has undoubtedly been shaped and probably warped by the newspaper press. The mild recommendations of Lord Leveson might have gone some small distance to redress that historical characteristic.

Power to the People?

Here's a condundrum of power. Swaggering, abusive media need to be checked by the state; but the state can also abuse power and itself need checking; and the media are an ingredient in democratic accountability. Similarly, professionals in the public service should have power, but may abuse and need to be held to account. Contributors to books such as *Public Service on the Brink*[4] seem to celebrate victimhood. In it teachers complain about inspection and tighter controls on teaching methods. But professionals, while deserving respect and autonomy, also need to listen. A positive response by teachers to the concerns voiced by Jim Callaghan 40 years ago, trying to open up discussion about the school curriculum to parents and the wider public, might have gone some way to head off the coming Thatcherite attack and the fragmentation of schooling described earlier.

It's a matter of balancing public officials' expertise against accountability. Some people push to extremes, arguing for direct control of public services by the people. This strain of thought has underpinned the move to directly elected mayors, favoured both by New Labour and now some Tories.

Instead of messy representative democracy with all its inescapable compromises and negotiations comes the desire to stamp the general will directly on affairs. This approach goes back to Jean-Jacques Rousseau and is reflected in the push to create city mayors to replace councils, in the belief a single powerful individual is better able to do what the people want. The same trend led to directly elected police chiefs and the resort to referendums, which boil down hugely complex questions into a deceptively yes or no. Like Brexit.

Bertolt Brecht conquered the dictionary of quotations with his mockery of an authoritarian government's need 'to dissolve the people and elect another'. For some, that's the last word on democracy: the people or the community can do no wrong, while only governments and officials can err.

The trouble with the doctrine is that all of the people some of the time and some of the people all of the time can be stupid, self-interested and stubborn. Community wishes can be short-termist and self-defeating: it's the duty of brave public managers, councillors and ministers, with the benefit of experience and expertise, to occasionally say so. Those who occupy positions of public power are condemned to be aware that not only is there a wider context but that in public affairs there are always contradictory aims and interests. The state exists to try to reconcile them. What the people say one day isn't necessarily what they want the next, and someone in a position of responsibility has to sort out the consequences. Again, it comes down to this question of balance between listening to the wider public, and applying expertise and knowledge beyond that available to the public.

Searching for Elusive Democracy

Things have to be done with people's consent because it usually means doing things *to* people. Power is unevenly distributed in our society so any decision-making forum risks reflecting that imbalance and propagating the fact that those with social and economic capital have disproportionate influence, especially in the planning process. A superficial appearance of equal rights may in fact reinforce that social inequality. For example, neighbourhood planning, advanced by the Tories, but previously also by Labour, is a good idea in principle, allowing residents more say. But it has been disproportionately used in rural and affluent areas and tends to be an instrument through which sectional and small group interests thwart the wider, common good – for example blocking house building, wind turbines or mental health clinics in their area.

Accountability is difficult. Take successive attempts at making the NHS more democratic: this has resulted in sparsely attended gatherings under such labels as Labour's Local Improvement Networks (LINk) and the coalition government's Healthwatch. Democracy in health is at risk of capture by particular patient interests, who want more spending on one condition. People rightly want to be given reasons as to why a service is underfunded or has been cut – and there may be good reasons, but the public might not like these explanations. So accountability must also be reciprocal, with people prepared to engage with complexity and choices regarding how to share limited resources – and, crucially, they must face up to questions about the need for raising tax.

During its term in government, Labour did nothing to make primary care – the part of the NHS closest to people's daily lives – more accountable. Instead it decided to inject voting into the provision of healthcare in the hospitals, ambulance and mental health services. Optimistically, it believed the community would mobilise in order to elect council members to local trusts. Virgin and other private health providers of course have no public interest governors.

As so often when the community is invited to participate, members of foundation trust councils and governors tend to be older and retired people; half their elections are not even contested. In the 2012 act, the Tories compounded confusion, giving trust governors more powers while, under pressure from their Liberal Democrat allies, shifting all of public health out to councils, ostensibly to introduce more democracy. Councils in England were told to set up new Health and Wellbeing Boards, which in theory join together council responsibilities for social care and public health with the NHS. Under austerity, councils have been severely embarrassed at taking on new health responsibilities because no sooner had they acquired public health than George Osborne sliced £2bn off its budget. Meanwhile, in a dark basement, the 2012 act also created Healthwatch – a set of local committees with tiny budgets, intended 'to give citizens greater influence over local health and social care services'.

It's an architecture more Gaudí than Sir Norman Foster, and designed semi-intentionally to confuse rather than involve the public who, in theory, were meant to be given more control. This is how the public sector suffers: complexifiction again, confusion and criss-crossing attempts at local democracy that still leave real power at the top.

Localism and Devolution

Devolution has weakened the UK state, making its reach and shape even more puzzling. Yet the state has been boosted within the devolved territories. Since 2000, Edinburgh, Cardiff and Belfast have broadly taken the view that public power is to be deployed for the good of the people. A positive, activist view of government has held across the parties, from Scottish Nationalists to Ulster Unionists, Sinn Fein, Labour and Plaid Cymru, even among Scottish and Welsh Tories. Cathays Park, headquarters of the Welsh government, feels like the seat of a (small) state. Edinburgh is home to a responsible and capable machine – albeit one that has still to resolve fundamental questions around who is to pay for the Scottish state. Nationalists tend to favour stronger states, though it remains to be seen whether the generalisation holds good in the US with Donald Trump.

Devolution, its advocates argue, has much further to go. Within England, it is not at the centre that public trust in the state can be refreshed and re-established but regionally and locally. 'Localism' has seen a curious union of left and right. Elements of the latter have long recognised that their purpose of shrinking the state could best be realised by splitting it up between local bodies, not necessarily elected. A bellwether for the right is the Taxpayers' Alliance, which declares itself in favour of councils gaining control over income and sales taxes. The reason is soon apparent. According to its chief, councils would 'be able to experiment with what services they offer ... they would focus on business-friendly policies'.[5] In other words, cut spending.

'Local' doesn't have to mean councillors, about whom Tories remain ambiguous, despite their party's enduring strength in England's shire counties and districts outside the big cities. Local government lost any role in probation and removal of social services is on the cards. Cameron said: 'Just as we've replaced failing local authority schools with great new academies and outstanding free schools, so we will say to any local authority failing its children: transform the way you provide services or those services will be taken over by non-profit trusts or other partnerships.'⁶ The treatment of children by their local authority is highly variable, it is true. Re-referrals to children's social care in 2015 varied from 3 per cent in one council to 44 per cent in another.

The line has been hard to follow. Rhetoric around the Cities and Local Government Devolution Act in January 2016 talks about freedom and local (state) activism. Yet austerity has relied on substantially reducing their grants while making local authorities take the pain and the blame for service cuts. Meanwhile, left-of-centre localism is also puzzling. It emphasises the failures of the central state while assuming that if councils had more control they would all be benign and progressive. In fact Tory councils are mixed; some have been enthusiastic cutters and, if given more power, might strive to do less, for example in Kent, Barnet or Wandsworth. Say UKIP were to come to power in an area where migrants have settled in significant numbers, such as Wisbech or Peterborough. Autonomy might feel good to the left in Greater Manchester or Liverpool, forever Labour, but at the expense of giving up on the victims of harsh social policies in rightwing-dominated Tunbridge Wells or Maidenhead.

Often you hear breathless talk about diffusing power and decision-making, 'unleashing the energy of citizens and communities', but less about how services are actually paid for. The trouble with localism is that the tax base in local areas is highly variable: Westminster could raise a fortune while Middlesbrough can't, yet needy Middlesbrough may need to spend more per head on services. That's why the central state has to be strong enough both to raise tax revenues and to redistribute money on the basis of need.

With apparent enthusiasm, former chancellor George Osborne agreed a deal in November 2014 between the NHS and Greater Manchester Combined Authority leading to an agreement to bring together £6bn worth of health and social care budgets. The conurbation centred on Manchester makes historical sense as a city region, thanks to the willingness of the predominantly Labour-controlled councils in the area to sink their differences. There is scope for joint management of transport, skills training and other services where scale matters.

But follow the money: the major obstacle to Greater Manchester becoming a city-state is resources, an area in which Osborne and his successors have been conspicuously silent. If the centre of Manchester and Salford Quays are looking up, the wider north west also contains Oldham, Burnley and Blackpool, areas still desperately seeking ways to escape deindustrialisation and decline. Their ability to levy tax is limited. The necessary concomitant of regional government is strong central government, able to transfer resources between areas, depending on each area's needs and ability to raise its own revenues.

The Northern Powerhouse is an odd mixture: a vision of state entrepreneurship at regional level combined with dogma, leading to the insistence on the untried model of a directly elected mayor for huge conurbations and withholding grants from, for example, Tyneside and the north east for being recalcitrant. Most of the promised extra money turns out to be rebadged from pre-existing commitments. The public has yet to get involved – in early 2016, two out of five adults in the north of England had never heard of the Northern Powerhouse. The conurbations get no additional powers over housing or buses or skills training. Right to buy is to be enforced everywhere, with no local option; ditto the forced 'emancipation' of academy schools from local authorities. Planning decisions are no less subject to override by Whitehall or, as in the case of HS2, are completely delocalised.

Conservative Central Office probably does not have a cunning stratagem but these various moves amount to divide and rule, pitting regions against one another and further fragmenting the sense of a common public commitment across the country. Earlier enthusiasm for devolving powers to Tory-voting Cornwall seems to have dried up once locals realised they might lose rather than gain grants. In Cornwall, a sparse population is expensive to serve. Its residents voted to leave the EU, despite being major beneficiaries of the EU's grants to impoverished peripheral areas. The key to devolution is money; for needy areas, self-assertion and complaints about centralism run the risk that the centre takes them at their words and ceases to redistribute resources their way.

Technocracy?

Scepticism about more local decision-making is not anti-democratic. The spirit of the age extols public participation, which surely means effort, discipline and commitment. Citizens may need protection from decisions that they made, the consequences of which they could not know in advance, but which government can forecast. Choice and personalisation are all very well, provided they are not recipes for selfishness or self-harm.

There's a danger that the public become infantilised. Elected politicians find it hard to talk honestly to citizens and tell them that they will only get what they pay for. If MPs and councillors promise the moon for no extra taxes, public managers should politely put forward the facts of the matter. Providing evidence for what has improved or got worse is a professional obligation. Telling the public plain truths is the bounden duty of a responsible public servant.

In this chapter we have tilted against the individualising, anarchic and anti-collective elements that may get bound up with democracy. Untrammelled political self-determination would be impossible without a cadre of expert managers – such as we currently have in the public service. Their self-confidence matters and they need to be more assertive. If roles are in flux, the post-Brexit shake-up must include those experts famously despised by Michael Gove – yes, public managers are experts – in making complex systems work.

Call it technocracy, or we can borrow from philanthropist Nicolas ·Berggruen, and talk about 'capable institutions that embody both the perspective of the long term and the common good'.[7] The formula is 'knowledgeable democracy with accountable meritocracy' – easy to say, so hard to do.

Chapter 11

The State of Things to Come

The Tories have had nearly 40 years to shape the state. Mrs Thatcher took up her chainsaw; John Major carried on with his own clumsy privatisations; Cameron and Osborne went at the task with renewed vigour, cleverly using the financial crash and recession as cover. The result more resembles the Bates mansion in *Psycho* (guess who is in the attic on the rocking chair?) than something modernist by Frank Lloyd Wright. But by and large, despite their despoliations, the state is still standing.

Great damage has been inflicted. Gables have buckled; the roof is holed. The welfare state has been subject to a malevolent propaganda campaign that branded benefit recipients, even the disabled, as shirkers. Against Tory traditions, the defence state has been battered too, even though the era of universal peace discerned by some when the Berlin Wall fell has failed to dawn. On the relationship between government and business, Tory ministers, including Thatcher herself, were deeply confused or panicked pragmatists. It's shreds and patches, some research support here, emergency tactical aid there, as in Port Talbot or over Nissan's car-making in Sunderland. Breakfast-lunch-

and-tea interventionists such as Michael Heseltine have been held firmly at bay.

During the Heath government in the early 1970s, the social services secretary Sir Keith Joseph had his 'turn' and announced he was no longer a Conservative but a liberal dedicated to dismantling the welfare state and pushing the boundaries of the market. That anti-state project has now lost some momentum. Its candles are still trimmed by devotees in thinktanks and a ragged rightwing chorus has struck up following the triumph of Trump. But the advent of Theresa May only added to the sense of exhaustion and the sheer incoherence of the project. Sympathetic columnists suggest 'the field is clear for the Tories to develop a new doctrine of the state, cultivating a distinctively Conservative blueprint of government'.[1] But what is that? The mainstream press and acolytes in social media still trumpet versions of anti-statism, but the further right you go in British politics, the less coherence there is in leaders' rhetoric and followers' demands. The implication of UKIP positions on migration, for example, is a huge expansion of surveillance, policing and border control, while at the same time the official party position is to cut taxes.

On the left, the Blair–Brown formula – which successfully brought Labour to power and kept it there – embraced contracts and markets: 'reform' was the quid pro quo for expanding public services. Its weakest link was tax. Neither leaders nor the party made any attempt to reach out to the British people to secure open assent to paying for the extra spending by fairer but also deeper taxation. Instead, Brown's fatal promise was something for nothing. Labour budgets cut income tax while raising less visible taxes. They never confronted people with the plain truth that they would only get the NHS or the schools that they paid for. Too little effort was made to counteract the post-Thatcher culture of individualism; indeed Blair reinforced versions of it in public services by emphasising personalisation and choice.

Labour failed to see that only the state could attempt to rescue or assist the victims of the globalisation Labour itself espoused. The apotheosis of free markets and open trade in the 2000s demanded simultaneous investment in regions, places and people who were losing out. Labour did make efforts. But Blair and Brown would not construct a politics around the state's duty to compensate losers by taking more from globalisation's winners.

Political rebellion by those victims partly explains the Brexit phenomenon, and the state must now guarantee them security in the broadest sense. In the words of the political philosopher John Gray, the old liberal ideology that saw state power as the chief enemy to freedom must be countermanded by reasserting the state's protective role.[2] It's time to go back to Thomas Hobbes and accept there will be a trade-off in which some liberties are lost. 'Balancing the claims of liberty against those of security will never be easy. Without security, however freedom itself is soon lost.'

On a less elevated level, we ended our book *Cameron's Coup* by asking whether people wanted to live in a country where services will fall further and further behind general living standards, widening the contrast between public squalor and private affluence. Perhaps a moment of truth will dawn when scandals break over disgusting and dangerous care homes for older people, or patients lying on trolleys in A&E as ambulances stack up outside. How do we want to live? What kind of country do we prefer – one in which the public realm is appreciated and supported or one where public service is denigrated and starved? The affluent may imagine that they can retreat to the private sector, but that will consume far more of their income than contributing towards decent public provision.

Post Brexit, the questions are not being put in that order or exactly in that way, but in the political upset at least the opportunity to ask them opens up. The public continue to want state provision of health, welfare, safety and other services, with sufficient regulation and intervention. Those demands for more not less government are now being joined by business interests. Here's McKinsey, the consultants, who in the past have propagated the standard rightwing view that public spending should be cut and services outsourced or privatised: 'As the competition for investment and entrepreneurial talent reaches global proportions, [government] support for nascent entrepreneurial clusters becomes a must-have.'[3] In consultant speak that is to say that city and regional authorities should identify opportunities in technology and business services (such as superfast broadband) and join together finance, start-ups, schools, colleges and transport. Other consultants also sniff a fresh wind. Deloitte's annual state of the state report – before 2016 a shrinkers' bible – admitted citizens want services that are 'appropriately funded'.[4]

But the road back is rocky. After decades when even Labour governments described tax as a 'burden', how do you convince people of the extraordinary value for money they get from the state? Thatcher's maxim – you will always spend the pound in your pocket better than government – sank deep into the psyche of our nation. It's time to remind people that what they buy in shops is worth so much less than those things they truly value in life – health, education, security, fine public spaces – and those things we all buy together.

The Figures

The basic question remains willingness to pay. Related to it is: what is the appropriate size for the state? How does our answer – around 43 per cent of GDP in net revenue spending – play out for taxpayers? To get seven-day, 24-hour NHS care as well as embanking those rising rivers, caring for the old and training tomorrow's workforce, we must be prepared to see income tax and other levies rise. People, including some in the squeezed middle and barely managing, will have less discretionary income, but higher social support. England, and the other countries in the UK with their degrees of fiscal freedom, must step across the bridge between the cost of decent services and tax revenues. One of the purposes of our book is to put that link in the centre of the picture. Politicians can't duck it; they have to put the unavoidable choice fair and square to voters, treating them as adults with a right to view the facts for themselves and make an informed choice.

The NHS needs real-terms funding increases of 3.5 per cent a year to 2030 at a bare minimum. To cope with the changing demography, health services will require a greater proportion of GDP to be spent on them, rising from 7.4 per cent to 8.8 per cent. Is that such a big ask? The Nuffield Trust's John Appleby says that such a rise would not put undue pressure on general taxation and would still be less than many equivalent countries. The Office for Budget Responsibility reckons most other things being equal, health spending in an ageing country will have to rise by 8 per cent of GDP over the four decades from 2020, or £156bn in today's money. A lot or a marginal addition (nearly £4bn a year)? That level of extra health spending comes from both the ageing population and technological advances and would apply regardless of the division between public and private sectors. So let's have an end to the interminable attempts from the right to push for health insurance or cash payments in place of our NHS: that's fools' gold, a recipe for hugely greater inequality in care, a ticket to bureaucracy and waste, and, as the chaotic American system shows, a way of spending far more money for far less value.

It's not just health. As risk mounts, from the Trump presidency in the west to the Kremlin in the east, so more will have to be spent on defence and security. At home, the aspirations of left and right, Brexiteers and Remainers, centre on economic success made up – depending on standpoint – of expanded trade, GDP growth or adaptation towards greater sustainability. They all depend on enriching the UK's human potential, which in turns points to spending more on early years and further investment in skills and proficiency.

That spending does not immediately involve extra taxation. But, after the trade-offs between policies and departments, after the efficiency savings are reaped (and they are perennially exaggerated), extra cash will be required. While indirect taxes have their place, that extra cash has to come from direct taxation of our incomes, wealth and property, and the 'we' reaches down the income distribution – you can't just foist revenue raising off on the rich. Put the proposition another way: people must share more of what they think of as their personal possessions in exchange for the wider social benefit they reap in return. Is that such an anachronism?

The Face of the State

The state can be more or less ingratiating. The face it shows citizens could help persuade people of the value they get from their tax pounds. Maybe it's too much to suggest all public servants should sport lapel badges saying 'At your service', or 'I am the state personified' but there are ways to connect frontline services to everything that is done behind the scenes in offices and departments. Academic Mark Moore suggests public value can be better projected: public managers should be more assertive, however inconsistent the political mandates they have to work under, however fickle the results of elections. They need to emphasise the legitimacy of their calling as professional managers and custodians of public resources on behalf of the people.[5]

We're not saying get rid of the noise and untidiness of elections and partisan manifestos. It's juxtaposing the hurly-burly with a calmer, non-partisan affirmation of public value. Take bins or any other public service in a place such as Kirklees, the West Yorkshire district centred on Huddersfield. Refuse collection is government in action and deserves acclaim (when provided effectively and economically). In the council chamber Labour has most seats but no overall control. If environmental services managers did promote their work more energetically, wouldn't Tory, Liberal Democrat and Green councillors claim the incumbents were seeking credit in order to get re-elected? That has been the line of attack by Tories since the 1980s, saying that publicity for the public sector – through newsletters and branding, for example – is tantamount to spending for political advantage. As a result they banned councils from publishing magazines promoting local services.

Tories have, at the same time, pushed Whitehall press offices into a more partisan position: a professional cadre of government press officers with their own code of fairness has been replaced in many departments by outsiders from the right-wing press acting as crude cheerleaders for their ministers. The response should be that in both central and local government protocols and conventions governing party political activity need continuous monitoring and strengthening, but also it should be understood that advertising what 'government' does is not partisan. Councillors and ministers who do not believe in the value of the state work they are elected to carry out should be politely asked to end their paradoxical occupation of their positions in charge of public services.

Maybe daily reminders of the necessity of the public sector could convince voters and residents to pay up. Regulators such as the Financial Conduct Authority or the Health and Safety Executive do not say often or loudly enough that without them, harm would ensue. Councils, the NHS, bodies such as the Environment Agency and Whitehall departments should not just project their work but present a generic front. It's all government. Credit is squandered when contractors' logos get in the way. The state does great good – and cynicism wins if that's not said out loud, celebrated and propagated. Here's just one small, quiet example.

———

The week before we visited Patricia and Bill Rose in their home in Oldham, they were at the end of their tether. Their boiler had broken down and they had no heating or hot water through a cold spell. In his late seventies, Bill suffered a stroke six months ago. As he sits all day wrapped up in jumpers in his chair by the window, he gets very cold.

'I didn't know what to do,' Patricia says. 'We've never asked anyone for anything, never claimed nothing, managed very well until now, but the plumber said a new boiler would be £2,000 and we don't have that.' By luck, a neighbour had seen a notice about Warm Homes Oldham and suggested they contact them to look for help. 'I wrapped Bill in shawls, with two hot water bottles and blankets round his feet to keep him warm while I went off to ask them about it.'

That chance suggestion has changed their lives – and very probably saved the local A&E from emergency visits and the council from future extra care. Warm Homes Oldham responded instantly, bringing round heaters, and the very next day their installers came to fit a new boiler, done in a day. Now the house is, as Patricia says, 'warm as toast, like it's never been'. Bill says, 'I feel a hundred times better. I was cold through and through to my bones, for months. The lads who took away the old boiler said it was so dangerous it's lucky it didn't kill us with the carbon monoxide. We had no idea.'

Founded four years ago, Warm Homes Oldham is an example of how the state's many arms can work in unison for everyone's benefit, including the taxpayers'. The NHS and the council combine to offer early preventative work that will save spending later. NHS clinical commissioners put in £250,000 a year while Oldham Council adds £50,000 and administers the scheme. It levers in the complex and dwindling Energy Companies Obligation, a limited fund that energy companies must contribute to, paying towards new boilers, loft and cavity wall insulation.

The Warm Homes scheme is available to low-income households with young children or elderly, sick or mentally frail people living in fuel poverty, defined as having to spend over 10 per cent of their income on keeping warm and lighting their homes. James Sommerville, the manager, says that they keep finding people cheated of hundreds of pounds a year by their energy suppliers, who leave them parked on needlessly high tariffs.

Now, thanks to this intervention, the Roses' energy bills should drop from £300 to £75 a quarter. 'We only ever had heating on for a couple of hours in the sitting room, never in the rest of the house, to keep the bills down. Now we can afford to keep it on.' They were given energy-saving advice that was good for them and good for the planet. They said they'd had no idea their gas fire was costing them far more than the central heating.

Warm Homes checked out the Roses' circumstances. They had never claimed the pension credit top-up nor did they have any idea they should have been claiming £25 a week for the non-stop care Patricia provides for Bill.

Academic evaluation of the scheme is positive, with good effects on general health and wellbeing and cuts in emergency admissions to hospital. All the clients we spoke to were full of spontaneous praise and, yes, warmth for the Warm Homes person who helped them: they keep that contact number permanently by their side for any future problems, a link with all the services they never had before.

Here is a prime example of what the good state can do, benevolent and practical, face-to-face friendly, not an impersonal bureaucracy only accessed online – but intervening before problems turn into crises that quickly ramp up demand for hospital beds and more expensive care.

Magic

From the Roses' cold front room to the security of the realm, we've tried in this book to make a general case for re-enfranchising and re-invigorating our consciousness and appreciation of government. That is not to prescribe exactly what government should do, or how or to what scale. We might find some Tory ministers enthusiastic about state capability – perhaps of the Michael Heseltine stamp – who do believe in state action, but restrict it to certain favoured areas, such as urban development. In similar vein, you might depict a Michael Gove figure as a sincere believer in education, albeit based narrowly on a Gradgrind three Rs notion of what matters.

In fact, Gove was prepared to invest in teachers and schooling – but wasted it on a damaging and quixotic pursuit of free schools and academies without clear mission or status. He crushed arts subjects, downgrading music and drama, instead pushing maths and technical subjects. But common ground between all parties should be belief in a government's duty and role to invest in education across all subjects.

A smart government would reject that arts/science divide and invest in both. At higher levels, the UK does STEM science well and should back winners. Equally, arts education is essential for Britain's booming cultural industries. What a crime to crush the life out of arts education, just at the moment when Tory ministers seemed to be realising the arts' potential, with Osborne approving commitments to Manchester for new theatre and exhibition space on the site of the former Granada Studios. The 2016 Budget committed £13m to Hull as UK City of Culture 2017 and promised funds for Shakespeare North in Knowsley. What's missing is a strategy to link schooling and nurturing young talent with future jobs. What's missing is a political commitment to a symbiotic partnership between individual genius and collective provision of all the springboards needed to develop brilliance into national success. Only connect the dots, and the state can make magical things happen.

―――――――――

'Nothing short of a miracle', said reviewers of *Matilda the Musical*, the Royal Shakespeare Company's blockbuster that by the end of 2016 had already been seen by over 2 million people across three continents.

It could never have been staged without government support. From first inception, transforming Roald Dahl's story into a musical took seven long years to perfect. 'It was the most difficult and expensive show, with so many children', says Catherine Mallyon, the RSC's executive director. 'It took nerve and it took resources. No commercial company would have taken on the risk or given it the creative time it needed to develop.'

She works from an office just across from Stratford-upon-Avon's splendidly rebuilt Royal Shakespeare Theatre, looking out over the river. The RSC is one-quarter state funded, with £15m contributed by the state. It puts £75m into the local economy through tourism and employment and it returns £7m in taxes to the Treasury. Like all the arts, the company has taken its share of the cuts, with more to come in the next round. Like directors across all the arts, Catherine Mallyon has to make the case over and over again for why the state should support something as ephemeral and ineffable, often regarded as elitist and expendable.

With *Matilda* the RSC took a deep breath after good reviews in Stratford in 2010 and took the huge risk of staging it themselves in the West End, at an investment of some £5m. 'We learned the lesson of *Les Misérables*', Catherine Mallyon says. 'We get only a tiny fraction of a royalty from that, although it was entirely our creation. But a commercial producer took it to the West End.' Instead, the RSC relied on benefactors who put up some of the money for transferring *Matilda*, and agreed to getting their money back without profits.

Success has its risks, she says. 'If only you did more of that you wouldn't need a state subsidy, people sometimes say. But you can't plan a formula for blockbusters, that's a recipe for failure.' Nor is that what the company is subsidised to do. She is determined that the RSC don't start to rely on the exceptional £4.1m *Matilda* brought in last year. 'We put the profits into a strategic development fund, not for running the company day to day.' But there's the nagging worry that too many people – politicians – might think they could dispense with their £15m Arts Council grant. 'One school of thought says we should pay any profits back to the Arts Council. But then I ask, will they pay us back for the ones that make a loss?'

What we see now in the glories of the London stage is the fruit of better-funded former times. Mallyon says, 'Those skills were all learned in years spent touring, or in small theatres, but that's hardly available to beginners now. We are returning to how things were in the 1990s. Everything was closing. The only plays in London had to have Hollywood stars – Madonna, or Nicole Kidman. The RSC itself was hanging on by its fingernails. I was running the Towngate Theatre in Basildon, when I had to turn the key on its doors as it was insolvent. It stayed dark for years.'

In these hard times, the only case for the arts that gets a hearing is one that offers returns in hard cash. And that's a case that can be made. Add up the fashion business, giant publishing conglomerates, international art dealers, galleries and auction houses, film, television, the BBC, video games, the advertising corporations, and this fast-growing cultural sector contributes over £77bn to the national economy.

The RSC can also lay claim to 'soft power'. English actors dominate Hollywood; the hugely popular *Game of Thrones* springs from talents nurtured by the British state. The RSC has been translating Shakespeare into Chinese and performing in China, while reciprocally translating a Chinese classic from the Shakespearean era into English to perform over here.

Everywhere arts venues are trying to tell their councils the same story. Walsall's famous New Art Gallery that opened in 2000 to revive this hard-hit ex-industrial area was a project funded by government, lottery and EU regional development money. But Walsall Council threatens to stop its funding and close it despite its good visitor numbers and the part it has played in reviving civic pride. Measuring impact is hard, but no harder than for family intervention by social workers and schools; it is unfair and short-sighted to single out culture for the chop when councils are under pressure.

The RSC tours deprived areas with productions such as *A Midsummer Night's Dream*, in which they brought local people in to act the rude mechanicals, and local children to join the fairies and sing. They go to schools where children have never been to the theatre. They teach teachers how to perform Shakespeare with primary-school children, and those teachers pass on the skills to others in neighbouring schools. They can prove their projects' worth, with measured effects showing how the most disengaged children have been enthused, improving their reading and writing through drama, raising their self-confidence and their ability to speak out in public.

For all the good the state can do through the arts, politicians have, at best, ambiguous feelings towards it. Some just show no interest, while others fear reprisal from *Daily Mail* philistinism. Catherine Mallyon observes their odd behaviour: 'We see ministers sneak in sometimes but they don't want to be noticed, they refuse to be photographed, afraid to admit in public the pleasure they get from the arts.'

Responsibilities of Servants of the State

An RSC director finds it relatively easy to speak out, but so must others, low as well as high. Where Thatcher's 40-year anti-state project may have scored its greatest victory is in reducing the self-belief and morale of public servants. What often tells against the version of the state we argue for is a loss of faith on the part of the state's own officials. Decades of antagonism from the rightwing and business leaders have undermined their professional self-confidence and pride. We are acutely aware that the reconstruction project outlined in this book depends on the quality and commitment of today's state employees and those to be recruited tomorrow. Cowed, hesitant or ideologically subverted, many lack a strong enough sense of their mission and purpose.

Yet on them rest the public's perceptions of the state. If staff resent their treatment at the hands of senior managers or politicians, if they are discontent with their pay and low in morale, the first people to notice are likely to be the parents, patients and the service users who are their everyday contacts. Outside work, a council worker, nursing assistant or HMRC official goes home or to the pub or on Facebook and talks about the conditions of their service to the community beyond: if they feel disrespected and downtrodden, struggling to keep going against unceasing cuts and management pressure for impossible efficiency savings, that's what people will hear. How often do civil servants boast about their job, proud of their organisation and of the wider public realm? If staff are treated grudgingly, then grumbling can become a habit.

The public gets the message about government more often from their own experiences at a reception desk than through listening to self-aggrandising speeches full of statistics. Polling analysts say staff demeanour and attitude help explain why Labour's great boost to public spending failed to win hearts and minds. Had Blair ministers been more positive about the services they ran, had they berated and belaboured public servants less, people might have appreciated the huge fillip given to services in those years. Playing the politics of increased spending so badly prepared the way for initial acceptance of Tory post-crash austerity amid claims that services were inefficient and feather-bedded.

Labour MP Alison McGovern gets to the point. 'The real life of the state undermines our argument for government action if the public don't like the attitude of the state that greets them.'[6] She argues that 'whenever the state disregards the people it is there to serve, this makes the Tories' argument for them. They can say: "See how you were treated by the government? There is too much government, the only relationship of respect is that of the commercial transaction."' She's right, because some staff in any organisation can be needlessly disobliging and obstructive, if badly managed.

But that's only a part of the story. When the public experience a depleted, hard-pressed service, staff should explain. 'Sorry, but we're understaffed and suffering cuts. With the best will in the world, we can't provide what's not funded.' But they are under strict instructions never to tell such truths by senior managers who are required to take Trappist vows on pain of sacking. A bit more honesty from professional public servants would open up discussion with the public about why services are less than optimal. The case for an active – and friendly state – rests on resources.

Responsibilities of Citizens

There are other hard truths the public should be told – about themselves as citizens. People rightly want to be treated with respect and honesty but they also need to recognise that the state isn't a grocery. Using public services is not the same as super-market shopping and it never will be, however it is resourced. Why can't booking a hospital appointment be as easy as booking an airline ticket, Blair asked? That was the wrong question, and it sent out entirely the wrong message. There is a good reason why everyone can't choose what they want from every public service as easily as Amazon dropping off your every whim by drone. It's an error of categorisation. Cameron and May pledged a 24-hour NHS and round-the-clock GP services as if the NHS were Tesco, welcoming all comers at any hour, regardless of priorities. Inevitably, Cameron would not cost these blithe proposals, making the glib assumption that what is already one of the most cost-efficient health services in the world (as attested by the Commonwealth Fund of New York) could be further squeezed.

The more people who shop, the more money the shop earns and the happier its shareholders. The more people demand a public service, the more overstretched it becomes because public resources are inherently limited. Principles of fairness apply, which are completely absent from shopping. Managers, ministers or local councillors have to decide how to allocate scarce public money fairly between very different needs, between ages, classes, regions, between present spending or investing in the future. That often means queuing; rationing is what all governments must do at every budget. A citizen can bang on the counter and in principle protest at bad service by going next door (assuming retailers are not in a cartel or have informal price fixing arrangements). But citizens demanding better public funding for their needs must make the case against a host of other priorities. To use a public service is to take part in a shared endeavour: my child's school, my ailment, my university fees, potholes in my street, bobbies on my beat – all these come at an opportunity cost to others. Me, me, me can never be the whole story. Misunderstanding the nature of public service leads to disappointment, risking disenchantment with the whole idea. Only by addressing the rationing choices openly do citizens become participants and co-operators in difficult decisions about the services we all own together.

Faith and Conviction

In this book we have tracked the decline, the cracks and the breakages in the state under a decades-long ideological barrage, now cast as pragmatic austerity. Liberalism, neo-liberalism, libertarianism, free-marketeering, it comes under many names but amounts to the same idea: disconnect the various organs of the state, and markets (plus charity) will provide. But the evidence from this brutal experiment says plainly that markets don't and won't fill the void. Since the 1980s, the state has been downsized and pulled back, allowing an explosion of inequality. Growing political disengagement has soured trust in government, leading to the country breaking apart in the 2016 referendum.

Over these decades collapsed industries went unreplaced, stripping away the livelihoods of whole regions and leaving trade grossly unbalanced. The prevailing wind blew laisser-faire and with it came the notion that governments can't repair such damage, can't 'pick winners' or build ambitious new towns round new economic functions as they once did in the post-war years. Belief in the power of positive government has dwindled to tinkering around the edges and providing a minimal safety net for modernity's victims. Our examples of where government can inspire, regenerate, create and encourage are tokens surviving on pocket money. What's needed is a spirit of investment and national self-belief on a grand scale.

The shift in mood reflected in the Brexit vote suggests a yearning for more than extra money in the family budget. Identity politics led many to vote for an idea of nation and collective identity far beyond enjoying (while worrying about the sustainability of) a higher rate of GDP expansion: purely economic arguments failed to sway enough people against Brexit isolationism.

Patriotism can be warped by demagogues but can also unite us in national endeavours. As George Orwell wrote in *The Lion and the Unicorn*, 'devotion to a particular place and a particular way of life' is a strong and natural drive, quite distinct from aggressive nationalism that seeks to impose a personal love of country on others. Of course, in today's UK, love of country has to be parsed through the constituent countries as well as Great Britain: belonging is plural not singular on these islands.

For patriotism, read pride in who we are together, abandoning precise boundaries for more ambiguous, flexible ones. Instead of borders, let's focus on what holds us together, what we can all point to as sources of self-belief, aspiration and celebration. Marketisers, outsourcers, asset-strippers and state-shrinkers are not patriots, they are surfing the world on seas of money. Theresa May seemed to recognise this, and yet has done so little to reshape a Tory party in thrall to bankers and hedge funds. The greatest lacuna in her thinking is about government. Waving a union flag is a Tory convention, but until Thatcher's project to destroy the state itself is buried, it's all hollow humbug.

What makes for pride is collective achievement, mostly accomplished by and through government. What holds us together are our common institutions, starting with the NHS and the BBC. We define our past and our prospects in public spaces, from Parliament Square up Whitehall to Nelson's column, the Royal Mile from Edinburgh Castle to Holyrood, Belfast's City Hall and Cardiff's Millennium Centre. Parks, science hubs, concert halls, Olympic stadiums, monuments, galleries, museums, swimming pools – add in anything here that gives you a sense of pleasure in collective identity, memory and common values. Contracts with Capita, Virgin, BUPA, Sodexo and the rest are written on water. The sale of gas networks, power stations and basic transport systems to foreign powers is a form of treason.

Relative to the 19th century, compared with 1945, the UK pursues the path of decline as an international power; even Brexit fantasists don't claim the UK as more than a second-order country. But it is still a country with tremendous human potential – our achievements in science and scholarship, commercial services, aspects of technology, art, broadcasting, sport and military derring-do should all engender continuing pride. Provided we invest. Provided we believe in our better selves.

There is a vehicle to organise that investment and a collective framework for that belief. It's the state. Years of chiselling away at its foundations and the crazy Gormenghast of tiers, bodies and agencies erected around it have taken their toll on public trust and, critically, on the public assent to taxation. However, enough respect and support for collective endeavour remains to build on. It has to be a joint effort, by the political class as by state employees and the public. Arguments about size and cost will – must – go on. But how much more effective the UK and its people could be if we called a halt to the antagonism and belittling of past decades and affirmed that government is good.

List of Acronyms

A&E: Accident and Emergency

ARC: Association of Revenue and Customs

CBI: Confederation of British Industry

CQC: Care Quality Commission

DfE: Department for Education

DVLA: Driver and Vehicle Licensing Agency

DWP: Department of Work and Pensions

EHO: Environmental Health Officer

EIF: Early Intervention Foundation

ESA: Employment Support Allowance

ESOL: English for Speakers of Other Languages

FRC: Financial Reporting Council

FOI: Freedom of Information

GDP: Gross Domestic Product

HEE: Health Education England

HMRC: Her Majesty's Revenue and Customs

HS2: High Speed Two

IFS: Institute for Fiscal Studies

LEP: local enterprise partnership

LINk: Local Improvement Networks

MCA: Maritime and Coastguard Agency

NAO: National Audit Office

NATO: North Atlantic Treaty Organisation

NI: National Insurance

NPM: New Public Management

OBR: Office for Budget Responsibility

OECD: Organisation for Economic Co-operation and Development

OFCOM: Office of Communications

OFQUAL: Office of Qualification and Examinations Regulation

OFSTED: Office for Standards in Education

PFI: Private Finance Initiative

PAC: Public Accounts Committee

PFI: Private Finance Initiative

RSC: Royal Shakespeare Company

STEM: Science, Technology, Engineering and Mathematics

TCPA: Town and Country Planning Association

TfL: Transport for London

UCATT: Union of Construction, Allied Trades and Technicians

UKIP: United Kingdom Independence Party

WI: Women's Institute

Endnotes

Introduction: Our Better Selves

1   https://www.theguardian.com/politics/2016/dec/03/poll-uk-trust-deficit-getting-worse-politicians-teachers-nurses?CMP=Share_AndroidApp_LinkedIn

2   https://www.theguardian.com/public-leaders-network/2011/mar/07/david-cameron-attack-civil-service

3   https://www.instituteforgovernment.org.uk/publications/whitehall-monitor-2017

Chapter 1: What a State We're in

1   http://www.bbc.co.uk/news/uk-wales-mid-wales-37223770

2   Jon Bakija, Lane Kenworthy, Peter Lindert and Jeff Madrick, *How Big Should our Government Be?*, University of California Press, 2016

3   http://www.oecd.org/eco/public-finance/The-effect-of-the-size-and-the-mix-of-public-spending-on-growth-and-inequality.pdf

4   Jared Bernstein, 'What's Slowing Growth?', *Washington Post*, 8 August 2016, http://wpo.st/Of3r1

5   Polly Toynbee and David Walker, *The Verdict: Did Labour Change Britain?*, Granta, 2010

6   https://www.theguardian.com/commentisfree/2013/jul/21/british-economy-still-in-bad-position

7   www.parliament.uk/briefing-papers/SN06642.pdf

8   Polly Toynbee and David Walker, *Cameron's Coup: How the Tories Took Britain to the Brink*, Guardian Faber, 2015

9   Institute for Fiscal Studies, 'Reforming the Tax System for the 21st
     Century, the Mirrlees Review', 2010, https://www.ifs.org.uk/
     publications/mirrleesreview/

Chapter 2: The Public Realm

1   https://www.dogstrust.org.uk/news-events/news/the-nations-
     stray-dog-numbers-fall-by-21-but-twelve-dogs-a-day-face-
     destruction-because-forgetful-owners-havent-updated-their-dogs-
     microchip-details

2   http://www.localgov.co.uk/Public-parks-generate-large-surplus-of-
     1.2bn/41901

3   http://www.localgov.co.uk/Welsh-council-urges-organisations-to-take-
     over-heritage-sites/41888

4   http://www.bbc.co.uk/news/health-37274562

5   https://www.hlf.org.uk/about-us/news-features/parksmatter

6   https://www.tuc.org.uk/sites/default/files/focusonhealthsafety
     report.pdf

7   https://www.theguardian.com/uk-news/2014/may/21/theresa-may-
     police-federation-power

8   Alan Murie, *The Right to Buy?: Selling off Public and Social Housing*,
     Policy Press, 2016

9   http://www.thecommissioningreview.com/article/70-nhs-staff-%
     E2%80%98confused%E2%80%99-over-healthcare-structure

10   https://www.tes.com/news/school-news/breaking-news/exclusive-
     sir-greg-martin-durand-will-close-if-funding-withdrawn

11   http://cep.lse.ac.uk/pubs/download/dp1455.pdf

Chapter 3: The State's Parlous State

1   https://www.nao.org.uk/wp-content/uploads/2016/12/Financial-
     sustainability-of-schools-Summary.pdf

2   http://www.localgov.co.uk/Report-calls-for-1bn-fund-to-transfer-public-
     assets-to-communities/41993

3   http://www.localgov.co.uk/Survey-shows-walkers-cant-use-one-in-ten-
     footpaths/42025

4 http://www.nurseryworld.co.uk/nursery-world/news/1159959/
   families-missing-out-on-health-visitor-checks

5 https://www.hsj.co.uk/newsletter/sectors/mental-health/hunt-vows-
   to-act-on-nhss-biggest-area-of-weakness/7011628.article?utm_source=
   newsletter&utm_medium=email&utm_campaign=Newsletter307

6 https://www.theguardian.com/commentisfree/2016/dec/21/
   prisons-unlocked-rehabilitation-david-laws

7 https://www.theguardian.com/science/2017/jan/06/forensic-
   science-cuts-pose-risk-justice-regulator-warns

8 https://www.lawgazette.co.uk/law/employment-tribunal-claims-
   plummet-by-100000/5058656.article

9 https://www.gov.uk/government/uploads/system/uploads/
   attachment_data/file/556396/rrcgb2015-01.pdf

10 https://www.nao.org.uk/report/local-enterprise-partnerships/
   http://www.ons.gov.uk/ons/rel/pse/public-sector-employment/
   q2-2014/stb-pse-2014-q2.html

11 http://www.conservativehome.com/thetorydiary/2016/12/how-
   do-you-solve-a-problem-like-the-railways.html

12 http://sciencebusiness.net/news/71719/Autonomy-will-make-
   universities-more-competitive

13 https://www.theguardian.com/cities/2015/aug/04/pops-privately-
   owned-public-space-cities-direct-action

14 Daniel Rodgers, *Age of Fracture*, Harvard University Press, 2011

15 Alan Milburn, 'The Voluntary Sector, a Partner in Reform', speech to
   the Association of Chief Executives of Voluntary Organisations
   (ACEVO), 8 May 2004

16 http://www.parliament.uk/business/committees/committees-a-z/
   commons-select/environment-food-and-rural-affairs-committee/news-
   parliament-2015/future-flood-prevention-report-published-16-17/

Chapter 4: Contracting Out

1 https://www.nao.org.uk/wp-content/uploads/2010/06/101168.pdf
2 'Outsourcers Target Healthy Returns from NHS', *Financial Times*,
   30 November 2016

3   http://www.instituteforgovernment.org.uk/publications/making-
    public-service-markets-work

4   http://www.publications.parliament.uk/pa/cm201617/cmselect/
    cmpubacc/633/63305.htm#_idTextAnchor008

5   https://www.publications.parliament.uk/pa/cm201314/cmselect/
    cmpubacc/473/473.pdf

6   http://www.nao.org.uk/report/compass-contracts-provision-
    accommodation-asylum-seekers/

7   https://www.nao.org.uk/wp-content/uploads/2013/03/Out-of-
    hours-GP-services-Cornwall-Executive-Summary1.pdf

8   https://ico.org.uk/about-the-ico/news-and-events/news-and-blogs/
    2016/11/127-days-in-the-job-and-preparing-for-gdpr/

9   http://www.justiceinspectorates.gov.uk/hmiprobation/inspections/
    northoflondon/

10 https://www.nao.org.uk/wp-content/uploads/2016/11/
    Commercial-and-contract-management-insights-and-emerging-best-
    practice.pdf

Chapter 5: The State of Business

1   'Where Have all the Bricklayers Gone?', *Financial Times*, 1 January
    2016

2   http://www.publications.parliament.uk/pa/cm201617/cmselect/
    cmtrans/740/74002.htm

3   http://www.parliament.uk/business/committees/committees-a-z/
    commons-select/transport-committee/news-parliament-2015/road-
    haulage-sector-report-published-16-17/

4   https://www.theguardian.com/business/2016/dec/25/showmens-
    guild-plays-vital-role-for-travelling-fairs

5   Simon Taylor, *The Fall and Rise of Nuclear Power in Britain:
    A History*, UIT Cambridge, 2016

6   https://www.theguardian.com/money/2016/dec/14/uk-4g-
    coverage-worse-than-in-romania-and-peru-watchdog-finds

7   http://www.nao.org.uk/press-releases/the-rural-broadband-
    programme-2/

Chapter 6: Staffing the State

1   https://www.oecd.org/publications/engaging-public-employees-for-a-high-performing-civil-service-9789264267190-en.htm

2   https://www.theguardian.com/business/2016/dec/14/peter-wilkinson-the-man-the-unions-say-is-driving-the-southern-rail-strike

3   http://www.cabinetoffice.gov.uk/news/dispelling-myths-and-stereotypes-about-public-sector-workers

4   https://www.theguardian.com/society/2016/jul/12/post-brexit-time-bring-in-technocrats

5   Peter Hennessy, *Having It So Good: Britain in the Fifties*, Penguin, 2007

6   https://www.theguardian.com/politics/2014/may/08/jeremy-hunt-homeopathy-studies-chief-medical-officer

7   https://www.theguardian.com/housing-network/2011/aug/08/david-walker-pay-disparities-in-social-housing

Chapter 7: The Efficient and Effective State

1   https://www.theguardian.com/society/2014/jan/28/data-public-services-election

2   https://www.instituteforgovernment.org.uk/publications/universal-credit-disaster-recovery

3   https://www.theguardian.com/public-leaders-network/blog/2011/jun/06/armchair-auditing-nao-scrutiny

4   Margaret Hodge, *Called to Account: How Corporate Bad Behaviour and Government Waste Combine to Cost Us Millions*, Little, Brown, 2016

5   https://www.instituteforgovernment.org.uk/sites/default/files/publications/IFGJ4801_Spending_Challenge_1409_V3.pdf

6   https://www.gov.uk/government/speeches/prime-minister-my-vision-for-a-smarter-state

7   https://www.gov.uk/government/speeches/francis-maude-announces-end-of-year-savings-2013-to-2014

8   https://twitter.com/goddersbloom/status/802445605251534848

9   http://www.echo-news.co.uk/news/local_news/9211106.Seven_police_stations_to_shut_to_the_public_as_part_of_budget_cuts/#comments-anchor/

Chapter 8: We Need to Talk About Tax

1 http://www.ifs.org.uk/mirrleesReview/design

2 https://www.parliament.uk/business/committees/committees-a-z/commons-select/public-accounts-committee/news/reports-taxation/

3 http://www.localgov.co.uk/Over-half-of-councils-targeting-debtors-homes-to-recover-unpaid-tax/42080

4 http://www.fda.org.uk/Media/Tax-gap-is-closing-but-further-8-billion-could-be-recouped-by-HMRC-providing-an-alternative-to-cuts-or-tax-increases-says-ARC-Budget-submission.aspx

5 Jenny Manson, ed., *Public Service on the Brink*, Imprint Academic, 2012

6 https://www.civilserviceworld.com/articles/interview/hmrc-chief-jon-thompson-relocation-going-digital-and-thin-lizzy-christmas

Chapter 9: The State Ahead

1 https://www.theguardian.com/politics/2016/nov/15/memo-about-whitehall-brexit-problems-was-for-internal-audience-says-deloitte

2 https://www.theguardian.com/politics/2016/nov/22/civil-service-unable-to-cope-with-brexit-bob-kerslake

3 https://www.theguardian.com/society/2016/may/19/englands-chief-medical-officer-warns-of-antibiotic-apocalypse

4 https://www.gov.uk/government/uploads/system/uploads/attachment_data/file/575973/The_Casey_Review_Report.pdf

5 http://www.cqc.org.uk/content/state-of-care

6 https://www.theguardian.com/society/2016/dec/27/home-ownership-figures-are-exaggerated-says-thinktank-resolution-foundation

7 http://www.oecd.org/regional/cities-will-become-inequality-traps-without-better-housing-transport-policies.htm

8 https://www.gov.uk/government/uploads/system/uploads/attachment_data/file/567242/national_cyber_security_strategy_2016.pdf

9 https://www.theguardian.com/uk-news/2016/dec/08/hostile-states-pose-fundamental-threat-to-europe-says-mi6-chief

10 https://www.theguardian.com/uk-news/2016/nov/21/royal-navy-risks-having-pathetically-low-total-of-ships-warn-mps

11 http://www.themanufacturer.com/articles/warren-east-rolls-royce-only-the-paranoid-survive/

Chapter 10: The State of Balance

1 https://www.gov.uk/government/uploads/system/uploads/attachment_data/file/60641/cabinet-manual.pdf

2 https://ico.org.uk/about-the-ico/news-and-events/news-and-blogs/2016/11/127-days-in-the-job-and-preparing-for-gdpr/

3 https://www.theguardian.com/media/2016/dec/19/rupert-murdoch-ive-never-asked-any-prime-minister-for-anything

4 Jenny Manson, ed., *Public Service on the Brink*, Imprint Academic, 2012

5 http://www.localgov.co.uk/TPA-Give-councils-greater-fiscal-powers-/42220

6 https://www.gov.uk/government/speeches/prime-minister-my-vision-for-a-smarter-state

7 Nicholas Berggruen and Nathan Gardels, *Intelligent Governance for the 21st Century*, Polity Press 2013

Chapter 11: The State of Things to Come

1 https://www.theguardian.com/commentisfree/2016/nov/21/philip-hammond-just-about-managing-chancellor

2 http://www.newstatesman.com/politics/uk/2016/11/closing-liberal-mind

3 http://www.mckinsey.com/insights/public_sector/Creating_growth_clusters_What_role_for_local_government?cid=other-eml-alt-mip-mck-oth-1407

4 Deloitte, 'The State of the State 2016–17', https://www2.deloitte.com/uk/en/pages/public-sector/articles/state-of-the-state.html

5 Mark Moore, *Creating Public Value: Strategic Management in Government*, Harvard University Press, 1995

6 Alison McGovern, *The Real Life State: Putting Dignity at the Heart of our Public Services*, Fabian Society, 2016

Index